Missing persons, political landscapes and cultural practices

Manchester University Press

Missing persons, political landscapes and cultural practices

Violent absences, haunting presences

Laura Huttunen

MANCHESTER UNIVERSITY PRESS

Copyright © Laura Huttunen 2025

The right of Laura Huttunen to be identified as the author of this work has been asserted in accordance with the Copyright, Designs and Patents Act 1988.

An electronic version has been made freely available under a Creative Commons (CC BY-NC-ND) licence, thanks to the support of the Tampere University Foundation, which permits non-commercial use, distribution and reproduction provided the author(s) and Manchester University Press are fully cited and no modifications or adaptations are made. Details of the licence can be viewed at https://creativecommons.org/licenses/by-nc-nd/4.0/

Published by Manchester University Press
Oxford Road, Manchester, M13 9PL
www.manchesteruniversitypress.co.uk

British Library Cataloguing-in-Publication Data

A catalogue record for this book is available from the British Library

ISBN 978 1 5261 7703 2 hardback

First published 2025

The publisher has no responsibility for the persistence or accuracy of URLs for any external or third-party internet websites referred to in this book, and does not guarantee that any content on such websites is, or will remain, accurate or appropriate.

EU authorised representative for GPSR:
Easy Access System Europe - Mustamäe tee 50, 10621 Tallinn, Estonia
gpsr.requests@easproject.com

Typeset
by Deanta Global Publishing Services, Chennai, India

To the memory of Jaakko and Juha

Contents

List of figures   *page* viii
Acknowledgements   ix
Abbreviations   xii

Introduction: towards the anthropology of disappearance   1

1. Enforced disappearance: politics of terror and paralysing uncertainties   37
2. Disappearing en route: missing migrants, ambiguous absences and exposure to death   60
3. 'Individual' missing persons: private agonies and ambiguities of citizenship   80
4. Material reappearances: dead bodies and mortal remains   100
5. Symbolic reappearances: photographs, memorials and ghosts   133

Conclusion: violent absences, haunting presences   157

Bibliography   163
Index   181

Figures

0.1	The map on IOM Missing Migrants Project shows the estimation of dead and missing migrants across the globe; the numbers shown here are from February 2024	*page* 13
1.1	A damaged family house near Prijedor in Bosnia-Herzegovina in 2001. A large number of family houses were destroyed in the area in the campaigns of ethnic cleansing between 1992 and 1995	44
3.1	The cover image of Hanneriina Moisseinen's graphic novel 'Isä – Father', presenting the disappeared father with his daughter, the author of the novel	85
4.1	ICRC Book of Belongings; clothes worn by the bodies in the mass graves in Srebrenica, here on display in the ICMP premises	114
4.2	ICRC Book of Belongings; items found in the mass graves in Srebrenica, here on display in the ICMP premises	115
4.3	Blood samples by family members of the missing in the fridge in the ICMP premises in Bosnia-Herzegovina in 2013	116
4.4	Decoded and transcribed DNA-information in the ICMP archive room, Bosnia-Herzegovina 2013	117
5.1	The memorial stone in Srebrenica-Potočari Memorial displaying the names of all the 8,372 victims of the genocide	144
5.2	Gravestones in Srebrenica-Potočari Memorial and Cemetery for the Victims of the 1995 Genocide	145

Acknowledgements

Writing this book has been a long process, and thinking about human disappearances an even longer one. I have actively worked on the subject of disappearances since 2011, and more than a decade of engaging with the issue and discussing it with others means that there are many people to thank, more than I can include here.

I want to start by thanking the Bosnians with whom I have worked and who have shared with me experiences that have been difficult, sometimes bordering on unbearable.

My very special thanks go to my dear colleague Anna Matyska, who read a version of each of the chapters and always made insightful comments that helped me forward. Without you, Anna, the book would certainly not be what it is.

I want to express my great thanks also to the whole DiMig research group, that is, the members of the 'Disappearing Migrants and Emergent Politics' project, funded by the Academy of Finland (2018–22). For four years we shared fruitful discussions, and this period significantly enriched my understanding of the subject. Without this group, I doubt that this book would exist. Thank you, Anna Matyska, Mari Korpela, Ville Laakkonen, Saila Kivilahti and Dimitri Ollikainen. Along with Anna, Saila also read several chapters and provided me with valuable comments.

Special thanks also go to my friend and colleague Ninna Nyberg Sørensen. Discussions with Ninna while developing my ideas on disappearances were critical in the early stages of this project, and I learned a lot from her while we were working together on an article comparing disappearances in Latin America and Europe; her profound knowledge of Latin America and her always critical and analytical approach opened my eyes to many issues. Thank you, Ninna!

My cooperation with Gerhild Perl and my discussions with her on migration, migrant deaths and disappearances have been very important and have contributed to my thinking over the years. Gerhild also read several chapters and made many useful comments that helped me to clarify my arguments. Likewise, Linda Haapajärvi, a valued colleague with whom I share many areas of interest, also gave feedback on various chapters. Thank you, Gerhild and Linda, for being such inspiring colleagues.

Kaarina Nikunen and Virve Peteri, my dear friends and colleagues at Tampere University, read a version of the introduction at a crucial moment and provided me with productive comments that helped me to move forward with the work at a time when I was rather hesitant about how to continue.

I started to develop the ideas for this book at the Tampere University Institute for Advanced Social Research in 2012–14, and the research seminar participants there were important in the early stages of the project. Later, the social anthropology research seminar group at the university became an important collegial and intellectual community for me, and many discussions with these colleagues over the years have contributed to this book. Moreover, two panels focusing on human disappearance at EASA (European Association of Social Anthropologists) conferences, one in 2016 in Milan and the other in 2020 in Lisbon and online, were both fruitful moments for developing ideas. Thanks to everyone who took part in these discussions.

The workshop 'Social disappearance: explorations around a travelling concept from Latin America to Eastern Europe', at the Forum Transregionale Studien in Berlin organised by Estela Schindel and Gabriel Gatti, contributed to enriching my understanding of the complexity of the issues involved in human disappearance. Thanks to all the participants, the workshop was inspiring and produced thought-provoking discussions.

When the manuscript was close to completion, I participated in a workshop titled 'Social and political responses to the missing and dead: conflict, migration and beyond', organised by Lia Kent and Simon Robins in Bangkok in the summer of 2023. The workshop helped me to clarify some of the arguments presented in the book, and it further enriched my understanding of the complexity of the phenomenon. Many thanks to Lia, Simon and all the workshop participants.

Thanks to Megan Caine for her great work with language editing, and for helping me to find ways to express things that are sometimes hard to put into words! I also want to thank the editorial staff at Manchester University Press for a smooth and friendly publication process, and my colleague Tuomas Tammisto for help with the map. Moreover, sincere thanks to the three anonymous reviewers for Manchester University Press – their comments and suggestions have certainly improved the manuscript.

Needless to say, any mistakes or misunderstandings in the book remain solely my responsibility.

Acknowledgements

Finally, I want to thank my family – my husband Timo and my daughter Xin – for their presence, love and support, and for always making life joyous and meaningful!

Tampere, 15 March 2024
Laura Huttunen

Abbreviations

AM data	antemortem data, data on a person collected before death
EAAF	*Equipo Argentino de Antropología Forense,* the Argentine Forensic Anthropology Team
ICMP	International Commission on Missing Persons
ICRC	International Committee of the Red Cross
ICTY	International Criminal Tribunal for the Former Yugoslavia
IOM	International Organization for Migration
PHR	Physicians for Human Rights
PM data	postmortem data, data on a person collected after death

Introduction: towards the anthropology of disappearance

While I have been working on this book, Russia has attacked Ukraine and started a war, an armed assault on both the military and civilians. In such circumstances, people invariably go missing, soldiers and civilians alike, both from their loved ones and from the knowledge grid of the state. Some of these missing are soon found alive and are reconnected with their families; some of them are found dead; and some remain missing, unaccounted for, for months, years or even decades. Some of them are never found, never reconnected with their families; in the state bureaucracies, their disappearance remains a question mark, to be bureaucratically considered as death at some point, but for their family members they remain in an open-ended liminality. The pain and horror[1] of disappearance is blurred by the pain and horror of injury, violence and death. I argue that disappearance has a particular place in human culture, imagination and politics, and that the pain, and power, of the disappearance of a loved one is different from the pain, and power, of death.

People go missing for various reasons, and for varying stretches of time. Sometimes people disappear only from their loved ones, and sometimes only from the bureaucratic gaze or state matrix, with their whereabouts known by trusted friends or family members; often they disappear from both contexts. Some people disappear of their own free will, to escape from unbearable circumstances. Some disappear in natural disasters or fatal accidents, some as victims of crime. Invariably, both civilians and soldiers disappear in the chaotic circumstances of war and armed conflict. Some people are intentionally disappeared by the state: totalitarian and military governments as well as various paramilitary and criminal organisations have used enforced disappearance as a tactic to control the population and create submissive citizens or subjects though fear and insecurity. All these instances of disappearance have something in common: they break up the normal flow of life and create an absence, often marked by harrowing uncertainty and distress among those left behind. In research literature and policy documents, such absent individuals are referred to as 'missing persons' or 'disappeared persons'.

Mary Douglas famously argued in *Purity and Danger* (1966) that humans as cultural beings think and act through categories; things that fall between categories are inherently problematic, anomalous or polluting. People who go missing are 'matter out of place' in Douglas's sense: they are not where they are supposed to be. They are inexplicably away from their normal lives, their work, their communities and/or their families. But they are matter out of place in a more symbolic sense as well. I will argue throughout this book that people who remain missing for protracted periods of time are placed between life and death symbolically, emotionally and even bureaucratically, and that such a position is utterly disturbing for those left behind. As Douglas argues, such anomalous positions are powerful because they disturb the established social, cultural and symbolic order. Reading this productive force of the absence of the missing is at the core of this book.

Anthropologists are rather reluctant to claim universals. The huge variety of cultural forms and social arrangements observed by ethnographers suggests that there is always the possibility of another way of doing, thinking and living human lives. In this book, however, I suggest a kind of universal in human life: people need to be alive or dead – socially, culturally and bureaucratically, they need to fall into one of these two categories. There are different understandings of how to define the line between life and death, and the ontological status of the dead may be differently conceptualised, but the line is there. The dead may be active in the social world of the living, as ancestors or spirits or in memorial practices, but dead they are. Of course, there are categories that fall between the two, but these in-between categories are often deeply problematic; heated debates around the euthanasia of fatally ill people and the treatment of certain medical conditions such as brain death (Lock, 2002) are indicative of this problematic zone. This grey area between life and death is also the cultural zone that gives rise to mythic creatures such as vampires, ghosts and zombies – those who are simultaneously dead and alive, embodying a peculiar, sometimes threatening, form of life.

My claim of universality immediately needs to be qualified. In many cultural contexts, death is regarded as a process rather than a single event, and many scholars have emphasised this dimension. Such an approach makes the line between life and death inescapably fluid. While accepting this approach, I still argue that the disappeared are a problematic category: if a person is regarded as in transition between life and death, the transition should be contained and codified culturally and socially. As Victor Turner (1977) suggests, liminality in the ritual context – the context in which the notion was originally used – is a dynamic state of being, a middle phase between past and future statuses, and thus forward-oriented. In a similar sense, the liminality of inexplicable absence is always geared towards closure,[2] towards the return of the disappeared – towards their reappearance, either alive or dead. Sometimes they reappear as ghosts or restless spirits, or in more symbolic forms such as pictures and memorials that embody the symbolic in material form. This persistent reappearance in sometimes unexpected forms indicates what I call the 'impossibility of disappearance' (cf. Gatti, 2014): the disappeared never just vanish without a trace. In this book, I will develop these intertwined notions – the claim that disappearance is an 'impossible' social category and, consequently, that disappearances almost inescapably bring about reappearances, in one form or another.

I have twice been touched by the disappearance of a loved one in my personal life. Both my brother and my first husband died by drowning, and both were missing for several months – my brother Jaakko in 1993, my husband Juha in 2004. Those months of unexplained absence were the most difficult times of my life – the relentless agony caused by such absence is hard to describe to those who have not experienced it. Jaakko and Juha were both found and identified, and this experience of getting a missing loved one back has filled me with gratitude, alongside my profound grief at their deaths. These events sensitised me to pay attention to my interlocutors' missing family members when doing ethnographic fieldwork among Bosnians, to see both similarities and enormous differences between their experiences and mine. My curiosity and a need to understand the phenomenon were aroused, and I started to look beyond Bosnia to gain a wider understanding of disappearance as a social and cultural phenomenon. This book sets out both to understand the similarities and differences between disappearances in different contexts, and to make sense of the elusive category of the missing or disappeared.

Beyond my own experiences, this book has grown out of some twenty years of ethnographic engagement with the Bosnian diaspora between Finland and Bosnia-Herzegovina.[3] Rather early on, I became aware of the fact that many of the Bosnians with whom I was working and talking had somebody who had disappeared during the Bosnian war (1992–95). Many of these disappeared relatives, friends and neighbours have been found dead in mass graves in the intervening years, while others remain missing to this day. In the former case, my interlocutors would travel to Bosnia for funerals that took place years after the death; in the latter, the fate of the missing person remains unclear. These disappearances and reappearances caught my attention and raised a number of questions: who were the disappeared? Why did they go missing? What did it mean for those left behind? Where were they found? By whom? What kind of work was involved in locating these dead persons and returning them to their families? What does it mean to bury somebody some ten or more years after their disappearance and death? What are the political implications of all this in Bosnia, and beyond?

Between 2012 and 2014 I ran a research project focused on the disappearances in Bosnia-Herzegovina during the armed conflict in the 1990s – in Bosnia, the disappeared are generally called 'missing persons' by the powerful actors in the area, as I will elaborate below. I interviewed people whose loved ones had gone missing during the war, and I set out to understand the process of looking for and identifying these missing. On several occasions, I visited the International Commission on Missing Persons (ICMP), one of the key actors in ex-Yugoslavia in coordinating the work on the missing. I read hundreds of pages of documents produced by various institutions and organisations working with the missing and disappeared. I talked with people in Bosnia and in the diaspora about the disappearances, and also with those not personally affected, in order to understand the implications.

This book is deeply rooted in my ethnographic engagement with the Bosnian diaspora and with disappearances in the Bosnian context. Throughout the volume, I introduce empirical examples and observations from this field. However, the book is not about Bosnia as such. In order to build a more extensive understanding of the force of unaccounted-for absence, I bring in other cases and other contexts in which people disappear, or have disappeared, forcibly or otherwise.

In 2013, while working on the Bosnian disappearances, I spoke with a representative of the Finnish Red Cross; his role in the organisation was to work on the tracing service that provided help to people who had lost contact with their family members. 'At the moment, most of the search requests come from the families of undocumented migrants. Irregular migration is the context where currently large numbers of people go missing. And these missing are often very difficult to find', he said. This discussion helped me to redirect my work. Since 2018, I have been working with a group of colleagues on a project on disappearances in mobile and migratory contexts.[4] This cooperation is another intellectual 'rooting space' for this book. The project focuses on missing and disappeared persons in the contexts of tourism, labour migration and undocumented migration within Europe, and it has vastly expanded my understanding of disappearances in general.

In this book, I tease out features that are common to all disappearances, irrespective of the context. What kind of social category is a missing or disappeared person, and what kind of social force emerges when somebody goes missing? At the same time, however, I am well aware that the context matters, that people go missing for a wide variety of reasons, and that their disappearance affects those left behind in different ways. Different disappearances also give rise to vastly differing political responses, and vastly differing levels of investment in both the search for the individuals and the identification and repatriation of bodies to the families for burial in those cases where the disappeared are dead.

I will argue that inexplicable absences have an enormous power that affects the lives of those left behind; they affect social relations, bureaucratic procedures, political processes and cultural perceptions. Disappearances are a productive force in the Foucauldian sense (cf. Gatti, 2014; Perl, 2019a). In their introduction to the volume *Anthropology of Absence*, Mikkel Bille, Frida Hastrup and Tim Flohr Sørensen (2010) claim that absences of various kinds – not only of people – often have a special power and agency that affects people's lives in many ways. They claim that 'what may be materially absent still influences people's experience of the material world' (Bille, Hastrup and Sorensen, 2010: 4). The authors suggest that we should read 'social phantom pains' (Bille, Hastrup and Sorensen, 2010: 3–4), in reference to the well-known fact that a patient may feel pain in an amputated leg or arm for a long time afterwards. 'Social phantom pains' are the sometimes-unforeseen consequences of various absences and amputations in the social world. In other words, these authors posit that the relationship between absence and presence is always a complicated one, and that absences may possess a peculiar kind of productive agency. This book is an exploration of the peculiar productive agency that disappeared persons have regarding their surroundings, and of the ways in which the disappeared 'reappear', in one way or another, as a consequence of this agency.

My mapping of this terrain starts with the categories used to address the issue, followed by remarks on the global frame and spatial dimension of disappearances, thus anchoring the book in particular key places and areas. In this section, I will briefly examine the scope and limitations of the empirical cases discussed. After this, I sketch a historical frame for thinking about disappearances. Finally, I frame my discussion theoretically within the anthropology of death and suggest ways to think further towards anthropology of disappearance or, more generally, towards theorising human disappearances in humanities and social sciences.

The categories: enforced disappearances and missing persons

Who are the disappeared? Whom do we talk about when we talk about missing or disappeared people? The phenomenon is elusive and escapes our attempts to create unambiguous, clearly demarcated categories and fix them in place. It challenges the constant urge to 'know' and categorise that is characteristic of modern knowledge systems.[5]

In certain places, at certain times, large numbers of people go missing all at once, making the category of the disappeared socially and culturally important. Armed conflicts, totalitarian regimes, natural disasters and fatal accidents are examples of this. Under such circumstances, a need grows to name and define the category of the absent. In addition, individuals disappear from their social environments in less dramatic circumstances, and their unaccounted-for absence also needs to be addressed. However, categories are always porous, and the categories of the absent perhaps even more so, as events connected with disappearances are often infused with uncertainty and ambiguity. This resonates with Gabriel Gatti's understanding (2014) of the disappeared as an impossible category – a state of being that is beyond language and meaning-making in many ways.

To begin to understand whom we talk about when we talk about those who are inexplicably absent, I will take a look at the most prominent terms used to discuss disappearances in English. I will discuss the different ways in which the category has been articulated within certain frames of interpretation, and will subsequently embed these terms in the practical and political contexts where they have been used. In other linguistic contexts, there are other established terms and names that carry local histories – an important point that I will elaborate below.

As noted above, when referring to somebody whose whereabouts are not known to their immediate social environments for a prolonged stretch of time, the most common terms used in English are 'forcibly disappeared person' and 'missing person'. These terms have differing histories, and they have come to connote different aspects of protracted human absences. Even though many languages do not make a similar distinction – for example, in Spanish, *desaparecidos* is used for both, as is *personnes disparues* in French – the global prevalence of English in political, policy and academic arenas makes the discussion of English terminology worthwhile.

The systematic application of enforced disappearance by some Latin American states in the 1970s and 1980s, especially Chile, Argentina and Uruguay, led to the coining of the term 'enforced disappearance' and to the rise of legal frameworks that would address this new kind of human rights violation. The English term is a translation of the Spanish *desaparecidos* (cf. Dziuban, 2020). Chapter 1 of this book is devoted to analysing enforced disappearance as a violent necropolitical (Mbembe, 2003) practice of establishing power. In the legal framework, the role of the state is at the heart of understanding such disappearances, the key criteria for which are the deprivation of freedom by the state, or with the acquiescence of the state, and the refusal to provide information about the whereabouts and fate of the forcibly disappeared person. As a result of all this, the disappeared person is set outside the protection of the law, and is denied a legal personality that is protected by it (Frey, 2009: 67). As Frey argues, the elements of the violation as defined in the UN's International Convention for the Protection of All Persons from Enforced Disappearance (the Disappearance Convention) are virtually covered by other rights already guaranteed in international human rights law, that is, freedom from arbitrary arrest, freedom from torture and execution, the right to legal recognition and due process and the right to life (Frey, 2009: 52). However, enforced disappearance emerged so powerfully as a new strategy of terror, leaving deep wounds not only in the families of the disappeared but in the social fabric of whole societies, that it gave rise to the need to formulate new definitions. Even though the political regimes in Latin America have changed, 'enforced disappearance' lives on as a powerful term with global significance.

The Disappearance Convention was adopted by the UN General Assembly in December 2006. Even though the convention itself is a rather recent development, it has a long history. It was preceded by several legal instruments, all in the 1990s: a UN declaration, the Inter-American Convention on Forced Disappearance of Persons and an International Criminal Court statute establishing enforced disappearance as a crime against humanity.[6]

This category of 'disappearance' has had a powerful social life since the 1990s; it has become the term with which to call for legal responsibility and moral accountability. It enables questions to be asked about the intentionality and force behind disappearances in various contexts. But, as the definition of enforced disappearance was formulated in relation to the refined machinery of state-sponsored violence in the Southern Cone of Latin America, applying it to other contexts, such as that of disappearances along migrant routes (see Chapter 2), has at times been challenging.

'Missing person' as a term has a different history and a different scope of application. It is the most inclusive term: it is often perceived as including everybody who is inexplicably absent from their families and communities, regardless of the reason for the absence. The term is mentioned in international humanitarian law, which does not give it an exact definition but nevertheless endows a missing person with certain rights or, more precisely, endows their family with the right to know their fate. In the Geneva Conventions (1949 and the additional protocols), the ways in which 'missing person' is used do not suppose a perpetrator, or any intentionality behind the absence. In this sense, it is often perceived as a neutral term and, as such, as useful for humanitarian organisations, for whom only credible non-alignment gives them access to carry out humanitarian relief work in conflict zones. Moreover, in working with the search for victims of fatalities and large-scale traffic accidents, INTERPOL systematically uses the term 'missing person', as the focus of its work is to find the missing and identify the dead rather than name the perpetrators.[7]

Moreover, as Amber Dean (2015: 22) suggests, 'missing person' is a thoroughly social term, as it foregrounds those left behind, those searching for the absent person. The emphasis on relationality and the plight of those left behind is a further dimension that makes the term useful for grassroots and humanitarian organisations. The International Committee of the Red Cross (ICRC) and the International Red Cross and Red Crescent Movement, which have a long and influential history of working with disappearances in armed conflicts, among both the military and civilians, use 'missing person' consistently as the key term with which to address disappearances. This resonates well with their established policy of neutrality and political non-alignment. In its 2019 publication, the ICRC expanded its 2013 handbook definition to include migrant disappearances:

> While there is no legal definition of a missing person under international law, the ICRC understands missing persons as individuals of whom their families have no news and/or who, on the basis of reliable information, have been reported missing as a result of an armed conflict – international or non-international – or of other situations of violence or of any other situation that might require action by a neutral and independent body. This definition includes persons missing in the context of migration.
> *(ICRC, 2019: 30; cf. ICRC, 2013: 16)*

The family is a crucial actor in this definition: families should know where a person is. Moreover, it is families who have the 'right to know' (ICRC, 2013: 6). This understanding has been consequential and productive in the hands of the ICRC: its worldwide tracking/tracing system called 'Restoring Family Links'[8] has operated for decades. This system has helped people in conflict situations, and often in chaotic circumstances, to reconnect with family members with whom they have lost contact. Such a strong linkage of family with 'the right to know' may, however, be problematic in some cases; there are people who flee *from* their families, because of various forms of violence, abuse and coercion that take place within them. Recognising this, the Red Cross emphasises that it always asks the person traced whether they want to be reconnected with their family.

Such an emphasis on the plight of those left behind characterises the humanitarian approach to disappearances more generally. The focus is not on *why* somebody has gone missing but rather on the consequences of the disappearance for those left behind. The emphasis is on strategies to alleviate the pain of the families and to help with practical problems arising from the fact that a family member has gone missing.

The ICMP is another organisation that uses the term 'missing person' rather than '(forcibly) disappeared person', even though it was founded in circumstances in which force and violence were very much present: to find those who were missing as a result of the conflicts that followed the dissolution of Yugoslavia. The ICMP makes a distinction between being 'subjectively' and 'objectively' missing:

> Subjectively, a missing person is anyone whose whereabouts are not known and who is being sought by another person or other persons. The term 'missing person' acquires an objective meaning when a person is formally reported as missing.
>
> *(ICMP, website)*[9]

The ICMP definition points to the distinction between being missing from your loved ones and being bureaucratically and officially missing, the latter requiring a procedure of registration. The ICMP was active in advocating for and developing bureaucratic procedures to declare loved ones officially missing in the ex-Yugoslavian territories in the 1990s, during the period of the country's violent dissolution. Similarly, it has been active in formulating the law on missing persons in Bosnia-Herzegovina, one of the first of its kind in the world. Such a bureaucratic procedure is a vehicle for turning private agony into a legal status with consequences; in the ex-Yugoslavian territories, launching the search for a missing person, the legal recognition of somebody's status as such and the humanitarian policies addressing the practical problems encountered by the families left behind are all closely tied to bureaucratic recognition.

This kind of connection between private agony and public recognition is significant everywhere – albeit being a tense and complicated issue in many cases. The recognition of the disappearance by the police or other state officials, or other relevant actors such as powerful international organisations, is crucial for initiating the search, and the public recognition of disappearances is on the agenda of many organisations working with the issue. However, when the state is the perpetrator, a complicit agent or simply utterly indifferent to the issue, such public recognition is, of course, deeply problematic. In Chapter 4, I will briefly discuss forms of citizen activism that work to develop modes of searching for the missing and identifying the dead in circumstances in which there is little or no trust in the state or larger organisations.

Currently, significant numbers of people go missing in the context of undocumented migration, especially across the North African deserts and in the Mediterranean, as well as while crossing the Sonora Desert, from Central America to the USA. Organisations, policy-makers and scholars have applied both 'missing persons' and 'disappeared persons' when addressing migrant disappearances. In Chapter 2, I will discuss more closely the tensions around naming this kind of disappearance.

Individuals also go missing from their families in the affluent Global North,[10] and their disappearances do not seem to be connected with political persecution. They appear to be individual cases that have no connection to other disappearances (Chapter 3). When the police work with such disappearances, the term 'missing person' is routinely used (e.g. Shalev Greene and Alys, 2017). Also, many organisations working with families use this term, which is understood as both inclusive and relational. Families of the Missing, an organisation that supports families of people who disappear in armed conflicts across the globe, adopts a wide and inclusive definition:

> A missing person is someone whose state of being and whereabouts are unknown. Anyone in the wrong place at the wrong time can become a missing person. The circumstances vary, from armed conflict to natural disasters to human trafficking to religious or political persecution.
> (*Families of the Missing, website*)[11]

In this definition, anybody whose whereabouts are not known to their loved ones can be regarded as a missing person. The definition also emphasises the haphazard or random nature of the process that produces the missing: anybody who happens to be in the wrong place at the wrong time may end up disappearing – the missing person cannot be blamed for their situation.

Both terms in English have had a globalised social and political life, and they have both been applied by a variety of actors, for a variety of purposes over time. I will make observations about their application in the section below on building a historical frame for human disappearances, as well as in the empirical chapters. In Chapters 1, 2 and 3, I will follow the application of the terms in varying contexts where people go missing, while in Chapters 4 and 5, I will make observations about the ways in which the terms have been translated into actions aimed at bringing the missing back into the sphere of the social and cultural, that is, aimed at making the disappeared reappear.

In this book, I sometimes use the two terms – 'missing person' and 'disappeared person' – interchangeably. I take them to refer to different aspects of the same phenomenon, rather than indicating entirely different categories. 'Missing person' foregrounds the absence encountered by those left behind, while 'disappeared person' enables it to be linked with discourses of enforced disappearance and questions of accountability. Rather than claiming that one or the other is the 'right' term, I use them both so as to be able to probe different dimensions of disappearances. Moreover, I take it as an analytical question to ask how various actors that are engaged with disappearances apply the terms, including individuals, families, state actors, non-governmental organisations (NGOs) and other organisations.

Because we are talking about such a variegated group of people across the globe, it is impossible to give exact figures or even convincing estimates of the numbers that fall into this category, or of those who are touched by the disappearance of somebody close to them. What is clear, however, is that tens of thousands of people disappear from their loved ones every year, and millions are affected by human disappearances. Whenever possible, I will provide more exact numbers or well-founded estimations regarding missing and disappeared persons in various contexts.

Finally, a few words about the linguistic context. In some places, vernacular expressions referring to the missing or disappeared have been established in everyday language. In Bosnia, *nestali* is recognised by local people as a word referring to a specific category, that of those who went missing during the dissolution of Yugoslavia. In the Spanish-speaking world, the term *desaparecidos* has become so widespread that according to some, it is now subject to over-use. For example, Gatti (2020) depicts a situation wherein various marginalised groups, including homeless and disabled people, seek to make political claims by calling themselves *desaparecidos*. At the same time, the continued salience of the term in the Spanish-speaking world also attests to the long history of enforced disappearances there, reaching into our current age. It is worth noting that in Latin America, the term most often used for missing migrants is also *desaparecidos* – in Spanish there is no established translation for 'missing person'.

In Poland, *zaginieni* is a term that is well recognised by the wider public because the annual numbers of disappearances are significant (Matyska, 2020; Matyska, 2023a; Matyska, 2023b). In Finland, the situation is quite different. When I tell people in Finland that I do research on *kadonneet* ('the disappeared'), I encounter perplexed incomprehension; the term does not ring any bells for most people, even though the country does have its own history of disappearances, including those who disappeared during the civil war in 1918, and the soldiers who went missing during the Second World War.[12] These disappearances have not, however, been publicly discussed as such. This lack of vernacular wording should sensitise us to the context-bound nature of any concepts. The existence, or non-existence, of established terminology with which to address disappearances is indicative of their history in various areas – often a complex history of voices and silences, embedded in histories of power, politics and culture.

Spatial dimensions: where do disappearances take place?

Disappearances take place everywhere across the globe. However, there are some factors that make large-scale human disappearance more likely. First, armed conflicts invariably leave in their wake soldiers missing in action, but they also result in disappeared civilians, broken family connections and dispersed communities, that is, people who go missing in the chaotic circumstances. Secondly, totalitarian governments frequently use enforced disappearance as a strategy of governing with fear. Thirdly, natural disasters and fatalities, such as the 2004 tsunami in Asia, can create large numbers of missing persons and unidentified bodies in a matter of moments. Finally, in current times, routes of undocumented migration are dotted with both unidentified bodies and families looking for their disappeared relatives. There are many places where several of these factors coincide, such as Iraq, Afghanistan and Syria. But there are also places that do not appear in the news as frequently as these three, while still being plagued by significant numbers of disappearances, Pakistan and Turkey among them.[13]

One way of starting to map disappearances in our current times is to look at where the organisations involved with the issue work. On the ICMP's website, in a section headed 'Where we work', there is a list of areas where the commission is active: Africa, Asia, Europe, Middle East and North Africa, and the Americas,[14] and each of these continents or areas opens up to reveal a list of states. The Balkans was the original site of the ICMP's activity; the organisation was founded to tackle the issue of missing persons in the ex-Yugoslavian territories in the aftermath of the dissolution of Yugoslavia, and it still works there. However, it has enlarged its scope of action substantially, and now works in locations such as Iraq, Kuwait, Lebanon, Libya and Syria – all places with layered histories of disappearances. The organisation also works in South Africa, with the legacy of apartheid violence; in Namibia and Cameroon, with aircraft accidents; in Colombia, El Salvador, Chile, Brazil and Mexico, where criminal organisations, undocumented migration and state complicity are intertwined in complex ways; in the Philippines and Thailand, with the tsunami missing; and in the Mediterranean region, with an initiative to address migrant disappearances. The ICMP's map shows two things: the global occurrence of disappearances and the multiplicity of reasons behind them.

The ICRC's map[15] is a bit different: it concentrates on conflict areas. However, the organisation is currently extending its work to the Mediterranean and to the migrant missing. There are also many smaller organisations that work with migrant disappearances on a lesser scale in certain geographic areas, such as the Colibrí Center for Human Rights in the US–Mexico border area, and Missing at the Borders, an organisation that works in the Mediterranean, on both the European and North African sides. The existence and activity of such organisations indicates that disappearances are taking place on a larger scale in certain areas. These organisations and their differing activities are discussed more closely in Chapters 1, 2, 4 and 5.

The International Organization for Migration's (IOM) Missing Migrants Project[16] seeks to make migrant deaths and disappearances visible and, to that end, has been gathering data on the subject matter since 2014. It

Introduction

Figure 0.1 The map on IOM Missing Migrants Project shows the estimation of dead and missing migrants across the globe; the numbers shown here are from February 2024. Credit: IOM Missing Migrants Project.

presents another version of the world map: the IOM's Missing Migrants map has six yellow circles of varying sizes marking particular sites. The circles have figures written inside them, indicating the number of migrant deaths in certain areas and making visible the deadliest sites for undocumented migrants. The biggest circles are the Mediterranean with 29,032 deaths, followed by Africa with 14,385, and the Americas (the circle hovering over the US–Mexico border) with 9,008.[17] This map indicates that routes of undocumented migration are significant sites of disappearance. In Chapter 2, I will discuss further the different ways of counting migrant deaths and disappearances, as well as their geographical distribution.

Together, these three maps suggest that, even though people disappear everywhere, the factors mentioned above – armed conflicts, dictatorships and large numbers of people driven to migrate via irregular routes – almost invariably mean large numbers of human disappearances. Moreover, natural disasters and fatalities can produce, in a short time, a large number of missing persons and unidentified bodies.

In this book, the most important geographical contexts are Argentina and Europe, the latter including Bosnia-Herzegovina, Finland and the Mediterranean. I live in Finland, and my personal experiences of loved ones disappearing took place there. Bosnia has become familiar to me through my work as an anthropologist; I have worked as an ethnographer in Bosnia, and with the Bosnian diaspora in Finland. In addition, I have been part of a research team the members of which have conducted ethnographic fieldwork in the Mediterranean, and in Poland and among the Polish diaspora. Consequently, these sites figure frequently in the book.

Argentina has appeared as an important site throughout my work with disappearances.[18] Early on, when beginning to work in this field academically, I came across the vast literature on disappearances, and reappearances, in Argentina. The Argentinian history of both enforced disappearance and opposition to the cruel politics involved has provided a fruitful reference point and site for comparison when making sense of disappearances elsewhere. Argentina is also a place with a rich culture of acknowledging disappearances publicly, in both art and political mobilisation, and the practices involved in finding and identifying the disappeared were significantly developed there. Although it is the above key sites that I discuss more thoroughly in this book, I also offer observations from elsewhere, such as Zimbabwe, Rwanda and Cambodia, based on research literature, policy documents and information provided by NGOs and other actors in the field.

The scope of the empirical examples

The cases on which I focus in this book are in many ways organically connected to my own history, to both my personal and research trajectories. More importantly, they enable me to discuss key aspects of human disappearances, from purposeful enforced disappearances to 'individual' people going missing in stable rule-of-law democracies and to disappearances in contexts that expose people to deadly circumstances while not necessarily targeting them as individuals. Each of the cases discussed in this book has the potential to open up human disappearance from a specific point of view, while each naturally has its limitations as an example.

Although Argentina in the 1970s and 1980s is the 'classical' example of systematic, state-sponsored disappearances, and probably the most widely studied case of the phenomenon, by juxtaposing it with Bosnia-Herzegovina in the 1990s, and to some extent with other cases around the world, I can both open up the variation in the strategy across time and space and make observations about the specificity of the Argentinian case itself. The intentional application of enforced disappearances in Bosnia took place under very different circumstances to those in Argentina, and I read Bosnia in the 1990s both as an example of the application of the tactic of enforced disappearance in the context of power struggles in an emergent state and, simultaneously, as an example of human disappearance in armed conflicts. In the latter sense, it is a rather special example in many ways; disappearances are probably not as systematically employed in all armed conflicts, at least not to the same extent as in Bosnia and, moreover, the ways in which disappearances were dealt with after the conflict in Bosnia are globally unique, as will be discussed in Chapter 4. Thus, my examples do not pretend to exhaust these issues; quite the opposite – they suggest that much more research is needed to bring more nuance into our understanding of them.

My discussion of migrant disappearances focuses on the Mediterranean, and to a lesser extent on the US-Mexico border area. These are widely studied cases, even though discussed much more in terms of migrant deaths than disappearances. Both are examples of a heavily monitored border area characterised by huge inequalities between its two sides, and by intensive, militarised border-control machinery. Undocumented migration takes place in other parts of the world as well, in border areas that are different from these two, both politically and geographically. We need more data and more analysis of what occurs in those areas to gain a deeper understanding of the interconnection between mobility and human disappearances.

Finally, my focus on Finland as the site of 'individual' disappearances certainly has its limitations. Finland is a small state in northern Europe, with a rather well-functioning welfare state, a still rather homogenous population, and comparatively high degrees of trust displayed by citizens towards the state and its institutions. These circumstances undoubtedly colour the ways in which missing person issues are dealt with and the expectations concerning these – probably also my own view on the issue. Citizens' and residents' expectations of the state vary considerably across the globe, even in rule-of-law democracies. To illuminate this variety, I bring in examples from Poland and certain other places in Chapter 3, but these examples are far from exhaustive.

None of my empirical examples discuss disappearances in fatal accidents or natural catastrophes. The examples are necessarily limited – but it would be the same with any set of cases. All in all, my argument in this book is that human disappearances always take place in historically and politically idiosyncratic circumstances, and, consequently, my collection of empirical examples simply paves the way for further empirical research and conceptual analysis.

Histories of absence: from Martin Guerre to biomedical identification

The tragedy of missing persons is as old as mankind itself.
(ICMP website)[19]

Where does the history of disappearances begin? The quotation above suggests that the history of disappearances, and of the agony produced by them, stretches back to pre-history, to the very early times of humankind. But is there such a unified history?

Perhaps the question is the wrong one. Maybe we should historicise the significance of absence, of disappearing or being away from one's habitual surroundings without an acceptable explanation, and also the practices of enforced disappearance as a political strategy. Or perhaps we should historicise disappearance and absence as social phenomena, along with identification practices and ways of addressing and remembering the disappeared.

An exhaustive history of disappearances and missing persons is well beyond the scope of this introduction. Nevertheless, I believe that historicising disappearances is important; we need to contextualise them in time, as well as in place and in political and social context. In this introductory chapter, I suggest some frames for thinking about the specificity of disappearances and absences in our modern age, by juxtaposing our present time with certain historical developments. I will make observations about the historical significance of absences as such, and will sketch some developments in practices of identification and memorialisation. In addition, I will consider enforced disappearance as a political strategy and the development of the human rights discourse around it.

Historicising absence

It might be considered that the ancient practice of exile (Gorman, 1992) was a form of disappearance at a time when there were either no communication technologies across long distances or they were very slow and unreliable. People were sent from their families and communities to live far away, often for the rest of their lives, without the possibility of keeping in touch with those left behind. Such practices created a void, an absence in the families and communities of those exiled. This void can be compared with those created by more recent disappearances, but there is a crucial difference: the nearest and dearest of the exiled person usually knew why they were absent, and the excruciating uncertainty that marks more modern disappearances was not there.

Natalie Zemon Davies' *The Return of Martin Guerre* (1984) is a classic in micro-historical writing. The book depicts the peculiar case of a wealthy peasant who disappears from his family and community in mid-sixteenth-century France, and who returns unexpectedly to attend a court case against a pretender who has stolen his identity and lived as him for several years. The study is an intriguing story in many ways. In the context of the current volume, it is interesting as a piece of empirical work that historicises our understanding of absence and identification. The study points to illuminating discontinuities, but also to a number of important continuities in the effects of protracted absences, when read against modern-day cases of missing or disappeared persons.

Martin Guerre leaves his family and, according to historical sources, lives for almost ten years in Spain, serving two wealthy noble brothers and fighting in the Spanish king's army. What is clearly different from our times is the fact that the possibility of keeping in touch with his family across geographic distances was extremely low. Communication technologies were, if not totally absent, very rudimentary when compared with our present-day world, which is overwhelmingly ruled by technologies that enable real-time communication over long distances. There were no telephones, and the postal connections were considerably limited. As far as the remaining historical records can tell us, the family Martin left behind did not hear from him for about ten years – in stark contrast to the ways in which most people today keep in touch with each other – but still they assumed that he was alive. Even though he was disapproved of for leaving his family, such a protracted absence was not totally inconceivable.

There are, however, some significant continuities between the late middle ages or early modern times and our current times: the position of close family members is profoundly affected by such disappearance. In particular, if the disappearing person is the head of the family and/or the key breadwinner, their disappearance may be catastrophic. In sixteenth-century France, the position of a widow was different in many ways from that of the wife of a living but absent man (Zemon Davies, 1984), and questions of inheritance, the legal position of spouses and responsibilities regarding children are still concrete questions faced by families of disappeared persons today.

Moreover, the fact that the close family, other relatives and neighbours of Martin Guerre live with his absence for years, not knowing where he is, resonates with the experience of some families in the Global South today: people are often forced to migrate undocumented, and communication with families and sending communities can be challenging at times, leading to situations in which people in these communities do not know when to get worried. In such circumstances, the lines between hope, fear and shame often become blurred: hope for the absent one's return, fear regarding their fate or that they have actively decided not to return and shame over the possibility that they have abandoned the family (cf. Drotbohm, 2023). This theme will be further discussed in Chapter 2.

In this book, I argue that the way in which we understand disappearances today is affected by the possibility of sustained, intense communication over long distances. Moreover, I will tentatively suggest that our understanding is profoundly shaped by our modern conceptions of the individual, personhood and citizenship. Absence has become 'impossible' in ways in which it was not five hundred years ago, and the need to bureaucratically 'know' and to fix each individual case is a deeply modern-day notion, connected with modern state structures and ideologies of governance. However, even in these times of obsession with knowing, categorising and fixing in place, there are people who are more 'disappearable' (Laakkonen, 2022) than others. Disappearing undocumented migrants and unidentified dead bodies along migratory routes seem to fall outside this urge to know and fix; similarly, indigenous populations and certain other marginalised groups slip away from the matrix of citizenship in many places (Petryna and Follis, 2015). Such a lack of interest in certain disappearances is interesting in its own way, pointing to hierarchies of what Judith Butler (2009) has called 'grievability'.

Enforced disappearance as a political tool

Martin Guerre left his family voluntarily, as far as we know. Many present-day migrants who disappear en route also leave, more or less, voluntarily – even though 'voluntariness' is a contested conception in this context (see Chapter 2). However, a significant number of those who go missing disappear as victims of a purposeful political strategy.

As discussed above, the history of (the politics of) disappearances in Latin America during the second half of the twentieth century has significantly affected the ways in which disappearances are discussed and conceptualised today. As I have argued, the introduction of human rights legislation in the 1970s and 1980s was an important landmark in the development of the discourse of enforced disappearance (Frey, 2009). The emergence of enforced disappearance as a juridical category and its being conceived as a crime against humanity has also affected how disappearances are understood retrospectively in different times and places. For instance, the victims of violence during the Spanish civil war (1936–39), buried in mass graves, have become retrospectively read as *desaparecidos*, as victims of crimes against humanity and of enforced disappearance. Ferrándiz (2015) claims that it is only over time that 'disappeared' has been established as the category denoting those extrajudicially shot and clandestinely buried during the Spanish civil war, and only then through a 'transnational' route: the struggle over the memory of the civil war has been incorporated into global human rights discourses and politics of memorialisation.

Likewise, Layla Renshaw (2010) argues that in many places in Spain, the dead victims were not necessarily disappeared in the same sense as in Argentina. The nature of the violence was different: it often took place within local communities, and family members who were not killed were forced to witness it. As a consequence, the locations of the graves of the extrajudicially executed bodies were often known to the family members, but no public mourning or any kind of acknowledgement of the murders was allowed. As Renshaw argues, the victims were not missing or disappeared but unacknowledged; they were 'forgotten' in public remembrance and official narratives but their fate was known, and they were remembered within intimate spaces and family circles. Renshaw (2010: 53) points out that they were often called *fusilados* – meaning 'those who were shot' – by the older generation who had lived through the violence. Renshaw continues: '"those who were shot" is a definitely resolved term, allowing no ambiguity over the fate of the people' (Renshaw, 2010: 53). However, since the beginning of this millennium, Spanish Republican memory activists have begun to equate the *fusilados* with the Argentinian *desaparecidos* and the latter term has become an effective and productive tool in the hands of a younger generation demanding a radical re-evaluation of the history of the civil war, giving rise to a series of excavations and exhumations and a heated debate on the language used.

As the example of Spain shows, people had been forcibly detained and extrajudicially executed in many places and under many regimes before the South American military governments came to power. Some writers want to locate the beginnings of this strategy in the Nazi regime and the Night and Fog decree in 1941 (e.g. Gordon, 2008), and the Nazi regime certainly was a moment when a significant number of people were forcibly disappeared from their loved ones and placed outside the protection of the law. Others have pointed to the elaborate practices of detaining people and stripping them of their citizenship rights in the Soviet Gulag during Stalin's regime (see Anstett, 2011; 2014), but the extent to which these were cases of enforced disappearance in the sense we understand it today can be debated (e.g. Schindel, 2020a: 34–5).

We can ask, like Renshaw, whether the victims of extrajudicial killings during the Spanish civil war were forcibly disappeared in line with the definition in the Disappearance Convention or, like Schindel, we can ask the same question regarding the victims of Stalin's regime. What is clear, however, is that in both cases the extrajudicial killings and the anonymous, unacknowledged gravesites created both a landscape of silence and histories of living 'in the presence of absence' (Anstett, 2014: 189) or with the mortal remains of unacknowledged loved ones close at hand. In this sense, they created political and cultural worlds permeated with fear and grief, and probably also rage. Under such conditions, the absent often return as a ghostly presence, in rumours and stories, as I will suggest in Chapter 5.

Moreover, several authors have argued that the necropolitical method of purposefully disappearing victims that was deployed in South America has a global history that considerably pre-dates the 1970s: as a specific strategy of power, it has travelled from Indochina and Algeria to Latin America and South Africa (Robben, 2005: 180–4; Anstett and Dreyfus, 2014b: 8) and from the British colonial administration in Africa to the present-day practices in some African states (Millar, 2023). If the South American military governments were not the first to deploy enforced disappearance, they were certainly not the last either. The sad fact is that using enforced disappearance as a political strategy has continued and flourished in many places since the Latin American military governments of the 1980s (e.g. Eppel, 2014; D'Souza, 2015; Comaty, 2019; Kodikara, 2023; Millar, 2023).

Rather than trying to establish which was 'the first' regime to used enforced disappearance to stabilise its power, or to list all the consequent regimes to do so, I will work with two themes that have arisen from this discussion. First, I will pay attention the role of the state as the guarantor of citizenship rights – or as the denier of them to some. Secondly, I will work with the understanding that the human rights discourse around disappearances is a modern, post-Second World War frame that enables us to see past atrocities in a new light. The establishment of the international legal framework on forced disappearances, including the UN Working Group on Enforced or Involuntary Disappearances,[20] has also sensitised both political opposition and the general public to the practice and to organising against it.

At the same time, I will argue that there is something inherently modern in the way in which enforced disappearances have come to be used by totalitarian and military governments as a means to control populations through fear and insecurity. Such strategies would not have made sense under the kind of regime that Foucault called the '*ancien régime*', wherein the sovereign displayed their power in spectacles of force and punitive coercion (Foucault, 1977); it was feasible for them to execute subjects publicly and to leave dead bodies on display as emblems of power.[21] In the modern world, with its state-based international system, states need to publicly adhere to certain norms of conduct in order to be recognised as legitimate actors in the global arena. This pushes regimes into hiding certain forms of violence against citizens and other residents.

Practices of search and identification

The detailed history of the search for the missing and of identification practices is also beyond the scope of this introduction. Rather, I will draw some lines with which to frame the scope of the change that has occurred in identification practices and make some observations on search practices.

The search for a missing person is a highly context-dependent practice, and it is impossible to say anything general about it, either historically or globally. The best-known global actor here, with a long and influential history in searching for the missing in armed conflicts, is the Red Cross;[22] the organisation has worked in searching for both soldiers and civilians who go missing in conflict situations. It was the Red Cross that pioneered the work on the missing by compiling lists of prisoners of war during the 1870 Franco-Prussian war in Europe, and it has successfully promoted the practice of soldiers wearing badges in order to be identified when dying. Searching for missing civilians became institutionalised when the ICRC's Central Tracing Agency was established in 1960 (ICRC, 2019: 31). The possibilities of search in conflict contexts and beyond has been radically changed by technological development, ranging from aerial photography, which helped to locate the mass graves of disappeared Bosnian victims in 1995, to the possibilities of the police locating a missing person's mobile phone and of tracking information in various electronic systems, such as the international banking system and international border-crossing registers.

Likewise, the identification of both the dead and the living has changed enormously over the centuries. Martin Guerre lived at a time when there were no photographs, and painted portraits were extremely rare and limited to the upper class and the nobility; there were no fingerprinting techniques, let alone any other biometric or DNA-based methodologies. There were no passports, many people were illiterate and the personal handwritten signature had not acquired its later significance. When the court tried to assess whether the person claiming to be Martin Guerre actually was him, they tested his ability to remember events from Martin Guerre's life, and heard statements from people who had known Martin before he left. This is in stark contrast to present-day identification practices, which are characterised by the predominance of state-owned identity documents (Torpey, 2018) and heavy reliance on specialised techniques and procedures, many of them biomedical and understood to be objective and scientific (e.g. Dirkmaat and Cabo, 2012; Grünerberg *et al.*, 2020).

In Martin Guerre's case, there was a need to establish the identity of a living person, to decide who was the real Martin. Today, such identification would be much easier because of modern identity documentation – even though identity fraud of various kinds and for various reasons is a phenomenon that plagues our times as well (Reeves, 2013; Comaroff and Comaroff, 2016; Le Courant, 2019). The development of biomedical techniques to read the body in ever more detailed ways, such as facial recognition (Møhl, 2020), is to a large extent about developing strategies against such identity fraud and controlling mobility across state borders (e.g. Grünerberg *et al.*, 2020).

The gradual emergence of the nation-state-based international system, and the concomitant passport regime, has tied the identification of individuals to projects of governance undertaken by the modern state (Caplan and Torpey, 2001; Torpey, 2018). As Torpey (2018: 5–25) claims, the monopoly of legitimate identity documents has become one of the key characteristics of the modern state. Moreover, many states constantly gather knowledge about the citizens and other residents within their territory, ranging from medical records to taxation rates and criminal records. Consequently, we live in a world where modern nation-states seek to fix their citizens and other residents in a matrix of knowledge. In this book, I will try to make sense of the fact that some of the missing or disappeared, such as undocumented migrants, seem to fall outside such projects of 'knowing'. To be more precise, while alive and on the move, undocumented migrants are subjected to constant monitoring by technologies that trace their whereabouts, seek to fix their identities and do not allow them to enter the Global North; but when they die, they are rarely identified, and they slip through practices of knowing.

The identification of dead bodies is often much more challenging than that of a living person. Many of those who go missing from their loved ones turn up as unidentified bodies in mass graves or along migratory routes, and ascertaining their identities is often truly challenging. In practices of identifying individuals, we have moved astonishingly far from what was described by Zemon Davies. We live in an era that is dominated by what Ferrándiz and Robben (2015b: 6) call 'corpocentric practices': fingerprinting, DNA-based methodologies and 'osteobiographic methods', that is, reading information from the teeth and bones.

A similar argument is put forward by Élisabeth Anstett and her colleagues; in a recent large European research project, 'Corpses of Mass Violence and Genocide',[23] the team analysed, in historically and geographically varied contexts, practices of dealing with unidentified human remains (Anstett and Dreyfus, 2014a; Anstett and Dreyfus, 2015). One of the outcomes of the project has been the argument that the emergence of new technologies of identification of the dead has given rise to a 'forensic turn', that is, the expectation that exhumations and scientifically grounded identification are the default method of dealing with unidentified human remains (Anstett and Dreyfus, 2015; see also Moon, 2012). This resonates with Robben and Ferrándiz's claim that exhumations that attract a lot of public attention create 'new globalizing tidemarks' (2015b: 2) and thus affect the ways in which we understand disappearances and the unidentified dead, as well as the proper ways with which to deal with them.

Claire Moon (2012) argues that the 'forensic turn' is linked to several global trends, including the rise of human rights legislation since the end of the Second World War, the professionalisation of forensic anthropology and the institutionalisation of the application of scientific methods in human rights work. Forensic anthropology as a practice of identifying bodies and remains has its roots in the identification of the war dead after the Second World War and the Korean war but, later on, it became intertwined with humanitarian and human rights issues. One of the culmination points of this development was the publication of the Minnesota protocol in 1989, a handbook for the investigation of extra-legal, arbitrary and summary executions.[24] I will discuss these developments more closely in Chapter 4.

Interestingly, the rights of the dead and the treatment of human remains have also been discussed in other arenas. There is an ongoing debate about the right place for and the proper treatment of the bones, skulls and soft-tissue remains of Indigenous people and other colonial subjects that were collected for research purposes and transferred to museums in Europe, North America and colonial centres elsewhere. Some of these remains have been repatriated to their communities of origin and reburied in line with local traditions, while the fate of others is still being debated (Fforde, 2013).

Remembering and commemorating the disappeared

In all human communities, there are established ways of remembering and commemorating the dead. When somebody disappears, these established practices become disturbed. In some places, in certain historical moments, practices of commemorating the missing have emerged. Again, rather than trying to address the existing multiplicity of ways of remembering the disappeared in different times and places, I will make some observations on practices and developments.

There is a long history of soldiers disappearing on the battleground (the so-called 'missing in action'), and publicly memorialising such disappearances is an important landmark in the politics of memory around the missing. In Europe, the First World War was a significant moment in developing memorialisation practices; during the war, large-scale disappearance became a painful European reality. However, unlike in many other cases of large-scale disappearance, the Great War provided an understandable and even respectable framework for understanding the disappearance of a loved one, even though mourning without a body or a proper funeral was certainly painful and ambiguous for families in many ways. The war gave rise to the practice of remembering the Unknown Soldier, that is, publicly memorialising in respectful ways soldiers who disappear in battle. The national ceremonies commemorating the disappeared soldiers and the monumentalisation of the battleground of the Somme were landmarks in this development (Dyer, 1994).

In his encyclopaedic treatise *The Work of the Dead: A Cultural History of Mortal Remains* (2015), the historian Thomas Laqueur places practices of remembrance in a deep historical frame. He claims that we live in a time obsessed by the names of individuals – and names need to be commemorated beyond death. Laqueur maintains that humans have been on a historical journey that has taken us 'from a world of largely unmarked graves to one in which hopelessly disembodied names – and even more, bodies bereft of names – are unbearable' (2015: 13). In European and North American burial practices, engraving the name of the dead person on the gravestone has become important in commemorating the dead, and the practice has been borrowed by many memorial sites that commemorate the disappeared, including the memorial stone in Potočari, Bosnia, which lists all of the more than eight thousand names of those who went missing in Srebrenica in July 1995. The victims of Srebrenica and the ways of commemorating them will be further discussed in Chapters 1 and 4, and memorialising the disappeared more generally will be covered in Chapter 5.

Laqueur's work, while both encompassing and convincing, remains to some extent Euro-North-American-centric. There are places and cultural contexts in which it is common to bury people without putting names on the graves. This does not mean, however, that the dead are nameless – on the contrary, these are often family graves managed by kin groups, and the families know exactly who is buried in them. However, when people are buried far away from their communities in nameless graves – such as the unidentified migrant bodies in Tunisia described by Zagaria – the connection between the body and the memorialising practices is severed (for both points, see Zagaria, 2020).

There are also places where commemorating the dead and the disappeared does not seek to name and individuate the victims but rather to commemorate a category of victims. In Cambodia, for example, memorials to the mass atrocities display nameless bones and skulls of victims, making visible the scale of the brutality and commemorating the victims as a group or category rather than as individuals with names. These practices have given rise to disputes over the ownership of victims' bodies (e.g. Lesley, 2015). Museums and memorials will be discussed in more detail in Chapter 5.

While official monuments reflect the degree to which the state recognises certain disappeared, remembering the missing and disappeared is not restricted to such official sites: diverse memory practices flourish in their shadows. Argentina is an example of a society where practices of remembering the disappeared have multiplied, creating cultural sites that continuously address the history of disappearance in the country. There are museums, memorial parks and organisations, as well as a flourishing production of memoirs and artwork around them (Taylor, 1997; Fortuny, 2014; Gatti, 2014; Blejmar, 2016). This is what Gabriel Gatti has called 'the field of the disappeared' (Gatti, 2014). And beyond such publicly shared practices, many family members and others close to the disappeared create their own private, idiosyncratic ways of remembering, some of which I will address in Chapter 5.

From the anthropology of death to anthropology of disappearance and beyond: understanding human disappearances and reappearances in social sciences and humanities

Although death is always a possibility when somebody goes missing, not all missing persons are dead. With 'individual' disappearances in the Global North, most people are found within twenty-four hours of their relatives reporting them missing, and most are found alive (Shalev Greene and Alys, 2017). In addition, people reported as missing or feared dead by their relatives in migratory contexts or under oppressive governments sometimes return alive. Nevertheless, the longer the inexplicable absence lasts, the greater the fear among those left behind that the disappeared person is dead. Death as a possibility lingers whenever somebody goes missing, and this ghostly uncertainty feeds into the power that disappearances have as a psychological, social, political and cultural force that makes things happen at different levels, ranging from emotional reactions to taking action by organising the search and formulating political demands to find out the fate of the disappeared. Thus, the anthropology of death, together with larger social-scientific discussions of the topic, provides a useful frame within which to think about disappearances. Disappearances are always potential deaths and, as such, they evoke the cultural frames for encountering death and dealing with it.

Death, burial and culture

There is a rich anthropological literature on death. The classic texts address issues such as cultural variation in conceptions of death, and cosmological understandings of and ritual practices around death. While such questions have remained meaningful for modern scholars, questions of power and governance have emerged as central themes in the more recent literature on anthropology of death.[25] Who has power over life and death in various societal configurations? Who manages death and dead bodies? (Mbembe, 2003; Stepputat, 2014; Ferrándiz and Robben, 2015a; Rojas-Perez, 2017).

In all cultural contexts, there are established, culturally sanctioned ways of marking the transition from life to death – mortuary rituals, burial practices and ways of remembering and commemorating. Such practices are also connected to cosmological understandings of human life, the afterlife and a human being's place in the universe, and they frame cultural understandings of 'good death' and 'proper burial' (Metcalf and Huntington, 1991; Robben, 2004a; Forde and Hume, 2018; Kent and Garça Fedjó, 2020). When a person goes missing and is suspected to be dead, there is often a lingering agony connected with the thought that the death is a 'bad death' and that the person has not been properly buried (e.g. de León, 2015).

Many anthropologists, starting with classics such as Hertz (1960), suggest that death should be conceptualised as a process rather than as a single event. This process-like understanding points to many aspects. First, biologically, death is a process (Lock, 2002),[26] and in many cultural contexts where secondary burial is practised, this biological feature is closely connected with a cosmological understanding of the gradual journey of the soul or spirit to the afterlife. Moreover, the death of a person launches a social process whereby the survivors need to renegotiate their relationships to the deceased, to one another and to their new changed statuses (such as those of widow or orphan). Arnold van Gennep, in his famous essay on rites of passage, pointed out that not only the deceased but also the close kin go through a process of transformation (van Gennep, 2004 [1909]). Finally, in religious or cosmological terms, death is a process of transformation, from a living member of the community to a dead person, an ancestor or a spirit. However, when somebody goes missing, this process-like character of death becomes exaggerated, or painfully extended, often to the extent of becoming unbearable. In cultural contexts in which the dead have a prominent place in the community as ancestors or spirits, the ontological status of the missing person is unclear, and needs to be negotiated one way or another.

Mortuary rites (Huntington and Metcalf, 1991), like other rites of passage, transfer the individual from one social status to another, in this case from the category of the living to that of the dead. Arnold van Gennep (2004 [1909]) established the well-known approach to rites of passage, claiming that they all share a tripartite structure: separation, a transition or liminal stage, and incorporation. People who go missing for a long period of time do not go through this transitory process as expected, even if there are good grounds to assume that they are dead. They stay in between, in limbo, in a deeply problematic liminal space. However, van Gennep points out that the liminality of the transition period concerns not only the dead person but also their relatives and others close to them: the social position of both the kin left behind and the dead person changes, and both these changes need to be addressed (Van Gennep, 2004: 213). Mourning is the culturally marked period of transition for the living. According to van Gennep, 'during mourning, the living mourners and the deceased constitute a special group, situated between the world of the living and the world of the dead'

(Van Gennep, 2004: 214).[27] When a presumably dead person is missing, the family members' transitory, liminal phase is prolonged indefinitely as well. Although the family members are, in this sense, also liminal personae for as long as their loved one remains missing and the burial is not properly carried out, they and the communities of the missing sometimes develop unconventional ways to resolve the liminality.

However, as Hester Parr, Olivia Stevenson and Penny Woolnough (2016) argue, it is not only death that should be understood as a process; becoming a missing or disappeared person is also one. 'We might imagine a series of scenes as an absence unfolds', they suggest (Parr, Stevenson and Woolnough, 2016: 68). Recognising the absence of a person, becoming worried, reporting the absent person as missing and sharing the worry within the community are examples of such 'scenes'. These 'scenes of absence', however, are very different in different contexts; for instance, reporting a person missing in present-day Finland is quite different from what it was in the Argentina of the 1980s or the Bosnia-Herzegovina of the 1990s – or from what it is to report an undocumented migrant missing in today's Spain or Morocco.

Anthropological literature on death and death rites points to the vast variety of what we can call 'ontologies of the afterlife'. The ways in which people understand the condition of the deceased person, as well as the cosmological relationship between the living and the dead, also affect the experience of living with the uncertainty of a missing family member or loved one. As Jean Langford, among others, argues, Southeast Asian cosmologies rely on a continuing sociality between the living and the dead, and the spirits of the dead are understood to literally and tangibly receive the material care given to the body. Thus, not being able to materially look after the body disturbs this important sociality (Langford, 2009; 2013). This agony of not being able to care for the missing dead body characterises the experience of many families of the missing, not only those of Southeast Asian origin.

When the liminal phase continues for a long time, the question arises as to whether it is still useful to define it as liminality – for example, in Bosnia, some people have been looking for their missing family members for more than twenty years now. In such cases, liminality seems to lose its characteristics as a transitory phase and to turn into a chronic condition (Vigh, 2008). However, I insist that seeing the missing as not-properly-buried liminal personae helps us to understand the urge to find closure in the face of the pressing absence of the missing, on both a personal and a symbolic level. Disappearances may become chronic in another sense as well: in some places, at certain times, so many people disappear that disappearances are not seen as rare or totally unexpected, and they may even become 'normal' in a sense (cf. Vigh, 2008, on different ways of understanding normalcy). However, even if disappearances thus become ubiquitous and chronic in this sense, in most cases they are not seen as acceptable and 'normal' in a moral sense. Especially when disappearances are the outcome of violent political projects that purposefully target individuals, the families of the missing do not accept the absence of their loved ones even when they see their neighbours facing the same horror – both in Argentina in the 1980s and Bosnia in the 1990s, family members were disgusted by the violence of disappearances even though they saw them taking place all around them. In contrast, some maritime communities, where a significant number of people regularly die at sea and the bodies are not always retrieved for funerals, have developed rituals of mourning in the absence of a body and of accepting disappearance at sea as part of 'the normal' (e.g. Stewart, 2011). This reminds us again that disappearances need to be contextualised in order to be understood in their full social and cultural significance.

Necropolitics and the governance of death

Researching disappearances inevitably activates necropolitical questions about the management of death and dead bodies. Who exercises power over life and death? Who manages deaths and dead bodies in various contexts, including those where the bodies are found unidentified, far away from their families and communities?

The very term 'necropolitics' is understood differently by different writers. In his much-cited article, Achille Mbembe understands it as the 'subjugation of life to the power of death' (2003: 39). Inspired by Foucault's notion of biopower, he claims that 'the ultimate expression of sovereignty resides, to a large degree, in the power and the capacity to dictate who may live and who must die' (Mbembe, 2003: 11). Mbembe's notion of necropolitics is especially fruitful when seeking to make sense of enforced disappearances. He probes the nature of sovereignty in various contexts by asking, 'Under what practical conditions is the right to kill, to allow to live, or to expose to death exercised? Who is the subject of this right?' (Mbembe, 2003: 12). In Chapter 1, I will analyse more closely 'the practical conditions' under which the right to kill is exercised in two places, the Argentina of the 1970s and 1980s, and the Bosnia-Herzegovina of the 1990s. Moreover, Mbembe differentiates between actual killing and 'exposure to death' as acts of exercising sovereign power. I will pay close attention to this difference in my reading of various contexts of disappearance.

Other scholars, however, have understood necropolitics a little differently. They argue that not only the power to decide over life and death, but also the governance of the transition from life to death and the microscopic everydayness of death and the actions around it, are indications of aspirations to sovereignty.

Francisco Ferrándiz and Antonius Robben (2015b) define necropolitics as the analysis of how dead bodies are produced and managed, and of what kinds of political contestation over the management of bodies and mortal remains take place in various contexts. Such an approach resonates with Finn Stepputat's theorising on the governance of death. He claims that the governance of the transition from life to death is profoundly tied to claims of political power and sovereignty (Stepputat, 2014). This idea raises a whole set of questions that are relevant in the context of this book. Who invests in searching for the disappeared and identifying the unidentified dead in various contexts? To what kinds of political project are these efforts connected? These aspects will be discussed in Chapter 4.

Adam Rosenblatt (2015) argues that investment in search and identification can be seen as a form of care, thus expanding the scope of necropolitical practices from the violent to the caring. Departing from the work of Mbembe, Stepputat and Rosenblatt, I will argue that necropolitical power may be used in either a violent and destructive mode or a caring mode; the exposure of people to violent death is a necropolitical exercise of power in Mbembe's sense, while returning the located and identified dead bodies of the disappeared to their families for respectful burial may be read as a caring necropolitical trajectory (Rosenblatt, 2015; also M'charek and Casartelli, 2019; Reineke, 2022). In Chapters 4 and 5, which address reappearances, I will develop this idea of a caring mode of necropolitics.

Towards the anthropology of disappearance, or understanding disappearances conceptually

I have argued elsewhere, together with Gerhild Perl, that we need to develop an anthropological understanding of disappearance as a phenomenon that is socially, politically and culturally embedded, and foregrounds the deep relationality of disappeared persons (Huttunen and Perl, 2023). This book develops that argument further. Throughout the book, I explore human disappearance as a social and cultural force that affects cultural meaning-making, intimate relations, community life and practices of governance. It is a phenomenon characterised by liminality and ambiguity, and it points to the porousness of the line between life and death and, as such, can be harnessed by various political projects and used in aspirations of power. An anthropology of disappearance, as I understand it, develops the theoretical understanding of the phenomena categorised as disappearances, while simultaneously producing a sensitive, ethnographically contextualised understanding of their varying effects at different times and in different places.

In her insightful treatise on the connection between dead bodies and the political in post-socialist Eastern Europe, Katherine Verdery (1999) argues that dead bodies in their materiality have enormous power to re-animate the political, as they connect us with notions of kinship, time and space, and historical continuities and disruptions. When people disappear and the bodies are not there, the power of death, or potential death, takes different forms and gives rise to different practices. Conceptual and theoretical analysis of disappearance is an exploration of this.

While writing this book, I have found my colleague Ville Laakkonen's term 'disappearability' (Laakkonen, 2022) very useful or 'good to think with'. The term taps into Nicholas De Genova's discussion on 'deportability' (De Genova, 2002); Laakkonen argues that disappearability is a structural condition that makes some people more vulnerable to being disappeared by dint of their being less protected – or often totally unprotected – by legal statuses, racialised hierarchies and prevailing political projects. Probing the disappearability of different people at different times in different places runs through this book: people are not equal in this sense, as some are more disappearable than others, but nobody is definitely 'non-disappearable'.

I build my anthropological take on disappearances on an analysis of both the political and the intimate dimensions of the phenomenon. Taking inspiration from Paul Sant Cassia's work on disappearances in Cyprus (2005), I place the state and the kin – or state, family and community – at the core of the analysis. Throughout the chapters, I explore both the ways in which disappearances (and reappearances) are related to state power, and the ways in which they create 'disturbed intimacies' (Huttunen and Perl, 2023) in the private lives of those left behind. The spiritual and cosmological dimensions are also touched on, and these certainly deserve more focused work in the future.

The anthropology of disappearance – or the social-scientific approach to human disappearance more generally – that I suggest in this book looks in two directions. First, it takes an analytical stance towards the production of disappearances; I suggest that it is important to analyse the ways in which different political projects make some people disappear, or expose them to the unprotected zone of 'disappearability'. Secondly, my approach foregrounds the reappearances of the missing; in other words, it analyses the different concrete and symbolic ways in which the disappeared reappear, the contexts of the appearances ranging from the private realm and intimate practices to public and political projects of searching for, identifying and commemorating the missing and disappeared. Even though I suggest a unifying theoretical approach, convincing analysis of disappearance needs to be ethnographic in tone, sensitive to changing cultural, social and political contexts.

I found Gabriel Gatti's conceptualisations very useful when shaping this frame. Gatti suggests (2014: 59–64) that at the heart of disappearance is the separation of bodies and names or bodies and identities. Disappearance produces names and identities without bodies, and bodies without identities and names. At the same time, the disappeared are cut off from their social ties, from their families, kin and communities. Forensic anthropology or, more widely, search and identification efforts, seek to re-establish these connections. If disappearance is conceptualised as a 'de-civilising' process (Gatti, 2014: 28) that cuts individuals off from their social and cultural worlds, then forensics is a 're-civilising project' that seeks to re-embed bodies or remains of the disappeared in their social and cultural connections. Chapters 1, 2 and 3 of this book explore ways in which people become severed from their social and cultural worlds by disappearing, while Chapters 4 and 5 map various ways to bring the disappeared back into the social and cultural sphere.

There are people, both scholars and activists, who believe that addressing 'everyday' disappearances within the same frame as enforced disappearance is insulting and disrespectful towards the victims of the latter. I understand this viewpoint, even though I do not agree with it. My argument in this book is not that all disappearances are similar – they certainly are not. I contend that we can gain valuable insight into the nature of disappearance when taking a wider perspective and looking at different cases in relation to each other. Moreover, it is sometimes hard to say into which category of disappearance an individual case falls. Sometimes families left behind do not know whether the absent member is a victim of crime or of an accident, or whether they have, in fact, chosen to leave (cf. Dean, 2015: 23–6). Such ambiguity is exactly what makes disappearances so excruciating for those left behind, and it simultaneously makes them a very powerful and cruel strategy in the hands of oppressive power. My aim is to understand both the similarities and differences between various kinds of disappearance, and to show respect for all the disappeared, and all the families and communities affected.

The structure of the book

This book is structured around disappearances and reappearances, thus following my argument that the disappearance of a person almost always gives rise to a reappearance, in one form or another. Chapters 1, 2 and 3 concentrate on disappearances, and Chapters 4 and 5 on reappearances.

Chapter 1 focuses on enforced disappearance as an intentional strategy to gain power. In this chapter, I draw on my own empirical work among

Bosnians, and juxtapose disappearances in Bosnia in the 1990s with those in the Argentina of the 1970s and 1980s. Discussing the Argentina of those decades as an example of a refined machinery of terror that revolved around disappearances and comparing it with disappearances in Bosnia during the armed conflict allows me to sketch the contours of enforced disappearance as a political strategy in different contexts. Examples from other contexts are also brought in to produce a more nuanced understanding of the practice. The chapter spells out the specificities of enforced disappearance as a tool of terror and as a specific 'necropolitical' (Mbembe, 2003) strategy to gain power. It goes on to argue that the specificity of enforced disappearance as a strategy is a product of the practice of simultaneously hiding both the act of killing and the fate of the victims, thus creating a space of deep ambiguity and insecurity that affects the community and disturbs its political life.

Chapter 2 looks at disappearances in migratory contexts, especially along so-called irregular routes and among undocumented migrants. The elusiveness of this category is highlighted by discussing the ways in which the numbers of missing migrants are produced, and migrant 'disappearability' is framed within the tightening border regimes between the Global North and the Global South. The chapter argues that migrant disappearances often result from migrants being exposed to dangerous circumstances rather than from their being disappeared by an individuating 'disappearing agent' – as in the previous chapter – and the relationship between disappearing migrants, state power and international governance of migration is discussed. From these more structural frames, the chapter proceeds to consider the voids left by migrant disappearances, and also the 'disturbed intimacies' (Huttunen and Perl, 2023) and painful ambiguities among the families left behind.

Chapter 3 takes a further turn and looks at disappearances that are often regarded as singular, individual, apolitical, everyday and unconnected, with a focus on the Global North. What does it mean for families to live with the disappearance of a loved one in democracies of the Global North? How does the state in these contexts recognise its missing citizens and search for them? What similarities and differences emerge when these individual disappearances are compared with enforced disappearances under dictatorial states, or with migrant disappearances under vulnerable conditions? The chapter analyses both the void encountered by the families left behind and the ways in which the state recognises these missing persons. Finally, in order to understand the relationship between the state and the missing individual, it brings into focus the police's work in finding such individuals, thus marking the start of the book's discussion of reappearances.

Chapters 4 and 5 turn their full attention to reappearances. In Chapter 4, the focus is on the reappearance of the missing, either alive or as dead bodies or mortal remains, and on the political projects that seek to make the missing reappear. The chapter builds its argument on a juxtaposition of the book's three key sites of Argentina, Bosnia and the Mediterranean, and the active search projects taking place there: the Argentinian civil rights movements, the international community's investment in search and identification in Bosnia and the fragmented search and identification scene in the Mediterranean. Again, examples from other contexts are brought in to diversify the understanding of these practices. In each case, both the practical and political challenges of the search for the missing and the identification of the dead are discussed. The activities of different actors, ranging from individuals and families to states and organisations of various sizes, are introduced in order to build a nuanced understanding of the projects of making the disappeared reappear. Finally, the search for the missing and their identification and reburial are conceptualised as a caring mode of necropolitics.

Chapter 5 argues that if the missing are not found either dead or alive, they return in more symbolic forms: they are present as photographs, memories, memorials and political discourses, and sometimes they return in dreams, or as ghosts that haunt those left behind. The chapter discusses both the private practices of family members of the disappeared and projects focused on making the disappeared visible in public. Photographs of the missing reappear in public spaces, in demonstrations and political protests demanding accountability, while in the private space, the relationship with such photographs is more complex, as family members negotiate between ways of remembering and of keeping the absent present. Museums and memorials, as well as art and media spectacles, make those still missing present in the public and political realm while simultaneously building an interpretation around disappearances. Finally, many family members and others close to the disappeared report ghost-like reappearances.

The final chapter ties together the discussions and observations presented in the previous ones. It returns to the contours of the book's central argument, that of the 'impossibility of disappearance', or the idea that the disappeared tend to reappear in either concrete or symbolic forms. Moreover, the chapter reiterates the idea of developing the anthropology of disappearance as a scholarly endeavour.

Notes

1 'Horror' as a term has emerged in scholarly literature during the last decade, see e.g. Debrix (2017); also Auchter (2019). The word is often used in contexts that address violated and severed bodies that are on display, in one way or

another. Human disappearances are often, especially in armed conflicts and under totalitarian governments, marked by extreme forms of violence, even though the bodies are hidden from public sight. In such contexts, rumours and imagined scenes that circulate among the families and communities left behind are full of horrific images of tortured bodies, as will be discussed in this book. This is why I found the words 'pain and sorrow' to be too mild in describing the encounters with disappearances in many contexts, and I chose instead to talk about the 'horror' of the situation.

2 'Closure' is a debated notion in relation to human disappearances. When I suggest that human disappearances are geared towards closure, I do not mean that finding the missing person brings an end to the process, or that only 'successful mourning' (see note 27) enables the families of the missing to continue with their lives. Finding the bodies or mortal remains of the missing almost invariably raises questions of accountability, and individuals and communities affected by disappearances are creative in finding ways of dealing with the absence. 'Closure', I argue, should be seen as the next step in the process of making sense of the absence and culturally regulating transitions, rather than as the end point.

3 The official name of the state is *Federacija Bosne y Hercegovine* – in English most often Bosnia-Herzegovina. For the sake of fluency, I often use the shortened form 'Bosnia' when referring to this state or to the territory.

4 Ville Laakkonen, Saila Kivilahti, Anna Matyska, Mari Korpela and Dimitri Ollikainen are the colleagues working with me on the project titled 'Governance and Grieving: Disappearing Migrants and Emerging Politics' (DiMig, see Governance and Grieving: Disappearing Migrants and Emergent Politics, Tampere universities) (https://www.tuni.fi/en/research/governance-and-grieving-disappearing-migrants-and-emergent-politics) (accessed 14 February 2024).

5 Following Mary Douglas, I suggest here that categorisation is at the core of all human meaning-making. However, many writers posit that this tendency to categorise and fix is expanded and intensified by projects of modernity, see for example Gatti (2014: 15–31).

6 The UN Declaration on the Protection of All Persons from Enforced Disappearances was issued in 1992, and was followed by the Inter-American Convention on Forced Disappearance of Persons in 1994, issued by the Organization of American States. The International Criminal Court's 1998 Rome Statute established disappearance as a crime against humanity, when committed as part of a widespread and systematic attack on a civilian population. Finally, the International Convention for the Protection of All Persons from Enforced Disappearances was adopted by the UN General Assembly in December 2006.

7 Of course, sometimes there is a need to find those responsible for accidents but the putative crime in such cases is not 'enforced disappearance'. The unidentified missing are rather seen as unintended victims of, for instance, a failure of traffic safety.

8 Restoring family links, ICRC (https://www.icrc.org/en/what-we-do/restoring-family-links) (accessed 14 February 2024).
9 https://www.icmp.int/the-missing/who-are-the-missing/ (accessed 14 February 2024).
10 There are, of course, 'individual disappearances' in the Global South as well. The ways in which the state recognises these disappearances and the ways in which the local police work with them vary enormously, and mapping this landscape would be an interesting task, indicative as it is of the diverse relationship between state and people across the globe. Such an exercise is, however, beyond the scope of this book.
11 www.familiesofthemissing.org/the-missing/ (accessed 14 February 2024).
12 In Finland, the soldiers who went missing during the war are usually simply called 'the fallen' (*kaatuneet* in Finnish), a term that does not differentiate between those returned to their families and those still missing. Sometimes they are talked about as 'those who went missing during the war', but no specific term for the group exists. I will briefly discuss this group and its reappearance in Chapter 5.
13 For disappearances in Pakistan, see https://coioed.pk/; in Turkey, see Turkey – A Comparative Analysis of Enforced Disappearances and the Missing in Middle East, North Africa and Caucasus (https://enforceddisappearances.dealingwiththepast.org/turkey/) (both accessed 14 February 2024).
14 ICMP Where we work (https://www.icmp.int/where-we-work/) (accessed 4 February 2024).
15 Where we work, ICRC (https://www.icrc.org/en/where-we-work) (accessed 4 February 2024).
16 https://missingmigrants.iom.int/data (accessed 4 February 2024).
17 These figures are from 4 February 2024.
18 I had planned to do fieldwork on the practices of addressing disappearances in Argentina in the spring of 2020 but, like so many other plans, this one was scuppered by the COVID-19 pandemic.
19 ICMP The Missing (https://www.icmp.int/the-missing/) (accessed 4 February 2024).
20 tps://ijrcenter.org/un-special-procedures/working-group-on-enforced-or-involuntary-disappearances/ (accessed 14 February 2024).
21 Such displays were practised by some leaders right up to modern times, e.g. in Argentina (see Robben, 2004b). Interestingly, some groups pursuing power in our times, such as ISIS and certain criminal organisations (see e.g. Nyberg Sørensen, 2014), use tactics reminiscent of the Foucauldian '*ancien régime*': they carry out public executions, disseminate them on social media and claim the murders in their names. However, they do not seek to be recognised among the legitimate states in the present-day international order, nor do they seek the approval of the so-called international community; rather, they rely on the deep frustrations and disappointments of those who are marginalised by that very same community.
22 See Wylie, Oppenheimer and Crossland (2020) for the intertwined history of the ICRC and the International Red Cross and Red Crescent Movement.

23 Corpses of mass violence and genocide, A research program funded by the ERC (https://corpses.hypotheses.org/) (accessed 14 February 2024).
24 MinnesotaProtocol.pdf (https://www.ohchr.org/sites/default/files/Documents/Publications/MinnesotaProtocol.pdf) (accessed 14 February 2024).
25 Reference to a good selection of both classic texts and more recent scholarship is found in Robben (2004a).
26 Margaret Lock (2002) argues that, within the framework of Western medicine, biological death is a process. Yet within the Western imagination, there is a need to identify the exact moment of somebody's death, and for a long time the social convention has been that when the heart stops beating, the person is regarded as dead. However, organ transplantation practice has made it necessary to define another kind of death, i.e. brain death. Lock's analysis interestingly highlights the Western tendency to think about death as an event that can be pinned down to a certain moment, rather than as a gradual process.
27 Van Gennep conceptualises mourning as a culturally regulated ritual practice rather than as a psychological state. It is also possible to apply this idea to a psychological framework and to claim that mourning ties the mourner emotionally to the dead person, creating a liminal state. Only 'successful' mourning that is brought to an end frees the mourner from the liminality of mourning and opens up the possibility of new relationships, and a new take on life without the deceased person. On the psychology of 'ambiguous loss', see Boss (2007). For an anthropological take on trauma and mourning, see Robben (2018).

1

Enforced disappearance: politics of terror and paralysing uncertainties

I saw my husband for the last time on 24 April 1992. That was the time when the soldiers invaded our town. We were hiding in the woods, but we came back to the house to fetch some food that we still had there. Then, suddenly, the soldiers came to our house. They took us, me and my daughters, to a bus waiting nearby, and they kept my husband. Later we drove past our house. I could see my husband there, in the courtyard, between two soldiers. After that, nothing. I do not know what has happened to him. I never heard of him again.

(Sabiha, a Bosniak woman, born in 1965 in Prijedor, Bosnia-Herzegovina)

I begin my exploration of enforced disappearance as a violent political strategy with this interview excerpt from 2013. Sabiha, a Bosniak woman, was in her late forties at the time and had been living in Finland as a refugee for nearly twenty years. The interview took place twenty-one years after the disappearance of her husband, who went missing during the 1992–95 Bosnian war and the campaign of ethnic cleansing that swept across northern and eastern Bosnia during those years. Since her husband's disappearance, the painful uncertainty of not knowing what happened to him has haunted Sabiha's life.

Several characteristics of the event described in the short quote above point to its being the crime of enforced disappearance as defined in the 2006 United Nations convention:

> For the purposes of this Convention, 'enforced disappearance' is considered to be the arrest, detention, abduction or any other form of deprivation of liberty by the agents of the State or by persons or groups of persons acting with the authorization, support or acquiescence of the State, followed by a refusal to acknowledge the deprivation of liberty or by concealment of the fate or whereabouts of the disappeared person, which place such a person outside the protection of the law.
>
> *(International Convention for the Protection of All Persons from Enforced Disappearance, 2006)*

The connections between the circumstances of Sabiha's husband's disappearance and the definition in the convention are clear. First, as Sabiha describes, her husband was forcefully arrested by soldiers connected with the state power – albeit a seriously contested state power in the context of the armed conflict that ensued in Bosnia after the dissolution of Yugoslavia and the declaration of independence in the former federal state. Secondly, the arrest was followed by a constant refusal to acknowledge that the event had taken place and the continuous concealment of the whereabouts and fate of Sabiha's husband: despite numerous enquiries, she was never informed about what happened to him. The evidence of violence in the area that has been piling up since 1992 (e.g. Maass, 1996; Silber and Little, 1997; Wagner, 2008; Halilovich, 2013) suggests that most probably he was killed; large numbers of civilians were placed outside the protection of the law during the conflict, and it has emerged that most of them were killed and their bodies hidden. Despite the probability of Sabiha's husband's death, his ultimate fate remains painfully obscure.

Even though the above-mentioned convention was adopted by the UN General Assembly as recently as 2006, fourteen years after Sabiha's husband's disappearance, the international legal framework on which it is based had already been in the making for several decades, as discussed in the introduction to this volume. In this chapter, I will look at the practice of enforced disappearance in places where it has been applied as a conscious political strategy by, or with the acquiescence of, the government, or by those aspiring to state power. I will spell out the specificities of using enforced disappearance as a tool of terror, compared with openly killing those demarcated as enemies. I read enforced disappearance as a specific necropolitical strategy (Mbembe, 2003): a brutal strategy of aspiring to sovereignty through the exercise of the power to take life. However, I will expand on Mbembe's conception and argue, as have several other authors (Robben, 2005; Gatti, 2014), that the specificity of enforced disappearance as a strategy is the product of the practice of taking lives and simultaneously hiding both the act of killing and the fate of the victims, thus creating a space of deep ambiguity and uncertainty that affects those left behind. Moreover, the prevalence of uncertainty creates an atmosphere of fear and insecurity that disturbs political life.

My own empirical research is anchored in the Bosnian context but, before discussing this more closely, I will start by looking at Argentina, as the South American experience has so powerfully affected the ways in which we understand enforced disappearance today. The abundance of research literature on Argentina also enables me to draw the contours of the strategy of enforced disappearance. I will then introduce the Bosnian context and my own empirical material, looking at the similarities and differences between the two contexts, and follow this with a number of observations on disappearances in other places, and finally some concluding remarks on the specificity of enforced disappearance as a strategy.

In this chapter, I mostly use the term 'disappeared' when referring to the victims of the political projects described – the projects being easily recognised as those referred to in the legal framework on enforced disappearance. However, in Bosnia, the term that has been consistently used by the key actors in the area is 'missing persons' – first by the Red Cross, and later by the ICMP. The humanitarian roots of the Red Cross and the unclear situation in Bosnia when the ICMP was established have probably affected their choice of terminology. Despite this, however, the ICMP has participated in the process of demanding accountability for the disappearances and pointing to the responsibility of the wartime leadership, as will be discussed in Chapter 4.

Argentina: refined machinery of terror

The machinery of death and disappearance that was deployed by the military government in Argentina between 1976 and 1983 is perhaps one of the most refined examples of the particular technique of terror described in the international legal framework on enforced disappearance. This fact should not, however, come as a surprise, as the experiences in Latin America's Southern Cone are what initiated the process of establishing the norms of the international legal framework on enforced disappearance, and, indeed, of defining it as a crime in its own right. The way in which the strategy was applied in South America formed the very basis of certain legal definitions, as discussed in the introduction.

The Argentinian military government developed enforced disappearance into a full-blown strategy of terror, with military-style organisation, industrial efficacy and bureaucratically refined procedures. The strategy, however, did not emerge in a vacuum. Anthony Robben claims that enforced disappearance as a political strategy has a history in Argentina that predates the military rule (Robben, 2005: 263–4), but its application in earlier times was never as systematic or fully strategised as under the military junta of the 1970s and 1980s.

The junta's military coup in 1976 was preceded by a period of political unrest and an upsurge of left-wing and Peronist political movements. The junta justified its drastic political moves by claiming that there was a need to bring peace to the country and counter the leftist, Marxist movements. This period is often called 'the dirty war', as the country descended into warlike conditions: many civil rights were suspended, and arbitrary abductions, torture and killings became the modus operandi. Robben argues, however, that the period is best described as 'a war of cultures', as what was at play was the violent imposition of certain cultural frames and values, that is, a hierarchical understanding of a patriarchal and conservative-Christian social order in the face of liberal, leftist and secular ideas (Robben, 2005: 178–9). According to Robben, the junta wanted to govern the people's hearts and minds. 'The mind of the enemy ha[d] to be taken', as General Villegas claimed (Robben, 2005: 189), and enforced disappearance became a central strategy in this endeavour to colonise the minds of the citizens. As a consequence, approximately 30,000[1] people disappeared from their families, most of them brutally tortured and killed, and an atmosphere of fear and terror permeated society (Robben, 2005; Gatti, 2014).

'Subversive' was the key word used by the junta to define the enemy, and not only were activists and guerrilla combatants targeted but also a large group of 'ideologues and sympathisers'. The latter two categories were continuously expanded to include an ever-growing number of people ranging from teachers to artists and psychiatrists, from trade union activists to priests working with the poor. The circle of those defined as putative subversives was constantly enlarged throughout the years of military rule, creating a debilitating atmosphere of fear, insecurity and suspicion. Nobody knew for sure who might be targeted. The strategy was both individuating, in that it targeted named individuals, and collectivising, pulling large groups of putative victims into the sphere of fear (Robben, 2005: 185–8).

The actual enforced disappearances were carried out according to a plan. An effective, military-style strategy divided the country into five zones, each subsequently divided into sub-zones that were again split into areas and sub-areas. Each area was operated by a specific taskforce, under the command of the armed forces. The taskforces were responsible for the operations against those demarcated by the military as revolutionaries or enemies of the state; they would force their way into their homes, beat their families into submission, and blindfold and abduct the targeted individuals, taking them away in unmarked private cars. Although this was the tactic that was usually described by the families of the disappeared, some people were abducted when away from their homes, never to return. This strategy of invading homes was, in Robben's words, 'intensely private'; as the violence intruded on the private sphere of the home, it lethally shook the affected families' sense of safety and security and had an impact on Argentinian society as a whole. The strategy of enforced disappearance transgressed the vital demarcation line between public and private, and violated the realm of the private, the rooting space of the self in Argentinian culture (Robben, 2005: 208–10).

The 'modernity' of the politics of enforced disappearance was reflected in the orderly organisation of the raiding taskforces. The assault itself was divided into the raid and the search; the latter entailed the whole house being searched for weapons and other proof of subversive tendencies among the inhabitants, and in the process, the victims' personal property was thrown to the floor and damaged. Throughout the assault, the bureaucratic order was efficient: first, the police were informed about what was taking place so that they would not interfere and, afterwards, the details of the abducted person were recorded and sent to the zone commander, and then a detention card was drawn up indicating the 'degree of danger' they presented. Such bureaucratic orderliness is striking given the ultimate secrecy of the operation: none of this information was given to those outside the operational military force. Families who asked for information were told that none existed (Robben, 2005: 207–11).

The abducted were taken to special detention centres rather than to ordinary prisons, but the existence of these places was never acknowledged when families and friends came asking. The abducted were treated extremely inhumanely and violently, with torture and rape being the norm. They were absolutely excluded from the protection of the law; the 'state of exception' (Agamben, 2005) was complete. Many of the dead bodies of the victims were totally destroyed, either through incineration or by being dropped them into the ocean from aeroplanes (Robben, 2005: 268–70).

The strategies and conditions that prevailed during these years were revealed to the public after the fall of the junta in 1983. Some of the abducted survived the detention centres and were able to provide testimonies. The transitional government set up a commission to research the crimes committed by the junta, and the commission's report, *Nunca Más* (CONADEP, 1984), has been widely circulated. This report, together with several survivor testimonies and memoirs, has been extensively discussed in Argentinian society, bringing the brutality of the practices in these *chupaderos*, or detention centres, into the light of day (see Gatti, 2014; Blejmar, 2017).

In Mbembe's necropolitical terms, the Argentinian junta used its power over life and death ruthlessly. It directly ordered the killing of citizens it defined as 'subversives', even though the actual act of killing was to be conducted in secret. The government was the initiator of and the driving force behind these lethal politics. But killing the 'enemies' was not enough; the junta also tortured and humiliated the victims in countless ways. Moreover, it disappeared them; it amplified the horror of death by leaving families and communities in limbo, not knowing the fate of their loved ones. The state became an agent of terror and death and, simultaneously, by hiding the atrocities and denying access to knowledge, created a paralysing atmosphere of uncertainty.

Robben argues that there is no single, comprehensive explanation for the Argentinian Government's adoption of enforced disappearance as the prevailing method of seeking to establish power. Rather, he identifies nine different, somewhat intertwined, reasons or rationales: operational, judicial, political, symbolic, economic, historical, pedagogical, psychological and social (Robben, 2005: 278–81). Operationally, the disappearances instilled fear in guerrilla combatants and in others deemed 'subversives'. Judicially, the government destroyed the incriminating evidence – if there were no bodies, there was no evidence of the crimes, the reasoning goes. This judicial function backed up the political goal of misleading both domestic and 'world' opinion – the widespread condemnation of the open executions in Chile after Pinochet's military coup in 1973 was taken as a warning by the Argentinian junta.[2] Among the international community of states, the junta sought to maintain the facade of upholding the rule of law. Moreover, it wanted to affect the historical narrative that would be constructed and to prevent its political opponents from having a voice in this.

Symbolically, the destruction of corpses was aimed at preventing the victims from becoming martyrs. Moreover, denying them a proper burial excluded them from the social order and cultural sphere in a powerful way, disturbing the deep-rooted practices and understandings around death that existed in what is a predominantly Catholic country (Robben, 2005: 269–70). Pedagogically, the military was 're-educating' what it saw as the mistaken youth, as well as punishing, by disappearing their children, those parents who had not succeeded in raising 'proper' citizens. Psychologically, the abductions, the torture and the annihilation of the corpses gave the perpetrators a sense of victory and absolute control, while brutally forcing their power on the bodies of the victims and the targeted families. Socially, the disappearances created a culture of fear that repressed opposition and political activism – but only to an extent. As is well known, the Argentinian association of mothers and grandmothers became a powerful oppositional movement that has been emulated in other places affected by violent politics. This will be discussed further in Chapter 4.

In reference to Stepputat's (2014) argument that it is not only the necropolitical power of making decisions about life and death but also the management of death and dead bodies that is important in the claiming of sovereignty, I point to the management of the bodies of the disappeared as an indicator of the thoroughly violent character of the Argentinian military regime. The denial of a proper burial, as well as the total annihilation of many bodies, represents an attempt to materially and symbolically wipe the victims from the social and cultural spheres, to permanently inscribe the power of the regime in the lives of their families – taking total control of lives, bodies and minds. Élisabeth Anstett, working on the violence of the

Stalin era in the USSR, argues that '[i]t is possible to see that whenever the practice of confiscation of bodies by the state occurs, it is accompanied by the mobilization – or indeed the creation – of technological devices which are specifically designed to facilitate the hiding of bodies and which are distinct from techniques of killing' (Anstett, 2014: 192–3). Such devices were indeed created and mobilised by the Argentinian junta.

Gabriel Gatti argues that the junta's politics of disappearance was not 'barbarism' but rather a profoundly modern project. The rationale of counting, classifying and controlling is at the heart of modernity, paving the way for biopolitical forms of governance. According to Gatti, the Argentinian, and more generally Latin American, forms of modernity are built on fantasies of empty land being inhabited by Europeans with a civilising 'gardening' project to create perfectly controlled, civilised 'garden states'. In the hands of the junta, this classifying and purifying effect was turned against 'its best creation, the citizen-individual' (Gatti, 2014: 15–31). In contrast, as I will argue in the next chapter, in certain other places those forcibly disappeared or exposed to death are those who are excluded from the protection of citizenship in the first place, such as undocumented migrants.

Bosnia-Herzegovina: establishing power in the emerging state through genocidal terror

Even though the period of military dictatorship in Argentina is often called 'the dirty war', it was not a war in the more conventional understanding of the word. Rather, it was a period when the well-established state terrorised its own citizens. The conditions in Bosnia-Herzegovina, however, between 1992 and 1995 – when thirty thousand people disappeared – were what we more ordinarily conceive as war or armed conflict. The dissolution of Yugoslavia was marked by armed conflict in several of its former states, and Bosnia's declaration of independence in March 1992 was followed by the outbreak of the most protracted and destructive of these. The conflict was preceded, however, by a period of growing ethno-nationalist agitation (e.g. Malcolm, 1996: 213–33; Silber and Little, 1997).

The detailed history of the dissolution of Yugoslavia and the armed conflict in Bosnia is beyond the scope of this book. However, in order to understand the mobilisation of enforced disappearance as a strategy during the Bosnian conflict, some basic facts about the situation need to be taken into account.

In Bosnia, the protracted armed conflict left behind some hundred thousand casualties, huge material destruction, heavily damaged infrastructure and a difficult political legacy. The conflict was characterised by brutal

Figure 1.1 A damaged family house near Prijedor in Bosnia-Herzegovina in 2001. A large number of family houses were destroyed in the area in the campaigns of ethnic cleansing between 1992 and 1995. Credit: Laura Huttunen.

genocidal violence throughout, with the assault on Srebrenica in July 1995 being the most well-known episode – the very name of the town has become a symbol of such violence. The presence of notorious prison camps in the area, where people, many if not most of them civilians, were tortured, humiliated and killed, is well documented (e.g. Gutman, 1993; Maass, 1996). Some two million people (out of a population of 4.2 million) were forced to leave their homes, around half of them escaping abroad. Moreover, the country was divided by the Dayton peace accords (1995) into two entities, the *Republika Srpska* (Serb Republic) and the Federation of Croats and Bosniaks, thus forcing the ethnicised violence into the very structures of the post-war state. By the end of the 1990s, some forty thousand people had been reported missing in the area of the former Yugoslavia, thirty thousand of them in Bosnia.[3]

The ferocity of the conflict in Bosnia is often attributed to the ethno-national composition of its inhabitants. The population consists of three groups, all of considerable size: the (Bosnian) Serbs, the (Bosnian) Croats and the Bosnian Muslims, or Bosniaks, as they are currently called. In Bosnia, this ethno-national division coincides with a split along religious lines: the Serbs are predominantly Orthodox Christians, the Croats are Roman Catholics and the Bosniaks are Sunni Muslims – although in each group a significant proportion is not actively religious. None of these groups formed an absolute majority in the new emerging state, unlike in the other ex-Yugoslavian new states, and the conflict revolved around the nationality question, even though the '"inevitable" ethnic antagonisms were more the object and *modus operandi* of the conflicts than their cause [... and] this vulgarized version of events disappears numerous other forms of identification that added multiple other factions to the conflict', as Admir Jugo and Sari Wastell (2015: 147–8) put it. Moreover, it was not a civil war between equally constituted parties but rather a contestation between very unequally positioned groups, as the former Yugoslav army remained to a large extent in the hands of Serbia and the Serbs, and Serbian and Croatian nationalist politics in Bosnia were backed by the neighbouring (new) states of Serbia (then still Yugoslavia) and Croatia.[4]

My understanding of the Bosnian missing is underpinned by some twenty years of ethnographic engagement with the Bosnian diasporic community between Finland and Bosnia. Practically all the Bosnians with whom I have worked in Finland came to the country as refugees during or soon after the armed conflict. As I outline in the introduction, after starting to work with the Bosnians I quickly realised that the majority of my interlocutors had been touched – often multiple times – by the disappearance of a close family member, a relative, a friend and/or a neighbour. In my discussions and interviews with them, two narratives of disappearance are repeated: in the first, the interlocutor depicts a moment in which a loved one is captured and taken away by soldiers, never to be heard of again, or located years later as a brutally murdered body in one of the mass graves or unmarked surface graves that have been excavated in the area. The second is a narrative of being separated from a family member in the chaotic circumstances of the conflict, and of desperate attempts to re-establish the connection, often in vain. In both cases, a devastating sense of fear regarding the missing person permeates the life of family members left behind. Hariz Halilovich (2013) reports very similar stories being told by his Bosnian interlocutors.

A large proportion of the Bosnians with whom I have worked over the years are Bosniaks from either the Prijedor/Banja Luka area in north-western Bosnia or the eastern Srebrenica area that borders Serbia – the same violence-stricken areas from which Halilovich's interlocutors come. Both areas fall within what is now, in post-war, post-1995 Bosnia, *Republika Srpska* or the Serb Republic of Bosnia-Herzegovina; in the ultra-nationalist Serb leaders' project of building a greater Serbia, these areas were to be included in the new 'pure' Serbia (Silber and Little, 1997). Practically all my interlocutors from this area were affected by the brutal violence; sometimes they witnessed killings and sometimes they were told about them, but most often they have had the deaths of family, friends and neighbours confirmed in the post-war decades during the excavations of the area's mass graves (see Chapter 4). Some of the disappeared are still missing. In my interlocutors' accounts of the war years, death and disappearance become intertwined, and feed into each other to create an atmosphere of terror. This was undoubtedly the exact intention of the perpetrators: to create a sense of fear and anguish that was so overwhelming that it would drive the survivors away from the area – and prevent them from returning.

The interview excerpt with which I opened this chapter is from a woman of Bosnian Muslim, or Bosniak, origin who is now living in Finland. The events she describes took place during the onslaught against the Bosniak-dominated villages in the Prijedor/Banja Luka area by the ex-Yugoslavian armed forces under Serb command – events that are well documented in journalistic and research literature (e.g. Gutman, 1993; Maass, 1996; Silber and Little, 1997; Halilovich, 2013). In Sabiha's narrative, this is the decisive moment that divides her life into *before* and *after*:[5] before the disappearance of her husband, and after it. Her story is one among many told by my interlocutors that serve as witness accounts of moments of abduction, of seeing loved ones taken by the invading Serb forces, after which there is no information about their whereabouts for months or even years.

Following Gabriel Gatti's (2014) formulation that disappearance is the separation of identity or name from the body, and of the person from their family and the wider community, the moment in which he was separated from his family and community sets in motion Sabiha's husband's enforced disappearance. When I interviewed her, Sabiha still did not know what had happened to him or his body. Following Parr and her colleagues' (2016: 68) idea that becoming a missing person can be thought of as a sequence of scenes, I suggest that this is a decisive scene in the continuum of unfolding scenes that turned Sabiha's husband into a missing or disappeared person. Other scenes followed, including Sabiha reporting her husband missing to the Red Cross officials soon after the event, and her regularly contacting, over some twenty years, the ICMP – the key actor working with the issue in the Balkans, discussed in more detail in Chapter 4 – to enquire about her husband. At the time of the interview, however, none of her enquiries had clarified his fate.

In Sabiha's story, we can see how the extended liminality of a family member's disappearance can affect somebody's life profoundly. For Sabiha, her husband's disappearance and the fact of not knowing what happened to him have been an inescapable ingredient of her life ever since. She says: 'Not a day goes by without my thinking about what happened to him. He needs to be buried. I have to be able to bury him, otherwise there is no peace, not for him, not for me.' The question of proper burial is repeated in stories told by the families of the missing. This concern with burial reflects the fact that, by now, most family members have accepted that their missing loved one is probably dead but not properly buried. The probability of death is supported by what people saw for themselves during the war, as well as by news, rumours and images circulating in Bosnia and among the wider public.

Stories and visual representations of the fate of the missing started to circulate early on. The first mass graves had already been found by 1996, when the United States, in trying to uncover what had happened to the Srebrenica missing, used aerial photographs, originally taken for military purposes, to detect possible sites (Wagner, 2008: 55; Jugo and Wastell, 2015: 150–1). It emerged that the wartime Serb leadership wanted to hide the mass graves precisely so as to prevent the international community from finding them, in order to be in a better position in the negotiations over the country's future. As the work on these graves has revealed, the executions were ruthless and the treatment of the bodies appalling by any standards. Brutal practices of bulldozing bodies from one grave to another were used and, consequently, victims' bodies were often torn apart, with individuals' body parts being found in multiple sites (Stover and Peress, 1998; Wagner, 2008; Jugo and Wastell, 2015).

Since the first horrendous findings, several other such sites have been located, the latest as recently as October 2014, in Tomašica, near Prijedor in northern Bosnia – the area where Sabiha's husband went missing.[6] Photographs of the mass graves have graphically shown the conditions in them, the intermingled violated bodies without individuality, without dignity, heaped together in nameless places. Such imagery has ingrained the unbearable indignity of the graves in the minds of those searching for their missing. An insult to any culturally codified perception of proper burial, these graves placed the dead bodies beyond any culturally sanctioned understandings of dignity and decency, thus violating the victims' very humanity. The circulation of such imagery, and the rumours and stories about both the torture and humiliation of captives and the undignified treatment of dead bodies, have intensely fed Bosnians' need to be able to properly bury the missing, even twenty years on.

In Victor Turner's (1977) sense, the unidentified bodies in the mass graves are liminal personae *par excellence*: they are stripped of all markers of individuality – victims usually had their IDs removed before execution, all rank and hierarchy wiped away – and then dumped in unmarked mass graves, putrefied beyond visual recognition and intermingled in a way that makes DNA-based identification challenging. In summary, the bodies are equal and indistinguishable, two characteristics of Turner's liminal persons. Here, however, unlike in the examples discussed by Turner, the equality is of an appalling kind. Moreover, the bodies are ritually between stages, between death and proper burial, and this in-betweenness is a driving force behind the investment in search, identification and reburial in any such contexts. Brutality towards the already dead, as discussed in the Argentinian context, was repeated in Bosnia, seriously disturbing cultural and moral sensibilities and pushing victims' bodies symbolically outside the contours of the socially and culturally regulated space, converting them into naturalised matter that lay outside the political community of the emerging new state. This brutality can be read as a horrific attempt to achieve a form of sovereignty that would reach beyond life and death, and to mark the targeted groups as less than human.

Over the years, many of Sabiha's former neighbours and a number of her current Bosniak acquaintances in Finland have had their disappeared loved ones found and identified, while she has still been waiting for news. Of course, the unfolding events suggest to Sabiha that her husband is also probably dead, but, while there is no body, there is no certainty. Historical layers of disappearance and reappearance in the Balkans feed into this sense of ambiguity and uncertainty; Sabiha recalls that in her childhood, stories circulated in her village about men who went missing during the Second World War. Although these men remained missing for several years, and their families already thought they were dead, some of them did return. Sabiha remembers the story of one such man – he had been in Siberia in a prisoner-of-war camp, unable to return or even to communicate with his family. Such stories create a historical landscape of disappearance and reappearance, of hope and despair that feed into the open-ended uncertainty. 'I just think that he might have lost his memory, maybe he does not know who he is anymore, maybe he is in Serbia somewhere …', Sabiha muses over the possibilities (cf. Stover and Peress, 1998: 198–9).

Further east, in the Srebrenica area, the genocidal violence intensified a little later than in Prijedor/Banja Luka. Hariz Halilovich (2013: 68–74) claims that the conduct of violence in the Prijedor region became a blueprint for genocidal tactics that were carried out in eastern Bosnia, which reached their peak in the massacre of Srebrenica in 1995. Selma, a young Bosniak woman with whom I spoke in Bosnia in 2014, witnessed as a child the genocidal machine that was set in motion in eastern Bosnia some time before the notorious assault on Srebrenica. In her story, the 'scenes' of her family member becoming a missing or disappeared person are slightly different from Sabiha's. Selma was living with her family in a village close to Srebrenica when the hostilities broke out. As she remembers it, one day all the families from her village were gathered together and sent away; they were told to take only their most important personal items and to get on a bus that was waiting in the village square. She remembers a threatening, hostile atmosphere. She boarded the bus with her parents and her sister, and it started its journey towards an unknown destination. But after a while the bus was stopped, and soldiers with weapons came onboard and ordered all the men off, including Selma's father. That was the last time she ever saw him. Even when getting off the bus, her father was still trying to calm his family down, repeating that everything would be alright. Selma has no definitive knowledge of what happened to him. After such a moment, there is only emptiness, a void, a question that remains unanswered.

Selma, along with her mother and sister, continued her life as an internally displaced person in the Bosniak-dominated area of Bosnia, without ever knowing what really happened to her father, or to the other village men who were dragged from the bus. Selma describes her mother as being broken by his fate and never really recovering from it, her personality changing from that of a cheerful and loving person to one that is inward-looking, quiet and distant. Selma is also worried about her sister, who lives a rather isolated life in Sarajevo and has never really recovered from her wartime experiences.

Several years after her father's disappearance, Selma met a man who told her that he had been in a prison camp with him. He gave her a small picture of Selma herself, one that her father had carried in his wallet. The man did not give her any details of her father's fate but left her with the understanding that he was dead. For Selma, this was a kind of closure, a moment of accepting her father's death even though she did not know where the body was, or what had actually happened to him. She told me that she does not even want to know the details – the rumours and witness accounts of the fate of the abducted and disappeared that circulate in post-war Bosnia are enough for her to be able to imagine and paint the contours of his fate in her mind.

Selma's mother's relationship to the disappearance, however, has been different. She is still waiting for news, entertaining the idea that her husband is possibly alive, somewhere, somehow. She even moved back to the village near Srebrenica several years after the peace agreement, to the family home that her missing husband had built. His handiwork in the structures and composition of the house became an anchor for her, a way of secretly touching him. Selma describes how her mother lives there in poverty, in a landscape profoundly marked by its genocidal history, in the *Republika Srpska* where many of her Serb neighbours call her 'Turk'[7] and want to deny her the right to full citizenship because of her ethnicity. She stubbornly looks after the house as the last proof of her husband's existence, his continuous absence imbued with his ghost-like presence there.

Among Bosnians from the Srebrenica area, many stories of disappearance take a different form. Srebrenica has a specific place in the history of disappearances (and reappearances, as discussed in Chapter 4) in Bosnia.

The assault on the town in July 1995, near the end of the Bosnian war, is notorious for the disappearance of some eight thousand men and boys in a two-week period – most of them later found, brutally murdered, in huge mass graves. The proceedings of the war tribunal in The Hague,[8] together with several research reports, convincingly reveal the conscious, pre-planned deployment of enforced disappearance and murder as a strategy of ethnically 'cleansing' the area. The carefully planned and executed destruction of lives in Srebrenica is reminiscent of the militarily-cum-bureaucratically ordered organisation of death and disappearance in Argentina under the junta. The assault on Srebrenica, however, was preceded by a protracted siege of the town, which had already created an unpredictable and chaotic situation.

As a consequence, rather than their personally witnessing the abduction of their disappeared loved one, many women report being separated from the men of the family and never seeing them again, and both women and men talk about a connection that they lost in the chaotic circumstances. Among them is Esad, a Bosniak man from Srebrenica, who has lived in Finland since 1997. Esad had three brothers who disappeared during the assault on the town. When I talked with him in 2014, all his brothers had been found in the mass graves in the area and identified. None of the bodies, however, were complete or intact – they all had body parts missing, and in the case of one of the brothers it was possible to identify only one rib bone through DNA analysis. 'But at least we know that he died. And we could give him a funeral!' said Esad. He did not witness his brothers' abduction, as he managed to escape from Srebrenica just two days before the notorious onslaught that set the genocidal rage in the area in full motion – as rumours were circulating among the residents that something was going to happen soon, Esad decided to leave town. His account of his disappeared and reappeared brothers was framed by his own escape: he could not tell me about his siblings before he had narrated in detail, with breathtaking intensity, his long and dangerous escape from the enclave, through woods and Serb-dominated areas to Tuzla, a then Bosniak-dominated town. The emotional intensity of his escape story was fuelled by the realisation that, had he not managed to escape, he would have been in the mass graves along with his brothers. The disappeared and reappeared brothers were, for Esad and his family, embodied proof of their own vulnerability as members of the group that was placed outside the protection of the law by the wartime leadership.

Living for years without knowing where his brothers were and what had happened to them was excruciating, Esad told me in an interview. The violence of the genocidal politics, including the disappearances, had marked his life profoundly. He and his wife still had a house in Srebrenica, which they had reclaimed during the post-war project of returning property to its original owners, and they went there every now and then. The visits, however, were marked by unease and, eventually, they decided to buy another house near Sarajevo. Summer-holiday visits to Bosnia are very important for the couple, but a return to Srebrenica feels impossible. The fear instilled by the politics of death and disappearance still disturbs their relationship to place in Srebrenica, and more generally to the state in post-war Bosnia (cf. Halilovich, 2013).

All these stories of disappearance produce what I call 'disturbed intimacies' (Huttunen and Perl, 2023), relationships and intimate practices that have been distorted by disappearances. Here we have both Sabiha and Selma's mother, waiting for decades for news of their husbands and never remarrying. There is Selma worrying about her mother and sister, both visibly changed by the events. Then there is Esad, who avoids his family home in Srebrenica, and keeps on repeating his story of escape from the death trap of Srebrenica to the extent of making his wife anxious. I will develop this notion in the following chapters, in relation to disappearing migrants and missing 'individual' citizens in the Global North.

Written life-stories gathered in Finland in 1997 from people with migrant background include several by Bosnians who escaped from Bosnia during the war (Huttunen, 2002). These written stories give very similar accounts of the events as the interview narratives: they all include descriptions of scenes of soldiers invading towns and villages, Bosniaks being called 'Turks' and told to 'go back to Turkey', and the onslaught of systematic campaigns to drive Bosniaks from their homes, gathering men in camps or on buses transporting them to unknown destinations, and sending women and children away from the area. The stories describe ethnic cleansing in full motion, with ethnically demarcated people being targeted for violent expulsion, killing and abduction and enforced disappearance.

I suggest that both the Argentinian military junta and the warring parties during the dissolution of Yugoslavia were seeking sovereignty through brutal necropolitical acts, but that the preconditions for this were different in each case: the Argentinian state had a long history as such, and necropolitical violence was deployed to secure power for certain actors within that state, while the Bosnian state was in the process of emerging and establishing itself. Even though there was a war going on in Bosnia, it is important to note that most of those who disappeared were not soldiers on the battlefield, the so-called missing in action, but civilians who were targeted as representatives of their ethno-national groups. As Achille Mbembe points out, war is a specific context for necropolitical aspirations as, under such circumstances, aspirations to power and necropolitical strategies are necessarily intertwined. 'War, after all, is as much a means of achieving sovereignty as a way of exercising the right to kill', he claims (Mbembe, 2003: 12). In Bosnia, as part of the project of seeking to establish sovereignty during the conflict, an outright, brutal 'right to kill' was combined with enforced disappearances and the expulsion from the area of civilian populations of the 'wrong ethnicity'.

While the Argentinian tactics of enforced disappearance were intensely private, violently invading private homes (Robben, 2005: 208–10), the Bosnian version worked in both the private and public realms. People were sometimes taken from their homes, and at other times from public places such as streets, village or town squares or buses. The enforced disappearances were embedded within a genocidal strategy of driving the 'wrong' ethno-national group out of the area through deportations and executions. Moreover, the family homes of Bosniaks, passed down from generation to generation, were systematically destroyed (Huttunen, 2009). Through this violence, Bosniaks were concretely and symbolically wiped from both the landscape and the 'body politic' of the emerging new state. Everything was done under the pretext of armed conflict and military necessity. The efficacy of this strategy is exemplified both by Esad's decision to buy a house in Sarajevo rather than to return to his home in Srebrenica, and by many diaspora Bosnians' reluctance to return at all (cf. Halilovich, 2013).

As in Argentina, the strategy of enforced disappearance in Bosnia worked in two registers: firstly, hiding the bodies was an attempt to avoid juridical and moral responsibility for the crimes, especially in answer to the so-called international community. Secondly, the strategy deeply engrained fear and insecurity in the minds of the survivors, who were sent away from the 'cleansed' area. This fear, along with the sense of unspeakable loss and horror, made returning to live in the area scarcely bearable for the few who took the decision to do so, while for many, the mere idea of going back was unthinkable.

At the same time, however, for those who left the disappearances forged a new kind of link to their country and area of origin. The decades-long nature of the search for the missing in the ex-Yugoslavian territories, as discussed in Chapter 4, has kept these individuals connected with it, with some returning to the area for burials when missing loved ones have been found and identified, and others constantly imagining the fate and whereabouts of their disappeared. The Bosnian disappeared are most probably within the territory of the state, and this is a crucial difference in comparison with the fate of disappearing migrants. It is much more difficult for families of migrants to imagine where the body of a disappeared family member might be. This theme will be discussed in the following chapter.

Variations in necropolitics of death and secrecy

Enforced disappearance: ideal form

In this chapter I have looked at two cases, two political projects in which necropolitics, in Mbembe's (2003) sense of the word, is exercised in its most brutal form: state power (or those aspiring to state power) kills those subjects who are categorised as 'wrong', as ethnically or politically outside the desired nation. In the cases discussed, the necropolitical project took a specific form, that of enforced disappearance, as the victims were intentionally made to disappear, with the act of killing being hidden and information being denied to those left behind. The victims were placed in a 'state of exception', to use Agamben's (2005) phrase, or outside the protection of the law, in the terminology of the Disappearance Convention.

Enforced disappearance, as exercised in the examples discussed here, is an individualising strategy: it targets specific individuals who are demarcated as suspicious or 'wrong' in the categorising endeavour of those in power. In this sense, it differs from the necropolitical mode of 'exposing to death' (Mbembe, 2003: 12), which will be discussed in the next chapter in the context of migrant disappearances. At the same time, in both Argentina and Bosnia, the strategy was also 'collectivising': the circle of potentially targeted people was large and porous, feeding into a political climate that was imbued with fear. Many people could see themselves or those close to them as potentially included in the growing numbers of disappeared.

During the periods discussed in this chapter, both the Argentinian and Bosnian leaderships developed a classificatory system that divided people into those protected by the law and those placed outside its purview. In Argentina, the dividing line was between 'the subversives' and those upholding conservative-Christian values, and in Bosnia, the division followed ethno-national-cum-religious fault lines. The Argentine practice targeted 'its own creation', individual citizens (Gatti, 2014: 15–31), and expelled them from the sphere of protection; in Bosnia, the strategy was to exclude an ethno-nationally (and religiously) defined group from citizenship of the new state from the very moment it was established.

As a political project, enforced disappearance often reaches beyond the act of taking life; it works also on the bodies of its victims by torturing and humiliating the living abducted, and dishonouring and violating the dead bodies of the disappeared and denying them a dignified, culturally coded funeral. The latter disrupts deep-rooted cultural practices related to governing the transition between life and death (Stepputat, 2014; Laqueur, 2015). As Anstett and Dreyfus (2014b: 3) suggest, the treatment of dead bodies is an indicator of the ideological constructions behind a conflict; there is a connection between the rationale or ideological grounding that defines certain groups as targets of genocidal violence and the consequent handling of their dead bodies. In Rosenblatt's words: 'The violence against the dead bodies reaches across the boundaries of life; it is committed first against living human beings and then against their dead bodies' (Rosenblatt, 2015: 164). Both cases discussed in this chapter exemplify such practices.

However, not all forcibly disappeared persons are dead. Some of them are alive in captivity, and some of them survive the brutal circumstances. For example, in Argentina, some of the detained-disappeared survived and returned to tell their stories in public, as will be discussed in Chapter 5. This always-present possibility of the disappeared one being alive feeds into the indeterminate nature of their condition and gives rise to paralysing uncertainties in the intimate, political and social life of those left behind.

To sum up, in its ideal form, enforced disappearance as a practice has several defining characteristics. The first of these is intentionality: when enforced disappearance is practised, the victims are intentionally made to disappear. In this sense, it is an individuating strategy. Secondly, the state is a key component, either as the prime perpetrator or through various forms of complicity. Thirdly, it operates through a classificatory system that places some people outside the protection of the law. Fourthly, it reaches beyond death by working on the bodies of the victims; living victims are often tortured and humiliated, while dead victims are treated disrespectfully and are denied proper burials. The fifth point is secrecy and denial, hiding the action and denying families access to information while allowing fear to spread. In this sense, the tactic is also collectivising. Finally, this last characteristic allows those in power to intentionally affect communities via disappearances, spreading fear and insecurity and thus seeking to silence and cripple political opposition.

Enforced disappearance: variation across time and place

The Argentinian machinery of enforced disappearance is often presented as the epitome or the ideal model of the strategic use of disappearances – as in this book. However, I believe it is useful to make a distinction between enforced disappearance as a concept with which we describe certain practices and give them (political and judicial) meaning, and the practices themselves. The variety of political practices that can be labelled enforced disappearance is large, and the practices are messy and changing, taking place in idiosyncratic circumstances. In the introduction to this book, I place the Argentinian case in a historical frame: the legal concept of enforced disappearance, with its specific characteristics, was created as a consequence

Enforced disappearance

of the efficiency of the Argentinian model, thus reflecting the ways in which it was carried out in that country. As a strategy and a practice, it has a history of variations that significantly pre-dates the Argentina of the 1970s and 1980s, and it has continued to produce variations ever since the fall of the military junta in that country, as the Bosnian example shows. As Zuzana Dziuban (2020) suggests, referring to Mieke Bal's (2002) much-cited idea, enforced disappearance is a travelling concept that has been used across contexts, gaining new meanings along the way and affecting how certain events are seen.

The more closely the practice of enforced disappearance in different contexts is analysed and broken down, the more slippery it becomes. For instance, there is great variation in the degree of secrecy exercised, and the role of the state takes different forms in different places. Even in the South America of the 1970s and 1980s, there were variations in the ways in which enforced disappearances were carried out. In contrast to the refined secrecy exercised in Argentina, in Chile many of the abducted were openly executed (e.g. Wright, 2007). In Guatemala, where around forty-five thousand people disappeared between the 1960s and the peace agreement in 1996, the terror worked, to a large extent, through the public display of both violence and victims' bodies. There were kidnappings and abductions of individuals who never returned, but also full-blown genocidal massacres that swept across a countryside inhabited by indigenous populations. In most of these massacres, some witnesses were purposefully left alive to talk about what they had seen and to disseminate fear. The indigenous population had been excluded from the full protection of citizenship, or of the law, since the beginning of the conflict and, consequently, the majority of the victims belonged to these indigenous groups (Sanford, 2003; also Frey, 2009). What was similar to what had happened in Argentina was the undignified treatment of the bodies: they were thrown into mass graves without rituals, sometimes accompanied by conspicuously irreverent or sacrilegious practices, such as the tipping of rubbish into the pit (Sanford, 2003: 125). In this sense, the Guatemalan victims became liminal bodies between death and proper burial, as did those in Bosnia.

At certain times, in certain places, violence becomes so excessive and ubiquitous that the line between disappearance and death is blurred to the extent that the two are indifferentiable. In Cambodia between 1975 and 1979, and in Rwanda and Burundi in the early 1990s, the governments made no attempt to hide the genocidal violence that was targeting large sections of the local populations (e.g. Malkki, 1995; Hinton, 1998; Jessee, 2012; Lesley, 2015; Bennett, 2018; Bennett, 2019). In such circumstances, people certainly do disappear from their families, but the disappearances are only part of the overall breakdown of normalcy. The horror of excessive death engulfs the horror of disappearance. These deaths were not strictly speaking enforced disappearances as defined in the legal framework, but the genocidal violence left behind large numbers of unidentified human remains, thus giving rise to social, political and cultural challenges akin to those created by enforced disappearance. This will be discussed in more detail in Chapter 4.

Since the 1980s and the fall of the military regimes in Argentina and Chile, many other governments or groups aspiring to power have used the strategy of enforced disappearance, with endless local variations. Moreover, there are places where complicated histories of violence blur the line between the strategic use of enforced disappearance and other extrajudicial killings. Each case is embedded in idiosyncratic local circumstances. Dictatorial governments, such as Saddam Hussein's regime in Iraq,[9] have applied the strategy. More examples would be rather easy to find as, according to one estimation, in the first decade of this millennium, enforced disappearances were taking place in some ninety countries around the world (D'Souza, 2015: 78). Each case is a little different, and the way in which the components of enforced disappearance – as outlined above – have been carried out varies.

For example, in Zimbabwe, a complicated history of violence has left a legacy of unidentified and not-properly-buried bones, families not knowing what has happened to their loved ones or where they are buried and unsettled spirits of these not-properly-buried persons harassing families and communities. This history of violence extends from the colonial period up to recent decades, via the independence struggles and postcolonial periods of bloodshed, such as the 'Gukurahundi' violence. As a consequence, there are communities that are affected by the disappearance of some of their members, and large areas where the landscape is marked by the presence of not-properly-buried bodies or bones (Eppel, 2009; Fontein, 2010; Eppel, 2014; Fontein, 2018).

Likewise, disappearances during armed conflicts, including practices of purposefully hiding bodies, have complicated histories that predate Bosnia, in places such as Vietnam (Kwon, 2006; Kwon, 2008; Ngô, 2021) and Timor-Leste (Kent, 2011; Kent 2020). Since Bosnia, large-scale disappearance has been reported in, for example, Lebanon (Comaty, 2019) and Kashmir (D'Souza, 2015; Zia, 2016), to name just a few.

Several writers have pointed to the alarming rise in the numbers of disappeared people in some democratic states, including Mexico (Wright, 2018; Mandolessi and Olalde Rico, 2022) and India (Fletcher, 2014; D'Souza, 2015; Chaure and Hicks, 2021). The 'comeback' of enforced disappearances in Latin America in this millennium has given rise to a debate over the meaning and integrity of democratic governance (Wright, 2018: 329; Mandolessi, 2022: 10–13). Since the declaration of the so-called War on Drugs in Mexico by Felipe Calderón's government (2006–12), up to eighty-five thousand people[10] have been reported as disappeared by their families, and there is proof of state complicity, corruption and organised crime behind the disappearances (Wright, 2018; Irazuzta, 2020; Mandolessi and Olalde Rico, 2022). The complex relationship between the state, organised crime, impunity and corruption in the area has created a political landscape that Irazuzta calls a 'post-sovereignty governmentality' (2020: 98), one that makes many people 'disappearable' (Laakkonen, 2022). Enforced disappearances, meaning the purposeful disappearing of individually targeted victims, intertwine with disappearances that result from people being exposed to deadly circumstances. This is true for both the disappeared citizens in Central America and the growing number of undocumented migrants who travel through the area (e.g. Citroni, 2017; Nyberg Sørensen, 2018). The latter will be discussed more thoroughly in the next chapter. All in all, the unfolding crisis of disappearances in present-day Central America is challenging established ways of thinking about the state, citizenship, protection and disappearance (cf. Gatti, Irazuzta and Martínez, 2021) – a challenge that should be taken up in the further development of addressing human disappearances in anthropology, and in social and political sciences more generally .

Finally, what should we think about terrorist attacks that kill ordinary people and make some of them disappear (e.g. Edkins, 2011: 15–37, 84–106)? In this chapter, I have argued that one of the key characteristics of enforced disappearance is an aspiration to power that intertwines death with disappearance to create an atmosphere of fear that paralyses political activity. Terrorist organisations do aspire to power, and terrorist attacks indeed intertwine death with disappearance, creating atmospheres of fear and insecurity that potentially affect political life. What makes such attacks different from cases of enforced disappearance, however, is the way in which the victims are chosen. Terrorism is not an individuating strategy in the same way as most forms of government-sponsored enforced disappearance are, and even though there is certainly a classificatory logic behind the choice of sites for terrorist attacks, who falls victim to these atrocities is ultimately a rather haphazard matter. Moreover, terrorist groups do not usually seek to hide their responsibility for the deaths. Quite the opposite in fact: they are often keen to publicly claim responsibility for violent acts, sometimes even ones they did not actually perpetrate.

Concluding remarks

I have claimed, with reference to Gabriel Gatti, that enforced disappearance in the sense described in this chapter is a profoundly modern practice.

I see this 'modernity' as working in various registers. First, the bureaucratic orderliness and the factory-like efficacy of the deadly practices are modern in their character. Secondly, the classificatory logic behind the political projects of making people disappear is imbued with the modernist urge to know and control. Thirdly, the way in which states operate in the transnational state-based arena of the modern world order makes disappearance, rather than the outright execution of political opponents, a viable strategy. The modern world order is deeply affected by discourses of human rights and obligations defined by various international treaties. Even though the premises of human rights are sometimes debated, and accusations of human rights violations strategically used against political adversaries across the globe, the discourse is still powerful, and blatant violations of human rights often give rise to international public outcries. The Argentinian and Bosnian strategies of enforced disappearance discussed in this chapter attempted to create a situation in which the 'enemy' was disposed of violently and an atmosphere of fear created, while at the same time maintaining the facade of a legitimate state in the international arena.

Even though I argue that the disappearance of a loved one is always difficult for those left behind, the context of disappearance does matter. As the examples in this chapter have shown, the violent imagery and rumours that circulate in societies plagued by frequent disappearances or terrorised by totalitarian regimes flood the families' and friends' imaginations with paralysing ideas of what might have happened to those who are missing (cf. Wagner, 2008: 151–84). Moreover, if a disappeared person is found dead and is identified at some point, any relief is overshadowed by the anger and pain that result from knowing how the loved one died, and by the realisation that somebody has taken the law into their own hands and exercised their power over the victim's life. The politics of enforced disappearance create disturbed intimacies, but also disturbed relationships to the state and the political sphere.

Notes

1 There are different estimations of the number of the disappeared. The first report published by the National Commission on the Disappearance of Persons (CONADEP) in 1984 listed 8,800 disappeared men and women, and 172 babies and small children who were either abducted with their parents or born in captivity, but later, human rights organisations estimated that the true number was around thirty thousand (Robben, 2005: 321–3). In its 2003 annual report, the Argentine Forensic Anthropology Team (Equipo Argentino de Antropología Forense, EAAF) put the number at around ten thousand (EAAF, 2003: 20),

but the figure of thirty thousand is often repeated in the literature. As Robben (2005: 323) argues, the true number will never be known, as many bodies were destroyed, and the regime also disposed of many incriminating documents. However, a significant body of bureaucratic paperwork has survived into the post-dictatorship era, and this has enabled the identification of a number of the victims of enforced disappearance. This will be discussed in detail in Chapter 4.

2 'The Argentine military did at night what Pinochet's men had done during the day' (Robben, 2005: 279).

3 For statistics on the missing in the former Yugoslavia, see ICMP Western Balkans (https://www.icmp.int/where-we-work/europe/western-balkans/) (accessed 14 February 2024).

4 For overviews of the situation, see e.g. Malcolm (1996: 234–71), Silber and Little (1996), Lampe (2000: 365–415), Halilovich (2013) and Jansen (2015: 1–29).

5 There are, of course, other 'before' and 'after' moments in her narrative (such as those relating to the outbreak of the war, and to her coming to Finland) but this is the strongest: a compelling moment that begs for closure, even twenty-one years later (cf. Huttunen, 2024).

6 Tomasica – Mass Graves Database (https://massgravesmap.balkaninsight.com/tomasica-2/) (accessed 14 February 2024).

7 This epithet relates to the history of Bosnia under the Ottoman empire (see Malcolm, 1996) and conflates the present-day Bosniak population with the Ottomans. By way of this discursive move, today's Bosniaks are blamed for historical Ottoman-era injustices, and are simultaneously marked as foreign, as not belonging to Bosnia.

8 International Criminal Tribunal for the former Yugoslavia (ICTY), United Nations (https://www.icty.org/) (accessed 14 February 2024).

9 See e.g. Iraq: No Justice for Enforced Disappearances, Human Rights Watch (https://www.hrw.org/news/2020/11/16/iraq-no-justice-enforced-disappearances) (accessed 3 August 2023).

10 Different authors present widely differing figures for the number of disappeared in Mexico. The figure of eighty-five thousand comes from Mandolessi (Mandolessi, 2022: 1).

2

Disappearing en route: missing migrants, ambiguous absences and exposure to death

On opening the Missing at the Borders website,[1] you are faced with a picture of what appears to be a family: a woman holding a photo of two youngish men, with three children gathered around her. All four are looking intensely at the camera, and the viewer. The attached text says: 'People, not numbers. Every year thousands of people disappear while seeking to cross borders. We want to give a voice and dignity to their families. We want to give them the opportunity to express their sorrow.'

When you click on the 'Stories' tab, you are then faced with a column of pictures of grave-looking faces. In some of them there is one individual, while in others there is a pair or small group of people, presumably a family, holding a photograph – clearly of a missing person. Alongside each of these images there is a name (that of the missing person) and a quotation from a family member, such as 'I live in the constant hope that he'll come back. I always hope that one day he'll come knocking on the door' (Dalila Basset Hamdi). The testimonies are listed one after another, conveying a sense of a multitude of families missing somebody. Under 'Countries', Algeria, Tunisia and Morocco are listed – all countries with Mediterranean shores; the focus of this website is on those who go missing while crossing the Mediterranean Sea.

I start by clicking on one of the videos on the 'Stories' page – this one is titled 'Ali Ben Aldelhamid Ayari'. A serious-looking older couple stand holding a photograph of a handsome young man. The text on the screen states that the man's name is Ali Ayari and that he has been missing since 15 March 2007. The attached quote, attributed to Gemma Bensalem, the mother of the disappeared young man, reads, 'If we had been able to bury him, we would have accepted God's destiny. We would have visited him at the graveyard like everyone else. We are neither alive nor dead.' I open the video link and see the couple sitting there, as they start to tell the story of their son (in Arabic, with English subtitles). The family is Algerian. Ali had been unemployed and trying desperately to find work, without success. He had told his mother that he felt like he had no future. One evening he leaves home without telling his parents where he is going. When he has not returned by the next morning, his mother visits the family of Ali's friends, who are also young unemployed men. There she learns that the young men have taken a boat heading for Italy. Somebody in Ali's friends' family has phoned the travellers and managed to speak to them en route, reporting that they were saying that they were in a boat off the Tunisian coast when suddenly a loud noise interrupted the conversation and a young man in the boat shouted, 'Pray for us! Pray for our safety!' After this, the families never hear from the travellers again. His parents do not know where Ali is or where to start looking for him: 'Some say they are in Tunisia, others say they are in Italy.' The elderly parents are devastated, and they utter the words that are quoted in written form on the website: 'We have no more hope, we have no more life. Our hope is to see him again, then we can die! ... If we had been able to bury him, we would have accepted God's destiny. We would have visited the graveyard like everybody else ... We are neither dead nor alive ... We do not know whom to turn to.' The video ends with the couple standing again, the mother holding the picture of her disappeared son.

This short clip touches on many of the themes discussed in the previous chapter, such as living with protracted uncertainty and the compelling need to provide a proper burial for an absent one who turns out to be dead. Here the themes are brought into a new context, that of irregular or undocumented migration. The sense of harrowing liminality expressed by this elderly couple ('We are neither dead nor alive') echoes the experiences of the families of the forcibly disappeared.

In today's world, significant numbers of people disappear from their families while migrating. Migrants travelling without documentation, along so-called irregular routes, are especially in danger of disappearing, and this often means death, frequently with their families and communities not knowing what has happened to them. The reasons for these disappearances are widely diverse, from dying at the mercy of the sea or desert to being abducted by criminal organisations or detained by state officials, to getting sick en route and not receiving help – the possibilities are as varied as human life. With the tightening of border regimes in the EU, the USA and Australia, the numbers of missing migrants have been growing since the early 1990s, and painful uncertainty often marks the lives of families and communities in the countries of origin. Disappeared migrants frequently turn up as unidentified bodies somewhere far from home, but the link between a body and the family or community is hard to re-establish under current conditions. In such circumstances, names and bodies are constantly being disconnected from each other (Gatti, 2014), a phenomenon discussed in the previous chapter.

In 2019, two members of my research team, Saila Kivilahti and Ville Laakkonen, travelled to the Mediterranean – Saila to Spain and Ville to Greece – to carry out ethnographic research on the world of migrant disappearances. They talked with migrants themselves, many of whom had crossed 'irregularly' to Greece or Spain; with migrants' family members, and with organisations working on migration, migrant deaths or sea rescue; with forensic anthropologists and undertakers; and with both activists and ordinary people living in areas affected by growing numbers of migrants and of concomitant unnamed dead bodies brought to the shore by the Mediterranean Sea. Their work shows how difficult it is to operationalise research on migrant disappearances as a single ethnographic site (cf. Laakkonen, 2023b). It also reveals the complexity of this world, the ever-present possibility of death and disappearance, the multitude of actors and, ultimately, the enormous inequalities that exist in a world structured by huge economic disparities, a hierarchical migration order and racialising discourses (Laakkonen, 2022; Laakkonen, 2023a; Laakkonen, 2023b; Kivilahti and Huttunen, 2023).

In this chapter, I will explore this world. In the previous chapter, I discussed enforced disappearance as a purposeful political strategy of terror, targeting specific individuals marked by their political adherence or ethnonational profile. People who disappear from their families while migrating are not, in many cases, targeted as individuals; their disappearances are connected to a variety of actors, situations and circumstances. If and when intentionality is involved, it is often of a different quality when compared with the strategies of dictatorial governments and military persecutors; the responsibility is frequently much more dispersed and more difficult to pin onto certain actors or perpetrators than in the cases discussed in Chapter 1. However, the claim that migrant deaths and disappearances are just an unfortunate side-effect of border control is an often-repeated phrase that covers up a complex reality of direct and indirect violence. This chapter discusses the nature of this intentionality by tying migrant disappearances to the increasingly restrictive border regimes that push migrants onto evermore-dangerous routes. Beyond this, the chapter explores the complexities of the world of undocumented migration as a space that exposes migrants to death and disappearance – in other words, a space that makes undocumented migrants utterly disappearable (Laakkonen, 2022).

I start from the structural and political framing of migration in today's world, and from a brief discussion of how we can understand missing migrants as a category. I will also consider the numbers of migrant disappearances and the ways in which this statistical knowledge is produced. After this framing, I will proceed to discuss experiences of 'disturbed intimacies' (Huttunen and Perl, 2023) in communities of origin, paying attention to everyday life experiences and social relations. In this context, with its ever-present question of force and vulnerability, I am also interested in migrants' and their families' active agency in making plans and decisions. I rely on fieldwork material gathered by my research team members, material sourced from the internet, and other researchers' accounts to create an ethnographic sense of what is taking place at the grassroots level.

The migration order and the production of disappearability

The directions, routes and intensities of migration flows have varied significantly over the centuries of human history (e.g. Van Hear, 2005; Hoerder, 2019). Similarly, the danger of dying or disappearing while travelling has varied significantly from one time and place to another. The creation of the nation-state-based system with various, sometimes overlapping, border regimes (Green, 2013) is, historically speaking, rather recent, but this system, with its concomitant passport and visa regime (Torpey, 2018; Caplan and Torpey, 2001) is the structure within which migrant disappearances currently take place.

As shown by the extensive body of scholarship on the increasingly restrictive border regimes in our present times (e.g. Andersson, 2014a; Kalir and Wissink, 2015; de Genova, 2017; Cuttitta and Last, 2019; Stierl, 2021), current migrant deaths and disappearances take place in a world structured by policies and politics that enable some people to travel across borders without much trouble while others encounter endless bureaucracy, the latter often becoming a barrier that pushes migrants towards irregular modes of travel along perilous routes. Legal routes to the Global North for the citizens and residents of the Global South have radically diminished in number, and at the same time border control technologies, including biometric identification and technologies for detecting movement, have become ever more efficient. New technologies for the management of human mobility are being developed at growing speed to support the hierarchical migration order (e.g. Andersson, 2019; Grünenberg, 2020; Grünenberg et al., 2020; Møhl, 2020).

The key factor giving rise to undocumented migration in today's world is global inequality or, rather, a range of inequalities: inequalities in terms of freedom of movement, in terms of state protection and safety, and in terms of resources and possibilities for a dignified life – or for life at all. Some undocumented migrants are fleeing life-threatening circumstances while others are moving to escape poverty, environmental degradation or 'social death', such as unemployment and a lack of opportunities for building a decent life. Often these conditions become intertwined in people's lives, with administrative categories such as 'refugee' and 'economic migrant' referring to intertwined aspects of tangled realities (e.g. Nyberg Sørensen, 2018).

Many scholars and activists argue that migrant deaths and disappearances are not just a side-effect of tightening border security but rather a conscious strategy of prevention through deterrence. In this vein, Jason de León (2015: 13–14) argues that undocumented migration should be understood 'not as chaos but as a well-defined social process', and he refers to the current US migration policies as 'a killing machine':

> My argument is quite simple. The terrible things that this mass of migrating people experience en route are neither random nor senseless, but rather part of a strategic federal plan that has rarely been publicly illuminated and exposed for what it is: a killing machine that simultaneously uses and hides behind the viciousness of the Sonoran Desert.
>
> *(De León, 2015: 3–4)*

In other words, De León argues that prevention through deterrence means that allowing some people to die or disappear while migrating is a conscious political strategy. Migrant deaths and disappearances are allowed to happen, as they are seen to send a warning to those contemplating undocumented border crossing: do not come, you may die and disappear! (See also Rozema, 2011; Stierl, 2021.)

This strategy did not emerge fully formed, however; it has a history of its own. According to De León, it emerged in the USA first as 'an off-the-cuff homegrown preventive measure against the unsightliness of brown-skinned illegal fence jumpers and the subsequent chaos the Border Patrol caused by chasing them through poor Latino neighborhoods where it was impossible to figure out who belonged and who didn't' (De León, 2015: 5–6), but was later developed more consciously to create a preventive effect, as a fear-generating strategic tool. In Europe, 'hostile environment' politics as a conscious attempt to create deterrence for undocumented migrants is often attributed to former UK prime minister Theresa May (e.g. Hiam, Steele and McKee, 2018). Initiatives in several European states and also in the European Parliament to criminalise rescue operations in the Mediterranean and other sea areas[2] have combined to create deterrence (Mainwaring and DeBono, 2021). Such politics are actively developed elsewhere in the world as well, for example in Australia. Understood in this way, 'prevention through deterrence' resembles the politics of fear employed by military and totalitarian governments that was discussed in Chapter 1: it intentionally creates and spreads fear and insecurity (also Nyberg Sørensen and Huttunen, 2020).

Nevertheless, in democracies, political processes differ from those in dictatorial states; likewise, the strategic use of fear in political processes is necessarily different. The complex relations between intentionality, responsibility and migrant deaths and disappearances are conceptualised in different ways by different authors. Gerhild Perl uses the term 'organized irresponsibility' (Perl, 2019a; also Perl and Strasser, 2018) to analyse the processes that leave migrants at the mercy of the sea (cf. Follis, 2015) and of other deadly circumstances. Racist discourses and populist anti-migration rhetoric feed into the acceptability of migrant deaths. Within the system of organised irresponsibility, victims are not targeted individually and there is no single 'disappearing agent' (Gatti, 2020: 51) behind the deaths and disappearances in the same sense as in enforced disappearances. In Mbembe's (2003) terminology, the tightened border regimes, underpinned by prevention through deterrence, work through the necropolitical strategy of 'exposing to death', rather than outright 'taking life'. However, for undocumented migrants, being 'exposed to death' means being positioned outside the protection of the law and, and consequently, vulnerable to individualising violence from traffickers or individual state agents such as border guards. In the world of undocumented migration, there is a continuum between necropolitical acts of 'taking life' and 'exposing to death' (cf. Duhaime and Thibault, 2017; Schindel, 2020b).

Undocumented migrants often participate in or contribute to the effacing or fading out of their identities, which makes the situation even more complicated. Within the current migration order, migrants often hide their true identities in order to reach the Global North: they travel without, or with false, documentation; they borrow passports from others and assume stolen identities in order to be able to travel at all; and they often give false names to their fellow travellers (e.g. Le Courant, 2019; also Reeves, 2013). Such annihilation of fixed identities makes their identification even more difficult if the worst happens and they end up as dead bodies somewhere far from home.

The states from which migrants originate are also part of the complicated structure of exposing migrants to death. Some migrants flee from violence perpetrated by their states of origin, sometimes from the threat of enforced disappearance. Hierarchies within the states of origin also mould migration trajectories: members of the educated and well-off middle and upper classes in the Global South can often travel via legal routes while the less privileged are forced onto irregular ones.

The official politics and its effects have attracted a great deal of scholarly and activist attention, but understanding the multitude of unofficial actors and processes that exist around undocumented migration is equally important. There is an underbelly of agents engaged with migration, a grey area of legal, illegal and semi-legal actors that provide services to migrants who cannot travel via official routes – a whole field of actors and entrepreneurs that flourishes in the shadow of state policies and, to a large extent, because of them. There are the large international organisations, such as the IOM and ICRC, that work with migrants and affect migration processes, but there are also a range of smaller NGOs, kinship and friendship networks of help (Sanchez, 2014), criminal networks of exploitation (Rozema, 2011; Nyberg Sørensen, 2013), and small businesses offering their services (Berg and Tamagno, 2013; Lucht, 2013). Thomas Gammeltoft-Hansen and Ninna Nyberg Sørensen (2013) call this entangled network of actors 'the migration industry', pointing out that a variety of people benefit from migrants in one way or another. Also, those who are there to help migrants and to mitigate their predicament unwittingly enable the continuation of irregular migration.[3] Together, the official politics and the multitude of unofficial actors produce a complicated social world where migrants become disappearable, or susceptible both to individuating acts of enforced disappearance and to being exposed to dangerous circumstances.

Who are the missing migrants? Numbers and geographies

Numbers

Our times are obsessed with numbers. To make a phenomenon newsworthy or politically significant, we need numbers. The number of migrants disappearing while travelling is, however, extremely difficult to come by, and this very difficulty reflects the elusiveness of the figure of the migrant and, simultaneously, the vulnerability of those forced to travel undocumented. The fact is that the data on disappeared migrants will never be complete; it is always only an estimation.

The most readily available source of data on the topic comes from the IOM's 'Missing Migrants' project, which maintains a website with a constantly updated estimation of migrant disappearances at the global level.[4] At the time of my writing this chapter, in February 2024, the website claims that 61,780 migrants have gone missing since 2014. Of these, 28,900 are missing in the Mediterranean, 1,013 in Europe, 14,378 in Africa, 2,628 in Western Asia, 5,847 in Asia and 8,924 in the Americas.[5] Further into the site, we learn that the numbers represent people who are presumed to have died while migrating, most of them via irregular routes. Presenting them as missing, rather than dead, demonstrates the fact that most of those who die while migrating irregularly remain unretrieved or unidentified. As their families do not know what has happened to them, from their point of view they are missing. This highlights the slipperiness of the term: the dead and the missing as categories leak into each other.

It is useful to pause for a moment to consider how the number of missing or disappeared persons in various contexts is produced, and how this reflects the circumstances of disappearances. In post-war Bosnia, discussed in the previous chapter, the number of missing persons is based on reports made by family members searching for their loved ones via the international organisations working in the area, especially the ICMP and ICRC. The circumscribed geographical area involved and the (over time) well-established procedures for registering a family member as missing with a trusted organisation have produced rather reliable numbers (Chapters 1 and 4). Likewise, the number of missing citizens in Finland (Chapter 3) is based on search requests filed with the police by families. Again, the institution is well-trusted and the channels for reporting a missing person well-established.

In contrast, estimates of the numbers of disappeared undocumented migrants are based on a range of sources, with highly variable accuracy. While disappearance reports filed by family members are also a source of data for counting missing migrants, they provide a much more unreliable source in this case than in many others; the lack of transparent, trustworthy infrastructures for reporting a missing person in cases when the disappearance takes place transnationally; the lack of trust displayed towards authorities in countries of origin, as discussed above; and the precarious status of undocumented migrants in countries of destination all contribute to this unreliability (IOM, 2021). Moreover, the fact that families are sometimes afraid that they will be accused of letting their son or daughter travel without proper documentation and the required visas and permits makes them reluctant to contact the authorities (e.g. Perl, 2018: 94).

Rather than relying only on families' reports, the IOM seeks data from various sources: official coastguard and medical examiner records, media reports, NGOs, and other migrants and co-travellers of the dead and disappeared. All these sources, however, have their problems and limitations.[6]

Reports made by coastguards and medical examiners rely on official data, that is, death certificates for migrants' bodies that are retrieved from the sea, border rivers, ships, containers and elsewhere (see also Last et al., 2017). This data does not include bodies that are never retrieved, bodies that vanish without a trace in the desert, on the high seas or elsewhere – and there are good reasons to assume that such bodies comprise a significant number. Most of the bodies examined by officials in the EU and the USA remain unidentified, despite the now often routinely taken DNA samples. This means that they remain missing from the point of view of families. The search practices employed and their challenges will be discussed further in Chapter 4.

The testimonies of co-travellers are often an extremely important source of information for families of the missing, who often rely on unofficial contacts for obtaining knowledge (e.g. Kivilahti and Huttunen, 2023), but they are significant also in the production of published figures. Reports by co-travellers indicating that somebody, or some bodies, drowned or were left behind during the journey may be the only source of data in many cases: for instance, in the Mediterranean, boats used by undocumented migrants usually have no passenger lists, thus the only proof of a person's death is a testimony from a fellow passenger (Black, Dearden, Singleton and Laczko, 2017: 8–11):. Such reports, however, are a rather unreliable source of data for producing accurate numbers. Sometimes all the passengers drown, and there is nobody left to report the dead and the missing. Moreover, when some passengers do survive, they may be in shock and unable to give an accurate report, or be reluctant to give one at all for various reasons (Perl, 2019b). Finally, in many cases passengers in 'illegal' boats (or in other modes of transport, such as trucks and containers) often conceal their true identities even from their fellow passengers. Thus, survivors may be able to provide estimates of the numbers of people who have died, but not necessarily their identities.

There is also a geopolitics of knowledge on migrant deaths and disappearances. The so-called migration crises, such as the one in Europe in 2014 and 2015, and the Bay of Bengal crisis in 2015, attract attention from the media, civil society groups and other actors involved in the 'migration industry'. Such attention brings institutional actors to the area and gives rise to monitoring and data production, while other areas may remain unmonitored, resulting in a lack of data (Laczko, Singleton and Black, 2017). For instance, in North Africa, media attention is rather accidental, and there are no strong state-based institutions interested in gathering data on the issue. Instead, survey-based methods are employed to obtain an estimate of the number of deaths that have taken place during journeys across the region; in other words, migrants are interviewed, using questions concerning deaths they have witnessed while travelling. Such data cannot be verified, and the same incident may be reported twice while many probably remain unreported (Laczko, Singleton and Black, 2017: xiv).

Frank Laczko, Ann Singleton and Julia Black (2017) argue that the history of activism around enforced disappearances in Central and South America affects the quality of the data on missing migrants in the region. Although close cooperation between state actors and family organisations creates channels for search and identification – further discussed in Chapter 4 – large numbers of disappearances in this area remain uncounted. Mandolessi (2022: 9–10) claims that in present-day Mexico there is a 'forensic crisis', with some thirty-nine thousand unidentified dead bodies, many of them undocumented migrants.

I argue that the vagueness of the numbers reflects the vulnerability and disappearability (Laakkonen, 2022) of the people in question. In a world with ever more effective technologies and practices of governance, monitoring and counting, this group of people fall through the protective structures; when they die, they also drop out of processes of monitoring and knowledge production, even though they were heavily monitored when alive and attempting to move across borders.

Geographies

At the time of writing this text, there were two prominent geographical areas in the media and in public discussions on migrant deaths and disappearances: the Mediterranean region (extending to the North-African deserts) and the US–Mexico borderlands. In addition, significant numbers of people were moving in dangerous circumstances in Asia, the Pacific and the Horn of Africa (e.g. Taylor and Lee, 2017; Triandafyllidou and Ricard-Guay, 2019).

These areas, the Mediterranean and the US–Mexico border area, have two factors in common: firstly, they are places where the so-called Global North meets the Global South, that is, people's living conditions, sense of security and opportunities for a decent life are radically different on the two sides of the border zone (e.g. Vigh, 2009; Lucht, 2012; Perl, 2016; Schielke, 2019). Secondly, the areas are characterised by highly demanding natural conditions: deserts, voluminous rivers and high seas. Traversing these areas without proper equipment is truly life-threatening.

Jason de León, referring to Callon and Law (1995), theorises such areas with the concept of 'hybrid collectif'. This term refers to the total environment, including human actors, such as parliaments and politicians behind the legal frameworks, border guards, NGOs of various kinds, and coyotes and other smugglers, and also non-human actors, such as the animals of the desert, and natural conditions such as heat and wind (de León, 2015: 38–42). 'Hybrid collectif' as a term brings the material and sociopolitical worlds together. The argument is that the legal and political frame controlling mobility in today's world forces some people to travel undocumented, and the ever-tightening border enforcement pushes these migrants to travel through areas where people often die because of the circumstances, and where natural forces then often destroy the dead bodies completely.

Missing from whom? Entanglements of state, kinship and family

To approach the question of migrant disappearances analytically, and given the complex political frame discussed above, we need to ask the question:

from whom have they disappeared? Are the disappeared migrants missing from their families and communities? Or are they missing from the state? In which case, which one – the sending state or the putative receiving state? Or are they missing from all of them – families, communities and states? In this sense, the category of missing migrants is more complex, and more variegated, than that of the forcibly disappeared victims of violence discussed in the previous chapter, and the configuration of states, families and communities can take a variety of forms. As this group of disappeared migrants is extremely diverse, it is hard to say anything that would apply to everybody. Still, there are some features that help us to understand what produces their susceptibility to various forms of violence and, ultimately, their disappearability.

Undocumented migrants' relationship to state power is often contested and complicated, both in the sending countries and in the putative countries of settlement. What does it mean for migrants to be seen by the state, or to remain unseen by it? Is the state a beneficial, caring and protective agent for migrants, or is it indifferent, or even downright violent and threatening? Or is it interested in them at all?

The answer to these questions varies from case to case. To start with: undocumented migration is a global phenomenon, and the states from which migrants originate are profoundly different from each other; consequently, migrants' relationships to their state of origin vary. Some migrants escape to avoid oppression and violence on the part of the state of origin; others migrate because of a lack of opportunities, as discussed above. Beyond this, migrant disappearability is deeply connected with political structures and policy practices, not only in the Global North but also in migrants' states of origin. Some migrants are not registered as citizens in their countries of origin, which may be the result of a conscious politics of excluding certain groups from the protection of the state, for instance indigenous groups in some Latin American countries (e.g. in Peru, see Rojas-Perez, 2015); in other cases, being unregistered is the outcome of bureaucratic inefficacy (e.g. Hansen, 2023). In some states of origin, such as Algeria[7] and Guatemala (Nyberg Sørensen, 2018), there is a long history of state-sponsored enforced disappearance; in such a context, the line between previous and present-day disappearances becomes blurred, and a lack of trust characterises people's relationship with state authorities (see also IOM, 2021). In such cases, people may wish to remain unseen by their state of origin. Moreover, undocumented emigration is criminalised in some countries, and states of origin are directly involved in border enforcement; for example, several North African states have entered into agreements with the EU to keep migrants from leaving the country, in exchange for funding and other benefits (e.g. Andersson, 2014b; Perl, 2018: 92–3). In such circumstances, families of disappeared

Disappearing en route 71

migrants are reluctant to ask for help from the authorities. In other cases, the inability of states to provide decent living conditions pushes local people to migrate (e.g. Lucht, 2012; Schielke, 2015; Schielke, 2019; Zagaria, 2020).

The relationship to state power in the putative countries of destination is also characterised by tensions, and by oscillation between the hope of obtaining visibility, official status and state protection on the one hand, and of remaining undocumented and unseen on the other. The latter applies to migrants who consider an official status unattainable. In such circumstances, migrants often hope that remaining undetected by the state will enable them to work, earn money and return home at some point (e.g. Lucht, 2012). Thus, sometimes people disappear from the state and remain purposefully beyond or below its radar, while trusted family members and/or friends may know their whereabouts. In reality, this means working in extremely precarious conditions, which again makes them vulnerable and, ultimately, disappearable. In these cases, the notion of 'being disappeared' is rendered indistinct from that of undocumented and marginalised living: people live at the margins of the state and economies, 'unseen' by the authorities, unprotected by any legal status (e.g. Leppäkorpi, 2022) and often unrecognised in official records or statistics. Gabriel Gatti (2020) has called such groups 'the social[ly] disappeared'. These people are missing from the state gaze, and although they may be missing from their families at the same time, this is not necessarily so.

Of course, there are also those who want to disappear from their families. Domestic violence, abusive spouses or parents or otherwise unbearable circumstances may prompt people to leave without informing those left behind. Gendered power relations affect migration trajectories throughout the process (Schmoll, 2014). Sometimes people need to disappear to avoid violent debtors who have organised the journey for them, and not telling the family their whereabouts may be a way of protecting them. Moreover, disappearance by severing connections with the family and community in the country of origin may be a way of managing social relations (e.g. Drotbohm, 2023), especially in cases where the migrants 'don't make it', that is, when they are not successful in finding work and earning money in the countries of destination (Lucht, 2013). All this adds to the excruciating uncertainty felt among families left behind. Spouses of the disappeared may ask themselves whether their wife or husband has actually left the family and started a new life elsewhere.

Nevertheless, based on ethnographic accounts of irregular migration, we can assume that most migrants want to keep in contact with their families back home. For the majority, the idea of dying en route, without their families ever knowing what happened to them and with no rituals to mark their death, is a horrifying thought (e.g. de León, 2015; Kobelinsky, 2017). While such a possibility is an ever-present threat in many migratory contexts, well recognised by putative migrants and their families (Perl, 2019a; Zagaria, 2020; Kivilahti and Huttunen, 2023), when it actually happens it violently shatters any hopes invested in the dangerous migrant journey. Moreover, such a death is the opposite of what is understood to be a good or dignified death in most cultural contexts.

If we take seriously the claim made by Hester Parr, Olivia Stevenson and Penny Woolnough (2016) that it is the search that creates 'the missing' as a figure, then most missing or disappeared migrants are missing from their families rather than from the state (also Robins, 2019). In other words, it is families or close friends who recognise that somebody has disappeared from their everyday life, somebody has not returned from a trip or somebody travelling or living abroad has not contacted the family for a disturbingly long time. However, it is hard to know exactly when to get worried, as there can be many reasons why the undocumented traveller cannot be in touch. When families do get worried, it is often hard to know how to proceed and whom to contact, as their relationship to state power is often tenuous (e.g. IOM, 2021). All this makes migrants susceptible to disappearing.

To conclude, the missing or disappeared migrant is an elusive figure – in some sense even more elusive than missing persons in conflict zones or under military regimes. Some migrants are missing both from their families and from states, the sending and receiving ones. Others may be 'invisible' to the receiving states, living an undocumented life as migrants without proper paperwork, while their families know their whereabouts (on such a situation, see e.g. Lucht, 2012). In most cases, however, migrants are missing from their families and communities. Sometimes bodies disappear without a trace in North America's Sonora Desert (de León, 2015), in North Africa's desert areas or on the high seas (Dziuban, 2023), leaving an empty space behind, marked by unanswered questions and anxieties.

Disturbed intimacies and painful voids

In the vignette with which I opened this chapter, the parents of a disappeared young man describe an unbearable void; their son's unaccounted-for absence turns their life into a limbo-like existence. Their situation may well be described as liminal (Turner, 1977) in at least two dimensions: firstly, they mourn the fact that they have not been able to bury their son, that the transition from life to (presumed) death has not been taken care of properly ('If we could have buried him, we would accept it and mourn him'), with the son remaining in a liminal state between life and proper burial. Secondly, these circumstances push the parents themselves into a liminal existence, which they describe as a state between life and death ('We are neither dead nor alive').

This is just one of currently sixteen video-recorded testimonies of such experiences on the Missing at the Borders website. The testimonies were provided for specific purposes: to unveil the ongoing violence of migrant disappearances, and to raise awareness of the predicament of the families. The political dimension of this website and its significance in making the disappeared reappear will be discussed further in Chapter 5. Some of the interlocutors may harbour the hope that their testimony will help to find their missing one. At the same time, the testimonies give access, even if superficially and momentarily, to the private worlds of families of the missing.

The testimonies are evocative, each of them inviting the viewer to listen to a story of a family member embarking on a perilous journey across the Mediterranean towards Europe, and of their disappearance on that journey. Mothers, fathers, wives and children come in front of the camera, one after another, repeating similar kinds of experience: a loved one leaving, the connection with a migrating family member broken, an inability to reach the person, hopes of him (all the missing are men) returning, fear (and growing certainty) of his death, unbearable ambiguity, pain at not being able to have a proper funeral and a limbo-like existence in a state of not knowing. The testimonies take the viewer into a situation marked by nagging uncertainty and unresolved questions about the whereabouts and 'ontological status' (cf. Gatti, 2014; Katz, 2023) of the missing one.

There are several common features in all the testimonies. One is the way in which the motivation behind leaving for Europe is built. In most of the cases, the disappeared person is a young or youngish man and, in all cases, he was unemployed and unable to find decent work or training. A desire to build a future, to become independent from ageing parents, to be able to support parents and to get married – decent income is often a precondition of marriage in North African societies (e.g. Schielke, 2015; Zagaria, 2020) – along with hopes of getting an education or otherwise 'going somewhere' in life (Hage, 2009) are aspirations that were often repeated by the disappeared. At the same time, however, these aspirations are dwarfed by circumstances, by rampant unemployment and scarce opportunities for building a life in the home communities or elsewhere within the state of origin.

A couple of the disappeared were already married, and one of them had earlier been able to cross to Europe along regular routes and work legally in Italy. However, his work permit was not renewed and he was stuck in Tunisia, relying on the meagre income earned by his wife. In the testimonies, being unemployed and dependent on spouses, siblings or parents is presented as humiliating for married men, and such a situation pushes them towards taking the decision to migrate via irregular routes.

Migrant deaths and disappearances have a profound impact on the communities from which migrants originate. Ethnographic research on African societies describes communities drastically affected by changing visa regimes and diminishing numbers of legal routes for migration (e.g. Lucht, 2012; Andersson, 2014a; Perl, 2016; Zagaria, 2020). Similarly, migrant deaths and disappearances mark countless communities in South and Central America (de León, 2015; de Vecchi Gerli, 2022; Verástegui Gonzáles, 2022) and elsewhere. This body of research builds up rich social, cultural and political contexts for individual migration choices. Individual experiences of loss and indeterminacy, such as the one presented in the opening vignette, become embedded in societal contexts.

In her ethnographic study of Zarzis, a coastal town in Tunisia, Valentina Zagaria (2020) describes a community with a history of generations of migration to Europe, to provide for the family and the community. The diminishing possibilities of legal entry into Europe have dramatically changed these patterns. While the pre-1990s visa regimes allowed for legal circular migration between the EU and Tunisia, the current regimes almost totally prevent legal entry into Europe. This pushes the younger generation to travel via clandestine routes. Local young men and, to a lesser degree, women, are 'burning' (*harga*), that is, taking the irregular route to Europe, to escape what Zagaria calls 'social death', or the impossibility of building a decent life in Tunisia. The local sayings, '*Ya harga ya sharga*' ('either we *harga* or we choke') and '*gharga wala harga*' ('we drown or we *harga*'), reflect the cruel entanglement of death with promises of a better life (Zagaria, 2020: 130). This description resonates deeply with the testimonies on the Missing at the Borders website. At the same time, dead bodies of unknown migrants from further south are found at sea and buried in Zarzis, unidentified. Zagaria describes the moral ambiguities around both the unidentified dead bodies (discussed further in Chapter 4) and the local youth's desires to migrate.

Ethnographic accounts from other parts of the world describe similar experiences of living with excruciating absence. Jason de León (2015) describes the disappearance of a fifteen-year-old Ecuadoran male, José Tacuri. De León was contacted by José's family, and he followed their search efforts. De León's description of the situation calls to mind the experiences of the families discussed in the previous chapter; family members repeatedly say that there will be no peace until they know what has happened to José, and his aunt and sisters talk about their imagination running wild, depicting scenes of José having lost his memory, being in detention, working as a drug mule for a coyote who will not let him go. José's unaccounted-for absence disturbs the life of the whole family (de León, 2015: 265–79).

It is worth noting that while in the contexts discussed above, the motivation to travel arises from challenging situations but not from a direct threat to personal safety or life, migrants in other places are escaping from seriously life-threatening circumstances: ongoing armed conflict, environmental disasters or direct individually targeted threats of violence from the state or other actors.

Unlike the family members of the Argentinian and Bosnian disappeared discussed in the previous chapter, the families of disappearing migrants very rarely actually witness the moment of disappearance. Instead, failures in communication lead families to believe that something is wrong: either expected phone calls do not happen, or attempts to reach the absent person remain futile. When the lack of contact is protracted, it gives rise to painful ambiguity and to hopes and fears oscillating between the possibilities of life and death. Some families gravitate towards believing that the disappeared loved one is dead, especially in cases where there are rumours or convincing testimonies about a capsized boat or other life-threatening events (Kivilahti and Huttunen, 2023).

Returning to the testimonies on the Missing at the Borders website, I wish to highlight one more common feature: the uncertainty of how to proceed with the search. In the vignette with which I opened this chapter, the parents of Ali Ayari say that they do not know whom they should contact to find out the fate of their son, even though more than ten years have passed since his disappearance. The world beyond their horizon opens up as an endless sea, with no reliable institutions in it to help them to find Ali. In Chapter 4, I will take a closer look at search and identification practices. However, to understand the experience of the families of missing migrants, it is important to acknowledge the absence of established or trustworthy institutional routes through which to report a person missing in many of the places of origin of undocumented migrants (also IOM, 2021). Talking to state institutions seldom leads to solving the cases. Instead, in their testimonies family members depict a variety of strategies for discovering the fate of the disappeared loved one, which often turn into a detective-like gathering of traces: watching news reels and videos of migrant boats on television and YouTube in order to capture a glimpse of their missing family members; making phone calls to survivors of capsized boats; and using their networks of neighbours and relatives to obtain information – such a reliance on informal and familial networks is very common among the relatives of undocumented migrants, because the situation is marked by a lack of well-established, trustworthy search routes (Dearden, Last, Spencer and Cuttitta, 2020; Kivilahti and Huttunen, 2023). The search for knowledge is incessant and never-ending.

In some cases, families suspect the authorities of being involved in the disappearance, as discussed above. On the Missing at the Borders website, Amar Chelbi's family members in Algeria believe that he has been captured by the coastguard in Tunisia and that he might be alive in prison there, referencing the illegalisation of undocumented emigration from many North African states. 'Just tell us they [Amar and his co-travellers] are in Tunisian jails! We would have a peace of mind if we knew that they are alive!' exclaims Amar's brother, giving the testimony with his parents. He continues: 'We accept that they be sentenced to three or four years as long as we learn that they are alive!' and 'Let us see him!' But doubt and hesitation creep in, and he and his parents say that they need to be relieved of the doubt, of the not knowing whether Amar is alive or dead. 'If we would have had his body, we would have accepted God's destiny for him and we would have resigned ourselves!' they say, echoing many other family members repeating the need to be able to give their loved one a proper burial.

The father of Aymen Ben Smida, who has been missing since 6 September 2012, puts it like this:

> One day they say he's alive, the next day they say he is drowned. That means we're still stuck. If you have a death, on the first day one dies, on the second day one's buried. On the third day laughter comes back into the house. Step by step one forgets. We're still in the first two days [after eight years].

In such accounts, the painful liminality between life and death, or between life and proper burial as addressed in the previous chapter, is echoed. Aymen Ben Smida's father's account spells out the significance both of funerary rituals for those left behind and of the over-stretched liminality of living with an unresolved absence. Swinging between hope that the missing person could be alive and fear that they are most probably dead creates a liminal landscape of uncertainty.

Sometimes the ways in which intimate relations are affected by disappearances is described in rather nuanced ways in the testimonies on the Missing at the Borders website. 'I no longer cook the dishes he liked. My poor children. I took away from them all the dishes that Mounir liked', says the mother of Mounir Benstoh, who went missing in 2007. She also describes how she calls her other sons by his name by mistake. The viewer can only try to imagine life lived in such a continuous painful presence-of-absence. Many family members describe how holidays and festivities no longer feel joyous, or how the weddings of their other children feel like funerals – but not the funerals they wish to have for their missing ones, which would end the harrowing liminality. 'What is most painful is that he was not with me in our son's circumcision!' says the wife of another missing man.

The excruciating state of not knowing is similar to that experienced in the cases discussed in the previous chapter. 'His absence is ever-present', says one of the mothers of the absent young men on the website (Beya Boudoukha). 'When I hear a knock on the door, right away I think he's come back', says another (Lyamna Hamidi), but so far the hope has always turned to disappointment. 'Our lives are like a constant funeral', says a father (Abdelhamid Chelbi), but this is a funeral that seems to continue endlessly without bringing closure. A liminal existence emerges, reminiscent of the one described by families of the forcibly disappeared.

In all the testimonies, the protracted absence affects the intimate lives of the families in various ways. The wives of disappeared men utter the simple statement: 'I do not know if I am married or if I am a widow!' Such an indeterminate status affects women's identity and their understanding of their possibilities in life. At the same time, it affects their legal rights and duties, as property rights are regulated through kinship relations and legislation or customary law related to them (cf. Perl, 2018: 95–6; IOM, 2021). Without a death certificate for the disappeared person, family members are often unable to transfer ownership of property and gain access to it (cf. Perl, 2018: 95–6; IOM, 2021). The disappearance of a parent may seriously affect the future possibilities of their children; in countries where children are not automatically issued birth certificates, their access to healthcare and schooling may become limited (IOM, 2021: 37).

Moreover, sometimes families borrow money to arrange the journey of one of their members, believing they can pay it back when the migrant finds employment in the country of destination. Migration is often a joint family effort (Zagaria, 2020), even though there are also examples of people – especially young men – travelling without their families knowing. If the traveller then dies or disappears, the debt falls on a family that is often already financially disadvantaged (IOM, 2021: 36–7). This struggle with economic hardship is compounded by worry and grief, and sometimes also stigma; in some places, being 'abandoned' by a migrant spouse or child may be seen as shameful (IOM, 2021: 35–6).

All this points to the fact that disappearance is an emotional predicament, but also a void that affects social and economic relationships and practices. Gerhild Perl (2018; 2019a), discussing the experiences of the families of twelve young men who died or went missing from the Moroccan village of Hansala, expands out from family members' emotional pain to other dimensions of loss. She convincingly shows how the families lose not only the person but also any hopes invested in them: hopes of income and security and hopes for a better future. The dead and the missing mean broken family lines and broken trajectories, in a geographical area where livelihoods have, for a long time, been dependent on migration and embedded in networks of kinship, care and remittances.

To sum up, migrant disappearances create voids in their communities of origin, and these voids have many dimensions. Disappearances cause emotional strain for family members and others close to the missing person but, beyond that, they also have profound practical and legal consequences that affect the legal statuses and economic circumstances of those left behind. A disappeared person is a void in a system of relations – kinship relations that are often relations of care and support, and economic relations of providing for family members. Finally, absences that turn into presumed deaths are culturally anomalous, and the lack of cultural frames for addressing the situation adds to the families' burden.

Concluding remarks

In this chapter, I argue that when we talk about migrant disappearances, we talk about a complex phenomenon. In today's world, undocumented migrants die and disappear because of tightened border regimes and technologically monitored border enforcement strategies that push them onto perilous routes and dangerous means of travel. At the same time, it is important to recognise migrants' own agency: they are not passive victims of such politics but people making active decisions about their lives. They choose to embark on migrant journeys, and sometimes people disappear intentionally from their families in order to regulate their social relations.

However, it is equally important to understand that migrants' agency takes place in a world structured by enormous global inequalities, and that sometimes people migrate simply to survive. The greatest common denominator among disappearing migrants is their vulnerable position in socio-economic and political terms, along with powerful structures of inequality. Often agency entails the possibility of exposing oneself to deadly danger.

I argue above that it is justified to claim that there is a kind of intentionality behind migrant deaths and disappearances, as they are often instrumentalised as deterrents to prevent putative future migrants from embarking on the journey. However, I also claim that the intentionality is of a different kind when compared with the politics of enforced disappearance exercised by authoritarian governments. Unwelcoming visa regimes and violent border enforcement create spheres of abandonment that expose migrants to deadly circumstances, with undocumented migrants being made vulnerable to death rather than being targeted individually. However, in the world of unprotection and organised irresponsibility where undocumented migrants move, they are also susceptible to being individually targeted by various actors, and the line between 'taking life' and 'exposure to death' (Mbembe, 2003) becomes blurred. As a consequence, migrant disappearances create disturbing voids in the families and communities of origin.

Several migration scholars have pointed to the fact that the deterrence of migrant deaths does not actually work as intended: rather than stopping migrants seeking entry into the Global North, it only pushes them onto deadlier routes (e.g. Andersson, 2014a). Alongside this academic critique are other moments of recognition, political initiatives for change and groups working in solidarity with migrants (e.g. Perl, 2018), which will be discussed further in Chapter 4. Although such discordant voices show that prevention through deterrence is not a universally embraced and accepted political strategy, the deadly consequences of the current migration regime remain unchanged, for the time being.

Notes

1 Missing at the borders (https://missingattheborders.org/en/) (accessed 8 March 2024).
2 See e.g. How rescuing drowning migrants became a crime, *The Guardian* (https://www.theguardian.com/news/2020/sep/22/how-rescuing-drowning-migrants-became-a-crime-iuventa-salvini-italy) and Abuse and 'vilification' of migrants on the rise as borders close, Reuters (https://www.reuters.com/article/us-human-rights-conference-asylum-idUSKCN1NK0KE) (both accessed 5 July 2023).
3 I want to emphasise that with this argument, I do not mean that help and support should not be given to migrants en route. Rather, my point is that such help is not enough if we do not reconsider the whole structure of the migration order.
4 For other projects counting migrant deaths, see Human Costs of Border Control (https://www.borderdeaths.org/) (accessed 14 February 2024).
5 https://missingmigrants.iom.int/ (accessed 14 February 2024).
6 The IOM publication series *Fatal Journeys* 1–4 'Fatal Journeys: Tracking Lives Lost during Migration', IOM Publications Platform offers a great deal of interesting data on migrant deaths and disappearances, and sets out both the challenges of gathering the data and suggestions for improving it (https://publications.iom.int/books/fatal-journeys-tracking-lives-lost-during-migration) (accessed 8 August 2024).
7 e.g. Algeria – A Comparative Analysis of Enforced Disappearances and the Missing in Middle East, North Africa and Caucasus (https://enforceddisappearances.dealingwiththepast.org/algeria/) (accessed 14 February 2024).

3

'Individual' missing persons: private agonies and ambiguities of citizenship

> In missing person investigations there is always a balance between the search for a person and the person's right to remain unfound.
>
> (Apps, 2017)

Most of the research literature on missing persons and disappearances focuses on conflicts, crises and political terror. However, there are individuals who go missing, from their families, and from the state, during peacetime and often in their familiar environments, in the affluent, post-industrial and politically rather stable societies of the Global North that are governed by the principles of the rule of law. These seem simply to be individual cases, embedded in private tragedies and idiosyncratic circumstances. There are no apparent necropolitical projects, in Mbembe's (2003) sense, behind these disappearances – that is, projects designed to intentionally take the lives of the subjects, or expose them to the possibility or probability of death. In this chapter, I address such cases; they are what Jenny Edkins (2011) calls 'people who go missing under more everyday circumstances' and whose disappearance seems to be unconnected to any others.

I use the descriptor 'individual' for these disappearances. However, I write the term in quotation marks for two reasons: firstly, every disappeared person is an individual, and is missed as that unique individual by those left behind. My intention is not to claim that the missing persons discussed in previous chapters are somehow less individual, as persons embedded in complex social worlds (cf. Edkins, 2011). Secondly, at least some cases that are understood as individual disappearances are connected to various inequalities within the societies of the Global North, even though this connection is not always apparent; nevertheless, we tend to view these missing persons as individual cases, and they are not seen by other citizens as forming a social category of victims or one of people disappeared for a particular reason (cf. Parr and Fyfe, 2012).

Even though these disappearances are apparently non-political, it could be argued that human life is always socially and politically situated. Some writers suggest that people with mental health problems or challenging socio-economic situations are over-represented in cases of 'individual' disappearance (e.g. Parr and Fyfe, 2012: 629–30) and many disappearances that are easily regarded as mere individual tragedies can be interpreted in larger sociopolitical contexts, with questions arising regarding social policy, healthcare systems and other care networks. Amber Dean (2015) suggests another kind of structural reading of 'individual' disappearances: she argues that sexism and racism are part of the structures behind the over-representation of indigenous women among missing females in Vancouver (cf. Gilchrist, 2010). Likewise, Anna Matyska claims that disappearances are often connected to inequalities of class and gender (Matyska, 2023b; Matyska, 2024a). Thus, some 'individual' disappearances might be interpreted as resulting from 'exposure to death' (Mbembe, 2003); for example, inadequate, or lack of, care for people with mental health problems or for abused children exposes them to deadly danger.

However, there are also people who seem to be rather privileged, or at least do not clearly fall into categories of marginality, but still disappear from their loved ones. In this chapter I discuss disappearances of people who are citizens of democratic states and whose families rely heavily, if not exclusively, on the state when searching for them. Rather than trying to analyse the ways in which the (possibly marginal) socio-economic position or the racial or ethnic background of the missing person could explain their disappearance, I focus on the relationship between that person and the state, alongside the effects that such disappearances have on the private and familial lives of those left behind.

My empirical focus in this chapter is Finland, which I read as an example of a rather stable, liberal democracy. I will make some comparative observations with other countries in Europe to diversify the analysis, but the chapter does not pretend to be an exhaustive description of disappearances in democracies; rather, it is a suggestion of how to conceptualise the relationship between the state and the missing in such cases. Although anthropological wisdom tells us that there is no universal 'state' (Sharma and Gupta, 2006; Lazar, 2013) – the relationship between the state and its citizens varies from place to place, in post-industrial democratic societies as well – the key point in this chapter is that citizens in democracies expect the state to adhere to the principles of the rule of law.

As in the previous chapters, I will look here at both the ways in which the family left behind, and others close to the missing person, deal with the disappearance, and the ways in which the state relates to them. First, I will briefly contextualise 'individual' disappearances, and follow this with a detailed reading of the pain experienced by the family of an 'ordinary' man who went missing in Finland. I will then expand out to the state and its search practices nationally and internationally, and to mapping the tensions in these practices. Thus, this chapter is geared towards the 'reappearance' of the missing through police work, with the focus on the police making visible the relationship between the state and the individual. The depiction of search practices in these rule-of-law democracies will also serve as a reference point in the next chapter, where I discuss various political projects in other contexts that are designed to make the disappeared reappear. Moreover, I juxtapose my analytical findings with those in the previous chapters to consider both the similarities and some dramatic differences between these 'individual' disappearances and disappearing undocumented migrants and victims of violent state politics.

Contextualising 'individual' disappearances

Different methods are used to produce statistics on missing citizens in different countries and, consequently, it is challenging to present comparable figures. Sometimes the numbers of 'missing person incidents'[1] are presented, that is, how many individual cases the police have investigated, while at other times what is counted is how many people remain missing for longer than a certain pre-defined time.

With this caution in mind, I take a brief look at the numbers of missing persons in certain countries and regions so as to start to map the phenomenon. Within the EU, there are approximately ten thousand unresolved missing person cases each year,[2] while in the USA the number of reported missing person cases revolves around five or six hundred thousand annually.[3] In Britain, every year some three hundred thousand people are reported missing to the police; 99 per cent of these cases are resolved relatively quickly, but some absences remain unaccounted for for longer, and about 1 per cent of the cases – some three thousand each year – remain 'cold', that is, the individuals are missing for years or even decades (Shalev Greene and Alys, 2017). In Poland, around twenty thousand people are reported missing annually (Matyska, 2020; Matyska, 2023b); this number increased after the country joined the EU and Polish people started to move as a workforce within the region. In Finland, out of a total population of about 5.5 million, some seven to eight hundred people are reported missing each year, and forty to fifty of these remain missing for longer than a couple of weeks. Even when taken only as a preliminary mapping, these numbers show that disappearances do touch large numbers of people in post-industrial democracies, and affect the lives of family members, friends, colleagues, neighbours and communities around the world.

As in the previous chapter about migrant disappearances, here the question of intentionality behind the disappearance also becomes crucial. Did the missing person leave intentionally? Did they want to leave because of circumstances that had somehow become unbearable? Or, is the missing person in a vulnerable situation? Are they a child or an older person, are they suicidal or with mental health problems, or is there something else that would render them incapable of making their own decisions? The police always consider these questions when somebody is reported missing. This consideration is at the heart of police work on disappearances (Holmes, 2017) and it reflects the liberal state's dual role in relation to its citizens, as protector of an individual's rights, including the right to privacy, and simultaneously as protector of their safety. However, I will argue below that this tension is multifaceted; while some of the missing indeed do disappear on purpose, and such intentional disappearances often become a strategy for managing tensions in family relations, misreading other disappearances as intentional leads to a failure by the police to protect the safety of the missing. How to address this issue is a key point of contention between the state and the kin.

Human rights discourses emphasise the families' 'right to know' the fate of their loved ones in cases of enforced disappearance. When a person goes missing from their family in a democratic society, this right is often questioned, and is balanced out by the individual's right to make decisions about their life, including about their whereabouts and whom to inform. This gives rise to tensions between the kin, the state and the missing person (Matyska, 2023a; Matyska, 2023b; Matyska, 2024a; see also Sant Cassia, 2005), and to questions about the 'ownership' of missing person cases. Who is the legitimate guardian of the missing person's rights and interests? What are the rights and duties of the state on the one hand, and of the kin on the other? And what are the rights and duties of missing persons themselves?

There is a branch of scholarship that aims to help the police in democratic states to effectively find people reported missing, ranging from writing on the psychological and medical profiling of the missing to the use of various methods and technological equipment in the actual search (e.g. Shalev Greene and Alys, 2017). The quote with which I open this chapter is from an article that addresses disappearances of British citizens abroad, and is representative of this branch of literature (Apps, 2017). While such scholarship is concretely aimed at helping to find the missing (and using public funds effectively in search operations), it simultaneously illustrates the role of the police as the guardian of citizenship rights and the representative of the state in relation to citizens in missing person cases. At the same time, this literature makes visible some of the tensions inherent in the search process.

The father who never came back

In 2013, Finnish musician and visual artist Hanneriina Moisseinen published a graphic novel called *Isä*, which translates as 'Father' in English. The book is based on the artist's own experience, and it relates the story of the disappearance of her father when she was ten years old. Moisseinen's father disappeared inexplicably while on a short work-related visit to an island in eastern Finland with a group of workmates. He was never found, and his fate never determined. Moisseinen gave several media interviews at the time of publication of the novel, reasserting that the story was autobiographical. I read the novel as a story that unravels, in an exceptionally detailed and evocative way, the experiences of families and others left behind when somebody disappears. The book shows how experiencing the disappearance of somebody close to you is a process, or a series of 'unfolding scenes' (Parr, Stevenson and Woolnough, 2016: 68).

The novel combines pictures and text, and it focuses strongly on the personal and private realm, beautifully conveying the ways in which the disappearance of one of its members profoundly changes the life of an 'ordinary' family. There are some references to the police work in the search for the father, and some questions about its adequacy, but the importance of the community in defining the significance of the disappearance is much more prevalent in this narrative. I will suggest some ways in which to interpret the relatively understated role of the state in Moisseinen's story of disappearance and search.

The novel opens with a cutting from a local newspaper. It is the news article that reported Moisseinen's father's disappearance at the time it happened, in the matter-of-fact style of news reporting that gives the details of the disappearance and describes any distinguishing marks. The article ends with a plea for the reader to contact the local police should they know anything about Mr Moisseinen's whereabouts. The police's phone number is then given, anchoring the storyline of the novel in the real world and reminding us that behind every unremarkable piece of news there is a whole social world affected by the events. However, at the same time, the phone number anchors this disappearance within a framework of legal protection; for this disappearance, there exists a framework for search. The disappearance is recognised by the state, and the search is begun soon afterwards. In this sense, the disappearance differs from those discussed in the previous two chapters.

In Moisseinen's book, the reader is introduced to the world of the story through pictures of the Finnish wood-and-lake landscape; endless woods and a labyrinthine landscape of lakes unfold before the reader's eyes. This opening sequence conveys a sense of a wilderness-like landscape, with

Figure 3.1 The cover image of Hanneriina Moisseinen's graphic novel 'Isä – Father', presenting the disappeared father with his daughter, the author of the novel. Credit: © Hanneriina Moisseinenen 2013.

endless nooks and crannies, caves in the rocks and mounds in the forest in and behind which to hide and endless stretches of water in which to drown; the series of pictures illuminates the fact that this open landscape is impossible to cover thoroughly when searching for somebody. The attached text says:

> The boreal forest zone is great and quiet. In its lakes and marshland countless people have drowned over time. People have been disappearing in the woods as long as there has been settlement in these parts./ Some have disappeared on purpose. Others by accident. Some have been found alive, some dead. Some have been lost for good./ People have fallen through fragile ice and their bodies may have been found much later. People have perished in the cold, been frozen in the snow when drunk, people have been killed, some have gone away in search of a better life./ Many are those in these parts who have taken

their own lives./ But what could have happened if a person disappears and is never seen again alive or found dead?[4]

The last page of this visual overture is a map of where the father went missing, showing again the location's vast watery labyrinth. The area that was covered by the search team is marked on the map: it is tiny, leaving out swathes of wood and water stretching in all directions. This five-page sequence is a compelling visual representation of the overwhelming sense of helplessness that many families of the missing feel, the sense of the impossibility of the task at hand, the vastness of the space and the paralysing number of possible hiding places.

The story that follows is a depiction of the 'unfolding scenes' (Parr, Stevenson and Woolnough, 2016: 68) of Moisseinen's father becoming a missing or disappeared person. The first part, titled 'Life before the disappearance', depicts the life of an ordinary Finnish family with two children, foregrounding memories of the father as an important figure in his daughter's life. There is nothing here that hints at the approaching tragedy; there are no particular problems, enmities or difficulties; life just goes on in its (in hindsight) beautiful everydayness. On his last morning at home, the father leaves early on his trip, while the rest of the family are still asleep. They wake up to the new morning, with no idea that they will never see him again – neither alive nor dead.

Then comes the dramatic section. The phone rings, and the mother answers. She is told about the disappearance by her husband's workmates and goes into a state of shock. The daughter comes in, and the disquieting news is conveyed to her. She reacts with concrete questions, 'Can we stay in this house? We have just moved in and renovated the house!' showing an early instinctive realisation that the disappearance is going to affect a whole range of issues in the life of the family, touching the very foundations of life.

The following section is introduced with dark colours and titled 'Life after the disappearance'. Again, various scenes follow one another. While coming to terms with the initial shock, the family members ponder whether the police have really considered all the possible explanations for the disappearance. Soon the daughter starts to imagine the possible course of events, the various ways in which her father could have died; there are pictures of him floating in dark water, pictures of dark, frightening human figures threatening him in the twilight of the woods. Such haunting images and painful thoughts about the putative fate of the missing are repeated in the stories of family members in other contexts as well (e.g. Wagner, 2008). Then comes a scene with adults talking behind a closed door, and the anguished child listening to her grandmother lamenting the disappearance of her son. The deep relationality of the missing person is embodied in the variety of people who mourn his disappearance.

New scenes follow. The father's absence becomes visible in everyday situations. The daughter goes to the bathroom and sees the hook where his towel used to hang. The empty hook becomes a subtle visibilisation of the painful absence. Another scene: the daughter goes to the school nurse for a check-up. The graphic novel format allows the author to place thought bubbles above the daughter's head, including anguished thoughts about her father and a fear that the nurse may ask her something about him. The scene ends with the nurse commenting on the daughter's periods, saying: 'You can talk about this with your mother – with your father you can talk about other things, but this is women's matter.' Painful thoughts about the absent father are present in the most mundane situations, a constant reminder of his absence.

Yet another scene shows the mother drinking alcohol, with her eyes depicted as black holes. She is too preoccupied with her own grief to be able to listen to her daughter, and the daughter becomes anguished over questions such as, 'What if my mother dies of grief, where can the children live then? Who will take care of them?' When the girl goes to school, people repeatedly ask her: 'Any news of your father?' But the questions are not always friendly and supportive, and shame emerges as an ingredient of life; disappearance is a strange and, as such, shameful event, and it sets the family apart from the 'normal' families in the community. The disappearance profoundly disturbs the life of the entire family, and radiates out from them to the whole community.

For the first year after the disappearance, everybody expects the father's body to turn up in the spring when the ice on the lakes melts, as the most probable explanation for his disappearance is that he has drowned. In one scene the daughter thinks: 'What if his body will not be found in spring? What if it turns out that he left us?' Such sweeping uncertainty characterises most instances of disappearance – the ambiguity of hope and fear colours the situation, and the possibility that the missing loved one has left voluntarily is a deeply wounding thought for those left behind, as discussed in the previous chapter.

The novel also makes visible another common theme in the stories of families of the disappeared in all contexts: the ghost-like imaginary appearance of the missing person in unexpected situations (to be discussed further in Chapter 5). In this novel, the daughter repeatedly thinks that she sees her father in various places, in the midst of her everyday life; in the comic-strip frames, we see the figure of a man who looks exactly like the missing father sitting in a café window, and in a car passing by. But when the daughter approaches, she realises that the person is not her father, but a total stranger.

This was a familiar theme in my discussions with Bosnians who had a family member who had disappeared: they told me about rumours and stories about somebody having seen the missing person somewhere, about family members imagining that they had seen them but realising the very next moment that it was somebody else. The haunting presence of the absent person punctuates the everyday life of their families and friends.

In the book by Moisseinen, spring comes and ice melts from the lakes, but the father's body is still not found. A kind of ritualisation of the death takes place as the daughter goes to the lakeshore to sing for her father. But he does not answer. 'He is silent', writes the author, and the ritual does not end the troubling liminality of absence, while his ghost-like presence continues in various forms. 'You have your father's eyes', says a schoolmate, in an unfriendly way. The idea of children bearing the features of a disappeared parent and embodying their presence is another theme that comes up in discussions with family members of the disappeared in many contexts (cf. Gatti, 2014: 77–95). I will explore this theme further in Chapter 5.

When discussing the effect of the disappearance on their lives, both mother and daughter in the book point to the absence of a grave. Dead people are buried in graves, and family members can go there to mourn, to remember, to light candles and leave flowers. The families of the missing get nothing, just emptiness. 'Disappearance is a black hole that eats up all light and joy', the daughter says. Such comments by the protagonists point to the importance of rites of passage and cultural scripts for transitional moments (cf. Katz, 2023; Matyska, 2023a).

Seventeen years later, the daughter, now grown up, travels to Argentina. It is interesting that she goes to Argentina in particular, a country with a history so deeply marked by disappearances, albeit not mentioned in the book. She goes to the marshland in the south of the country, even though she is warned against doing so: 'You may disappear there, many people have … .' But she does go, driven by an inexplicable need to get 'as near to disappearance as possible'. She goes hiking in the vast landscape, sleeps there, and returns with exhilarated relief: 'I did not disappear!' After this she is ready to go back to Karelia, her home district in eastern Finland, to talk with her mother. The last section of the book shows mother and grown-up daughter talking together about the father and his disappearance, sharing the pain that they were not able to share when the crisis was still acute.

At the end of the story, daughter and mother conclude that, in a way, the worst has already happened: they have never found out what occurred and have never recovered the body. There had been fears that something shameful would come out, for example that the father had abandoned his family for another woman. However, now they conclude that not knowing anything at all about what happened is the worst possible outcome. But still, the ethos of the story is that they survived. The book ends with a letter from the daughter to her disappeared father, a loving letter, but one full of sorrow: sorrow about forgetting, sorrow about losing out on the chance to grow up with him by her side. The latter kind of grief indicates the peculiar timescapes of disappearance: while those left behind grow older, the disappeared one stays frozen in time.

The book is a beautifully conveyed story of the way in which the disappearance of one of their members profoundly changes the life of an 'ordinary' family. The missing father is never found and the disappearance remains unexplained. Visually, the book convincingly delivers the paralysing realisation that there are endless possibilities regarding his whereabouts: pictures of the wilderness-like forest-and-lake landscape of eastern Finland, a sparsely populated part of the country with an endless variety of sites rarely visited by humans, places for a dead body to remain hidden. At the same time, it is a story of the life-shaking power of disappearance, of the ways in which it can change the lives of everybody in the family, but finally it is also a story of learning to live with the pain. I read this graphic novel as a convincing voice telling us that 'unpolitical', 'individual' disappearances also leave life-long traces in the lives of those left behind. It shows that those close to the missing do not simply stay in a 'frozen' state (cf. Parr, Stevenson and Woolnough, 2016) when facing the liminality of disappearance; on the contrary, the story depicts a painful, complicated and temporally extended process of negotiating with the anomaly of unaccounted-for absence, and shows how the family members actively mould their relationship with the disappearance.

In this story, the disappearance is reported to the police, and the missing father is searched for. Unlike in the previous chapter, the protection of the law and the recognition of the missing person as a deserving citizen are there, but still questions and anxieties arise: do the police take the family's worries seriously enough? Is there enough investment in the search? In Kivilahti's (2016) interviews with family members of missing persons in Finland, the same theme is repeated: even in a country like Finland, where people usually have a high level of trust in the police as an institution, when a loved one goes missing the family members repeatedly express the feeling that the police are not doing enough. Likewise, in the British context, Parr and Stevenson (2015) argue that the relationship between the police and the families of the missing is often marked by tensions.

The main protagonist in Moisseinen's story comes to accept the disappearance of her father and the lack of closure; his disappearance becomes accepted as a 'permanent state of being', something to live with (cf. Katz, 2023). In this sense, Moisseinen's story is radically different from the experience of 'pervasive missingness' and the lonely, 'deeply individualised', incessant struggle to discover the truth experienced by many family members of those forcibly disappeared, exemplified by the protagonist in Atreyee Sen's article on the mother of a young man disappeared by the Indian state during the Naxal uprising in the country (Sen, 2023). I argue that this difference relates to the circumstances of the disappearance – intentional violence and brutality towards forcibly disappeared victims of state violence leaves families with a radically different affective and political landscape, and makes it impossible to accept what has happened in the way that the protagonist of Moisseinen's story does.

Thus, I suggest that even though the disappearance of a loved one is always painful and creates personal, social and cultural ambiguities and anomalies, being convinced that the disappeared person is being searched for to the greatest extent possible, and that the state recognises them as a rightful citizen worthy of protection, mitigates the pain of families and others left behind. Trust in the state, even if contested and questioned to some extent, leaves room for people to face the personal pain and come to terms with the absence.

'Disappearance is not a crime': the ambiguous status of the missing citizen

'We have to remember that disappearance is not a crime', said a Finnish police officer when interviewed about police practices and procedures regarding missing person reports. This sentence resonates with Apps's (2017) observation with which I open this chapter.

In 2021, my research team interviewed representatives of the Finnish police about their work with disappearances and participated in a search and rescue training event in the Finnish Lapland.[5] Here, I analyse the work of the Finnish police as an example of police operations regarding missing persons in rule-of-law democracies, and I argue that it is shaped by a tension that is at the heart of citizenship in liberal democracies: on the one hand, a fully capable adult citizen should be able to make decisions concerning their own life, including their whereabouts and whom to inform about them; on the other hand, the state should protect its citizens when they are in need of protection. If there is reason to believe that a missing person might be in danger, for example as a victim of criminal assault, the police should intervene. Moreover, children, older people and people with vulnerabilities, such as mental illness or specific disabilities, are entitled to the protection of the state. The 'Janus-face' of the state as both a controlling and caring actor (Caplan and Torpey, 2001) becomes visible when somebody goes missing.

In the interviews, the Finnish police reflected frequently on the dual role of the police and the importance of assessing both whether the missing person is in need of protection and whether there is a need to launch a search. When a person is reported missing, the police carry out an evaluation of the situation: is the disappeared person in danger? How imminent is the danger? Are they an adult, capable of making their own decisions? If the missing person is a child or an older person (over seventy years of age), suicidal, with health problems including mental health issues, disabled, or otherwise vulnerable, the situation calls for an immediate response. When the police make the decision to launch a search, the infrastructures and procedures for doing so are already there, well-established both within the country and also outside its borders through international police cooperation networks. This differs radically from situations in which an undocumented migrant goes missing, as discussed in Chapters 2 and 4.

In Hanneriina Moisseinen's story of disappearance, the vastness of the landscape in eastern Finland is one of the paralysing factors that the family of the missing man face. Finland is a sparsely populated country, with large areas of wood, lake, and bog and swamp land with just a few human inhabitants, especially in the north and east. There is a culture of hiking, foraging for berries and mushrooms and hunting and fishing in this wilderness, and Lapland attracts large numbers of tourists to its trekking routes, both from the urban centres of southern Finland and from abroad. In these circumstances, dozens of people annually become lost and, as a consequence, there is a rather well-developed system of searching for such people.

The training event in which we participated in the Finnish Lapland was exactly about such a search in open terrain. It was coordinated by the local Red Cross, but the police were the key actor in the event. Besides the police, the border guard, emergency services, representatives of the Finnish army, medical personnel and dozens of volunteers, many of them already experienced search and rescue activists, were taking part. It was an intensive two days of cooperation between these different groups and was designed as a training session for both younger police officers and volunteers.

Four of the volunteers were made up to look like injured trekkers, and they hid in the wintery, snow-covered woods. The police led the search and rescue operation, and the other actors, including the volunteers, were effectively organised to work under them, and to thoroughly comb the area in line with the Managing Search Operations (MSO) technique used by the police. Moreover, advanced technology was deployed, including a drone transmitting images from the landscape and a thermograph that could show footprints in the snow and thus suggest the direction of travel and possible whereabouts of people moving through the terrain. Eventually, the four 'injured trekkers' were located and transported in an army truck that had been converted into an ambulance. The first day of the event was the actual exercise in the wilderness, and the second day was spent discussing and analysing the exercise together, learning from experiences, successes and mistakes. Such exercises take place several times a year in Finland, in different parts of the country. Participating in these events, and also in actual searches, is a kind of 'hobby' for many of the volunteers with whom we talked.

The Finnish search and rescue practice is an example of well-developed, well-functioning cooperation between the police and volunteers. It has evolved over decades into a flourishing network of activists cooperating with the police and prepared to invest their skills and free time in search operations. The Voluntary Rescue Service (*Vapepa, Vapaaehtoinen pelastuspalvelu*[6] in Finnish) is a network that brings together people active in different sectors; reindeer herders, rescue dog activists, orienteers, divers, scouts, sailors and others join forces when there is a need to find somebody in distress in the wilderness. Each group brings its own expertise to the situation. For example, the reindeer herders in Lapland are indispensable participants in the areas where they are active; they know the landscape, they have the equipment needed to travel in the rugged terrain, and they are frequently on the move across considerable distances. Likewise, trained dogs are of great help when searching for somebody in the wilderness. These are just a few of the specific volunteer skills that are incorporated into the search process.

What we saw during the event was the state acknowledging its role as the protector of citizens, legal residents and tourists within its territory, and incorporating civil society efficiently into this project. The large-scale application of advanced technology was conspicuous, indicating the level of investment in the search. While the state invests expensive technology, police and army resources and the workforce of health professionals, the volunteers invest their own time and effort. This smooth and effective way of interlocking civil society activists into the search structures indicates a relationship of trust between the state and civil society. Unlike in the previous (and following) chapters, here we see well-structured, well-planned cooperation between the state (the police) and civil society organisations, all investing significantly in the search and rescue effort. The search and rescue teams emerge as assemblages of various actors, knowledge and equipment (Parr and Fyfe, 2012: 62–8); as technology becomes more advanced, and the relations between the state and civil society evolve, these assemblages change over time.

When the disappearance does not take place in the wilderness, the assemblages of search take on a different form. In our interviews with the Finnish police, the officers described a number of techniques that were used for following traces left by a missing person, also outside Finland. The way in which society these days relies on various electronic systems with global reach makes it possible to follow the 'digital footprint' (Parr and Fyfe, 2012: 625) of every person, that is, the various kinds of trace that people leave behind in such systems while just living their lives. The significance of such technology-based tracking and tracing systems has grown in recent years. Social media presence and mobile phone usage are easy to track as long as the phone is working and in use. Withdrawing money from a bank account, paying for something with a credit card, buying plane tickets, crossing international borders – all these small acts leave traces in the electronic systems. In Europe, passports are required only at the Schengen borders, thus enlarging the area within which a person can move more easily without leaving traces, but the banking system effectively records all legal transactions within the Schengen area as well. Access to such systems by the police is circumscribed by various statutes and decrees that guarantee the privacy of individuals in democracies, but nevertheless, when warranted, the police do have this access.

Searching for a missing person becomes more challenging for the police when the individual is abroad or is thought to be. The police can operate only within the state they represent; their warrant for operations is curtailed at the national border. However, when the state recognises one of its citizens abroad as being in need, the police have rather well-developed channels for cooperation across national borders. A similar kind of assessment takes place as in domestic disappearances: the police make a judgement as to whether the person is missing purposefully, and whether they are vulnerable and in need of protection (e.g. Apps, 2017). When they are convinced that the missing person is indeed in danger, they can rely on a range of established procedures and structures. The local police, who receive the missing person notifications, can activate well-established cooperation networks via INTERPOL when searching for information. One Finnish police officer mentioned the case of a teenager who was reported missing by his parents early in the morning, and was found in an airport in Paris that same afternoon. Such an effective and speedy search was enabled by the well-functioning cooperation network.

Of course, cooperation is not always easy, and there are tensions and doubts in the relationship between the police and the families of the missing. Even though the police have guidelines for working on missing person cases, in reality the search is often messy, and it depends on many factors. As Parr and Fyfe (2012: 626) argue, 'searching for missing people is always a contingent process, inescapably related to the specificities of reporting mechanisms and details, risk assessments, available resources, officer decision-making and family liaison'. The families and the police evaluate the situation from different viewpoints; while the police work with generalised understandings of risk and a statistics-based assessment of the profile of the missing person, the families rely on intimate knowledge and long-shared histories. Rather frequently, the families accuse the police of not taking their worries seriously enough and not investing enough in the search, and they often carry out their own search actions alongside the official investigation. And even in Finland, despite the well-functioning cooperation that exists between the police and civil society, there are some private actors who prefer to work independently from the police.[7]

Tensions between the state and the families in democratic societies become more visible when a large number of people go missing at once, such as in terrorist attacks or fatal accidents. Jenny Edkins (2011) analyses the ways in which the state interacted with its citizens who were looking for their missing loved ones in two extraordinary moments: in New York in 2001, after the terrorist attack on the World Trade Center, and in London in 2005, after three explosions on the London underground, both of which resulted in a significant number of missing persons. According to Edkins, in moments such as these, when events threaten the political order, the state is more interested in re-establishing that order than in acknowledging the anxiety of its citizens and of others looking for their missing, and she calls for a politics that recognises the missing as 'persons as such', valuable in their uniqueness.[8] However, in the aftermath of the 2004 Boxing Day tsunami in Southeast Asia, Western states were very effective in defending their missing citizens' right to be searched for and identified and, as a consequence, the identification of the bodies of presumably Western tourists was often prioritised over that of locals (Cohen, 2009). These practices brought to light, once again, the global inequalities that make some people much more disappearable than other.

Moreover, the electronic tracking devices discussed above are useful only when the missing person moves along official, legal routes and operates within public bureaucracies and banking systems. The undocumented migrants discussed in the previous chapter often do their best not to leave any traces in such systems, in order to avoid deportation. As they have slipped out of networks of knowledge, when something drastic happens and they go missing, they become not only extremely hard to trace but also vulnerable, or 'disappearable', to borrow again Laakkonen's (2022) concept.

Tensions between state, family and civil society

Research literature on missing person cases from various countries (e.g. Parr and Fyfe, 2012; Lowenkron and Ferreira, 2014; Parr and Stevenson, 2015: Parr, Stevenson and Woolnough, 2016; Lewicki, 2020; Matyska, 2020;

Matyska, 2023b; Matyska, 2024a; Matyska, 2024b) suggests that there are almost invariably tensions between the police (as the representative of the state) and the family or kin of the missing person. Family members' criticism is often articulated through civil society and, in some countries, an active field of civil society actors working with human disappearances has emerged, giving rise to disputes between state, kin and civil society over the 'ownership' of missing person cases. However, unlike in the cases discussed in the previous chapters, in this chapter, the state is not accused of making its citizens disappear; rather, it is often criticised for not investing enough in the search.

Anna Matyska, working with disappearances in Poland and the Polish diaspora, depicts a slightly different landscape from the Finnish one. In Poland, the number of disappearances rose after the country joined the EU, and disappearances have now become a well-recognised social issue. At the same time, the level of trust in the police, especially in their equal investment in all missing person cases, is not very high. This situation has created a social landscape of various, sometimes competing, actors searching for the missing and seeking to safeguard the interests of disappearing persons and their families. Besides the police, the scene includes the well-established NGO, the ITAKA Foundation,[9] which has worked with disappearances since 1999, and several groups of volunteers that are not as established but are nevertheless active. Moreover, there are dozens of private detectives and clairvoyants who sell their services to families, especially those who are unhappy with the way in which the police work. Some of the clairvoyants, detectives and search and rescue teams work *in* Poland, while others work transnationally and on social media, serving those whose family member has gone missing outside the country. While in Finland the state and the police seem to incorporate volunteers effectively into their efforts, in Poland there is more competition and conflict between various groups, as well as more criticism of the police work (Matyska, 2023a; Matyska, 2024a; Matyska, 2024b).

A programme about disappearance has been running on Polish television for years and, rather than being 'true crime' entertainment, it is designed to present relatively recent, still unresolved, missing person cases and to urge the public to contact the authorities if they have any information. The programme is very popular, and it has become an important agent in relation to disappearances in Poland. It has helped to make disappearances a public issue that is debated among citizens and politicians to a much larger extent than, for example, in Finland (Matyska, 2024a). However, even though the field of actors is rather diverse, the expectation among citizens is that the state should protect all missing persons equally and listen to the worries of every family.

The field of actors discussed by Matyska seek to make the disappeared visible, both to their families and to the state. Pawel Lewicki (2020) discusses a group of Polish migrant workers within the EU who intentionally disappear from their families in order to regulate familial expectations, and whose visibility both to the state and to their families is rather fluid and transient. Lewicki argues that many transnationally disappeared Polish citizens are people with addictions and/or HIV who are living on the streets in Berlin (and elsewhere in the EU's metropolitan centres). Many of them choose to disappear from their families, because they have 'failed' to be successful according to the prevailing expectations: Poland still relies largely on the male breadwinner model, addictions and HIV are highly stigmatising, and the welfare system in relation to those marginalised by these conditions is near to non-existent. Even though these individuals have legally migrated to other EU countries, EU policies support the legal residence of only productive citizens, and those from other EU countries who are sick or addicted and unable to stabilise their employment fall through the protective structures.

Yet, as Lewicki argues, these people are not totally invisible – they are disappeared from their families and are often invisible to the state both in Poland and in Germany, but they become periodically visible to charities that work with HIV-positive individuals, and to the local (in this case German) medical system when their condition gets bad enough. Sometimes these glimpses of presence trickle down to the families, thus letting them know that their missing member is alive, if not necessarily well.

Lewicki's work also illuminates the ambiguities faced by the families of those who are transnationally missing. When a family member who resides abroad goes missing, it may be more difficult to judge when to get worried (cf. the previous chapter on migrant disappearances). Also, sometimes the family do not necessarily know whether the missing person has left the country. Realising that a family member has disappeared becomes harder when the (possibly) missing person is already away from their habitual environment and has no daily contact with their family in the country of origin. Time becomes a crucial factor in this realisation – the longer there is no contact with the absent person, the more worrisome the situation becomes for those left behind (cf. Kivilahti and Huttunen, 2023).

Concluding remarks

In the previous chapters, I have looked at varying relationships between state(s) and disappeared persons, ranging from the state's indisputable responsibility for the disappearances (in Chapter 1) to indifference and lack of investment in the search (in Chapter 2). In this chapter, another kind of relationship between the state and the disappeared emerges: the state recognises the missing as people potentially in need of protection and worthy of search. In Mbembe's (2003) terms, in the cases discussed in this chapter, the state 'lets live' and finds the missing worthy of protection. The relationship between the state and its subjects is, however, marked with tensions even in democratic, rule-of-law states. The state is not accused of targeting its own citizens, but at times it is criticised for not taking all disappearances sufficiently seriously, and for not investing enough in the search.

Among families left behind, these disappearances produce similar kinds of reaction as in the cases discussed in previous chapters, such as ambiguity, anguish and pain. However, the absence of necropolitical violence is certainly significant when family members seek to come to terms with the disappearance and possible death of the missing person, and the relationship between the state and its subjects is negotiated on more benign terms. The state shows its caring face more often here than in Chapters 1 and 2, even though there is always the question posed by the relatives of whether the state (or the police) has done enough.

However, my initial claim about 'individual' disappearances in democratic states being apolitical in nature needs elaboration; the existing research literature suggests that social class, gender, health and racial and ethnic hierarchies, among other factors, are related to a person's disappearability. Cuts in healthcare and social welfare systems may produce situations that expose some people to death and to the danger of disappearance. More research is needed to build an understanding of disappearability in affluent societies of the Global North.

In the previous chapter, I argued that undocumented migrants are searched for mainly by their families, and to some extent by certain NGOs and other non-state actors (see also Chapter 4). In this chapter, the missing are often searched for by both their families and the state, even though the relationship of each of these parties to the search itself is necessarily different. However, returning to the claim that the search produces the missing or disappeared as a category (Parr, Stevenson and Woolnough, 2016), the 'individual' disappeared discussed in this chapter are missing both from their families and from the state. The configuration of state, family and civil society thus takes on a distinctively different form from those discussed in Chapters 1 and 2.

Even though the state engages (in most cases) with the search for the missing in rule-of-law democracies, some scholars have pointed to the lack of cultural frames with which to address the disappearance of a loved one if they are not found (e.g. Katz, 2023). When a loved one dies, there is a blueprint for action that allows families and communities to go through a period of transition, but when somebody disappears and remains inexplicably absent, there are no pre-established cultural conventions that could help the families to come to terms with the situation. This lack of conventions and the stigmatising effect of the disappearance of a family member were depicted touchingly in Hanneriina Moisseinen's story of her father's disappearance. Thus, although the state acknowledging a disappearance and engaging in the search might mitigate the pain, it does not resolve the affective and ontological challenges that continue to haunt families and others left behind when a missing person is not found.

Notes

1. The same person may go missing on repeated occasions and thus be counted multiple times in these statistics, e.g. teenagers in foster care.
2. RE_Motions (https://www.europarl.europa.eu/doceo/document/B-8-2016-0939_EN.pdf) (accessed 16 February 2024).
3. Number of missing person files in the United States from 1990 to 2021, Statista (https://www.statista.com/statistics/240401/number-of-missing-person-files-in-the-us-since-1990/) (accessed 14 February 2024).
4. The English is from the original book, which has the Finnish text translated at the bottom of each page.
5. My research assistant Dimitri Ollikainen conducted four formal police interviews, and both Dimitri and I participated in the ethnographic plunge into the world of search and rescue. During our participation in the training event, we had several informal discussions with the police, as well as with other participants.
6. Vapepa homepage (https://vapepa.fi/en/) (accessed 14 February 2024).
7. In Finland, there is a nationally famous search activist called Reino Savukoski, who does not cooperate with the police but specialises in searching for bodies in water and has located many missing persons' bodies over the years. See Passaro (2022).
8. While I share Edkin's view on the importance of taking every disappearance seriously and treating family members and their pain with respect, I believe that this call for a politics based on 'the person as such' misses the point. The ability of bureaucratic systems, and of the police, to work with a variety of different cases is based not on idiosyncrasies and single cases but rather on creating reliable data and, at least to some extent, universalising categories. The police, organisations and other bureaucracies need to work with categories in order to be able to work at all – which does not mean that they should not be attentive to the needs and anxieties of individuals on the ground. To their family, friends and community, somebody who has gone missing is a unique person embedded in a dense social world; this knowledge of the person is certainly useful

to the police and other officials in their search for the missing, and should be listened to. However, the missing one can never be a unique person in this way to a bureaucratic structure that never knew them as an individual. Their task is not to mourn the unique individual, but to search for them as effectively as possible.

9 ITAKA homepage (https://zaginieni.pl/home-english/) (accessed 14 February 2024).

4

Material reappearances: dead bodies and mortal remains

In September 2013, a new mass grave was found in Tomašica, in northern Bosnia, about twenty kilometres southeast of the city of Prijedor. The first Bosnian mass graves of the 1990s were uncovered some seventeen years earlier in the Srebrenica area and, after the first discovery, new ones were soon found.[1] The Tomašica grave, however, was located after a rather long period of no new discoveries of this size and significance.

When the news of the Tomašica discovery emerged, one of my Bosnian interlocutors, Lejla, said to me in an agitated voice: 'Maybe this time! Maybe they will find him now!' We had talked on a previous occasion about her husband, who went missing in the Prijedor area in 1992; she had been searching for him for more than twenty years at this point. I was not quite sure how to interpret her tone of voice: was she hoping for his remains to be found? Or was she fearing that they would be? My guess is that it was both.

Some months later, Lejla's twenty-year-old daughter sent me a message. The body of her father, Lejla's husband, was indeed identified among the remains of the more than four hundred persons[2] found at the Tomašica site: 'My mother collapsed. She does not want to speak or eat or anything. She is devastated.' From our previous discussions, I knew that Lejla had wanted, more than anything, to find out what had happened to her husband, and to be able to give him a proper burial if he turned out to be dead. Yet when the news came, she was forced to accept the brutality of her husband's fate, and the fact that somebody had indeed intentionally executed him and buried him in an utterly disrespectful way in an unmarked mass grave. Because of the news circulating in post-war Bosnia, she had naturally anticipated this, but she was still devastated. Later on, little by little, Lejla recovered and returned to her everyday life. The following summer, the family buried the remains of her husband, together with those of others from the same village who were identified in Tomašica.

Lejla's reaction to the reappearance of her husband reflects the ambiguity and the diffuse, potentially disruptive, power of reappearances; when a disappearance is linked to necropolitical violence, the reappearance is a

Material reappearances 101

moment not only of relief and closure but also of giving up hope and facing the brutality of the violence against the disappeared. Humanitarian and human rights[3] projects of exhuming and identifying the disappeared have been met with resistance and objections in some places (e.g. Rosenblatt, 2015: 125–52), reflecting the multiple ambiguities surrounding reappearances. However, in most cases, the overwhelming desire of the families of the missing is to know what has happened to their absent one, and to know where they lie.

In the latter part of Chapter 3, the book's attention turned to the reappearances of 'individual' missing; in this chapter, the focus is on reappearances after atrocities, including migrant disappearances. My focus here is on the material reappearance of the missing, and I suggest that this means the ending of the liminal period of disappearance in the strict sense of the term, that is, as the middle phase in a rite of passage (Turner, 1977). In Chapters 1 and 2, I suggested that, from the point of view of families left behind, the missing and disappeared are placed disturbingly between life and death, or between life and proper burial. When the mortal remains of the missing are received, this clarifies their status as dead, and being able to provide a proper burial closes the ritual transition. However, the protracted liminal stage often radiates out in different ways to the period that follows, for example by colouring funerals in particular ways and by giving rise to continuous political struggles over accountability for the events that led to the disappearance in the first place.

I understand material reappearance as a two-stage phenomenon: first, the disappeared reappear alive or as mortal remains – in the latter case, they are often discovered by professionals searching for them, or by passers-by or people working on the land, such as construction workers. In the second stage, the dead disappeared person reappears for their families and communities only after a successful identification reconnects their name and identity with the remains.

I take inspiration from Gabriel Gatti's formulation of forensic work as a 'reconnecting' and 'reclaiming' project that also 're-socialises' and 're-cultures' those identified (Gatti, 2014: 57–75): if disappearance severs people from their social connections, from their names, identities, families and communities and sets them outside the social and cultural world, then identification reconnects them with this world. In this sense, identification 're-civilises' the mortal remains, at the same time as bringing to an end the harrowing liminality of disappearance for those left behind. A focus on forensic work here also allows me to discuss caring modes of necropolitical power.

The recovery and identification of Lejla's husband was made possible by one of the (numerically) most successful projects in the field of searching for and identifying missing or disappeared persons – according to the ICMP, approximately 80 per cent of those reported missing in the ex-Yugoslavian territories had been found and identified by the time of my writing this chapter. Such a high percentage is rare; in most places marked by large-scale disappearance, the numbers of the found and identified missing remain much lower. Here, I position the Bosnian success within a larger frame; I emplace it both within longer-term developments in humanitarian and human rights forensic work, and within a particular contingent historical condition.

As discussed in the introduction to this volume, we live in an era marked by a 'forensic turn', that is, an expectation that exhumations and scientific modes of identifying remains are the default form of addressing human disappearances and extrajudicial killings across different contexts. In this chapter, alongside the focus on reappearances, I comment on the emergence of our current understanding of humanitarian and human rights forensic work and follow the development of this work from Argentina via Bosnia to present-day migrant disappearances.

The multiplication of search, exhumation and identification projects globally has given rise to tensions and contestations around these projects and, as Zahira Aragüete-Toribio (2022) argues, these tensions are manifold. Is the main objective of the exhumations to produce evidence for court cases against the perpetrators, in projects framed as transitional justice, or to return the disappeared to families for dignified burial? Is the Western, scientific and DNA-based approach always the best, or should the universalist assumptions about the forensic method be decentralised? Aragüete-Toribio, among others, points to epistemic complexities around death and human remains that challenge the prevalence of DNA as the only tool for identification. In this vein, she calls for more place-specific approaches (Aragüete-Toribio, 2022: 6; also Eppel, 2009). Some critics question the very premises of the forensic approach, issuing a reminder that in many contexts it is not possible to retrieve all the remains, or even the majority of them. Moreover, the reappearance of persons and remains is almost always a more complicated question than just the retrieval and identification. These critical dimensions will be discussed in this and the following chapters.

In this chapter, I ask what kinds of actor configuration make the disappeared reappear in material form, as bodies or remains, and with what kinds of consequence. I emphasise the importance of embedding all empirical cases in their ethnographic, political and historical contexts. The chapter reflects the structure of the first part of the book: I start with reappearances in Argentina, and then move on to those in Bosnia and then to the challenges of searching for and identifying missing migrants. Moreover, I make a number of observations on search and identification practices elsewhere, to give the argument a more global frame. However, before addressing the empirical cases, I will briefly discuss what I call 'modes of material reappearance' and practices of identification.

Modes of reappearance and techniques of identification

> Always when I see the Red Cross people collecting money for some purposes, I drop a coin into the box. I will never forget what the Red Cross did for me and my family! I will always remain grateful to them!

The above quotation is from Jasminka, a woman of Bosnian origin and wife of Esad, whom I introduced in Chapter 1. Jasminka escaped from Srebrenica in early 1995, travelled through Croatia and Germany and ended up in Finland as a refugee, while Esad remained in the besieged town but succeeded in getting out just a couple of days before the fatal onslaught that started in July 1995. For months, they did not know each other's whereabouts, but they were reconnected by the ICRC's International Tracing Service after a period of excruciating uncertainty. This was in the 1990s, at a time when mobile phones were not as ubiquitous as they are now, and the Red Cross often played a crucial role in reuniting people separated by conflicts and disasters. The ICRC's International Tracing Service has a long and influential history of making the missing reappear by reconnecting people who lose contact in the chaotic circumstances of crises, as discussed in the introduction to this book.

Most families and friends of the missing dream of an outcome like Jasminka's, that is, their disappeared loved one returning alive, within a bearable time frame. Some missing persons do reappear alive; of the 'individual' missing who disappear in more everyday circumstances, as discussed in Chapter 3, most are found relatively soon and many of them alive. However, in many other contexts, most of the missing turn out to be dead, and are found only after a protracted period of searching and waiting, which can stretch for years and even decades.

Élisabeth Anstett (2014: 187–9) claims that the disappeared-dead tend to return, even if they are not being searched for. In Russia, where Anstett has worked on the Gulag victims, human remains of former prisoners of the Gulag system turn up in road construction sites and other places where the land is being dug up. Likewise, remains of dead migrants frequently turn up along migrant routes, such as on the Mediterranean shores. However, in most cases of material reappearances, the missing and the disappeared are actively searched for, and the powerful need to know what has happened, and to uncover the fate of the disappeared, has given rise to a variety of search practices. Consequently, in places marked by large-scale disappearance, a range of political and humanitarian projects that seek to find (or hide) the remains have emerged. These projects load the remains with significance – as evidence of crimes, as ancestors, as dead family members and/or as dignified human beings.

What remains of a person to be found depends on many factors, including the circumstances of death, the treatment of the body after death, the surroundings in which the remains have lain and the length of time between death and retrieval. Sometimes a whole, visually recognisable body is found; in other cases, bodies are in an advanced state of decomposition or totally skeletonised. There are also situations in which only a number of body parts, or a couple of bones or teeth, remain to be found. And then there are cases in which the fate of the disappeared is never discovered and the enigma remains.

Whatever way in which the remains are found, and whatever the significance given to them, in order to complete the 're-civilising' project of forensic work, the remains need to be identified. The simplest method of identifying a dead person is visual recognition, that is, a family member identifying the body. However, in the cases discussed in this chapter, the remains are often beyond visual identification because of their advanced state of decomposition; in such circumstances, family members may be asked to identify clothes or personal items found on the body. The longer the period between death and reappearance, the more transmuted the remains are and the more professional the methods needed in order for identification to take place.

The so-called traditional methods of identification rely on anthropometric measurements and comparisons of antemortem (AM) and postmortem (PM) data, such as dental records and other medical information. The availability of AM data is often limited in instances of disappearance, as will be seen in the discussions of the empirical cases below. Since the early years of this millennium, DNA-based identification has been the privileged mode of identification in many contexts (Wagner, 2008; Bennett, 2014; Smith, 2016). It has come to dominate the discourse on identification to the extent that a Finnish police officer told us in an interview:[4] 'If I fell down dead and collapsed now, they would need my DNA to identify me!' The prevalence of DNA as the only credible mode of identification has rearranged practices and social relations in projects aimed at making the disappeared reappear in various contexts, as DNA-based identification relies on specialised expertise, including laboratories and other equipment (Smith, 2016). Both Argentina and Bosnia have a special place in this development, while the current wave of migrant disappearances has given rise to new challenges to it. Moreover, citizen-led search and identification practices have challenged this increasing professionalisation – a point to which I will return towards the end of this chapter.

Argentina and Bosnia: landmarks in search and identification projects

Argentina and Bosnia are often named as specific milestones in the development of human rights forensics: Argentina as its birthplace and Bosnia as the site where the international community invested significantly in the search, giving rise to important innovations and unprecedented results (e.g. Rosenblatt, 2015). My focus on these sites is twofold: firstly, I explore them both as specific sites of reappearance from the point of view of the families and communities; secondly, I look at the ways in which the search and identification projects emerged in these places, and how these projects were shaped by the particular configurations of actors and politics, both local and international.

Argentina

Gabriel Gatti (2014: 61–2) describes a visit to the headquarters of the EAAF in 2005. During the visit, he was shown boxes containing the unidentified bones of victims of the 1970s and 1980s enforced disappearances, discussed in detail in Chapter 1. The visit took place more than twenty years after the fall of the Argentine military junta that was responsible for the enforced disappearances and deaths. These unidentified bones as liminal beings, remains without an identity decades after the disappearances, embody the complex history that has existed around search, identification and politics in Argentina since the 1980s.

Argentina is celebrated, and rightly so, as the first place where significant resources were invested in searching for the disappeared and identifying their bodies, and where these practices were intertwined with human rights politics and civil society engagement (e.g. Moon, 2012; Rosenblatt, 2015). Interestingly, however, in terms of the number of located and identified bodies returned to their families – in Gatti's (2014) terminology, bodies that have regained their identities – Argentina does not stand out as an exemplary case. According to a recent estimation, only about one thousand of the thirty thousand disappeared have been identified and reburied with their names.[5] Nevertheless, in terms of challenging the practice of enforced disappearance in ways that have been politically significant and globally visible, Argentina is certainly an outstanding example of the fight to make the disappeared reappear, and the country has shaped how we discuss the crime today, as explored in both the introduction and Chapter 1 of this book.

Family members' search for the Argentinian disappeared started while military rule was still in place. Anthony Robben (2005: 282–317; see also Burchianti, 2004: 138–9) describes how the search began as individual, unorganised attempts by family members of the abducted missing, who ventured into police stations, hospitals and morgues trying to find out about their disappeared loved ones; some even went to prisons and military bases to search for information, mostly in vain. The next step was to apply to a court for a writ of *habeas corpus*, but again they had no success, because the military coup had suspended constitutional rights. Eventually, so many demands were being made by the families that the Interior Ministry set up an office in August 1976 where people could register disappearances (Robben, 2005: 287), but it was not actually there to help in finding people but rather as a cover-up for the ongoing violence. Ironically, the corridors leading to this office became an incubator for the political movement of the mothers of the disappeared, Madres de Plaza de Mayo, which was to have a powerful role in bringing down the junta (Robben, 2005: 299–317).

Soon after, the Madres started their famous Thursday marches in Plaza de Mayo, Buenos Aires' central square, demanding to know the fate of their disappeared loved ones. Some of the group's leaders were themselves abducted but this did not stop the movement continuing. Other human rights organisations participated in the struggle from its early days but the Madres became its public face (Robben, 2005: 299–317), and the struggle has grown into a celebrated movement that has fascinated scholars, journalists and others over the years (e.g. Fisher, 1989; Agosin, 1990; Bouvard, 1994; Taylor, 1997). The Madres' insistent practice of visibly carrying photos of their disappeared children has become an iconic mode of protest, copied by numerous family organisations around the world in the search for their missing.

During the later years of the military rule, the first dead bodies and mortal remains of the dead-disappeared reappeared accidentally, despite the perpetrators' brutal practices that sought to destroy them completely. The discovery of a mass grave of four hundred unknown dead in a cemetery near Buenos Aires gave rise to demands that their identities be clarified. The first exhumations were carried out in 1982 and 1983 when the junta was still in power, but this was done in an utterly unprofessional manner that destroyed crucial evidence and created an atmosphere of continuing violence and sacrilege around exhumations in the minds of Argentinians. Television reports showed bulldozers disturbing graveyards, and bones piled up in undignified heaps; this fed into suspicion about and resentment of exhumations (Robben, 2005: 327). Such suspicion was later fervently stoked by a splinter group of the Madres (Asociación Madres de Plaza de Mayo).

The Argentinian practice of enforced disappearance was notorious for often destroying the bodies entirely, either by incinerating them or exposing them to chemicals, or by dropping them into the ocean from planes (e.g. Robben, 2005: 268–70; Schindel, 2014: 253–5). Thus, many of them will probably never be found; they are 'perfect disappearances' (Gatti, 2014: 64). However, a significant number of the disappeared who were killed in captivity were abandoned in public places and buried in unnamed 'N.N.' (*nomen nescio, ningún nombre*, no name) graves, with bureaucratic protocols recording the burials and registering death certificates (EAAF, 2003: 21–2). This bureaucratic meticulousness enabled later innovative identification work by forensic anthropologists and others.

The junta collapsed in 1983, and the newly elected democratic government set up a National Commission on the Disappearance of Persons (Comisión Nacional sobre la Desaparición de Personas, CONADEP) to gather evidence of the fate of the disappeared to be used in court cases against the former regime. The commission's report, *Nunca Más* ('Never Again'), was based on statements and witness accounts made by those who had survived the brutal detention system, and it brought the machinery of enforced disappearance into public view. With the fall of the military junta and the return to a democratic regime, the exhumations gained momentum; they had become more acceptable as they were now linked to legal proceedings against the perpetrators in the form of evidence for the accusations in the *Nunca Más* report (Crenzell, 2011).

Human rights forensics as the kind of practice we understand it to be today emerged in this conjuncture, with several different actors participating in its development. Both CONADEP and the Madres contacted forensic specialists in the USA to facilitate search and identification projects, the commission focusing on exhumations and evidence, the Madres on identification.[6] Cooperation with the US forensic specialist Clyde Snow turned out to be crucial. He started to train Argentinian students in Buenos Aires, and together they founded the Argentine Forensic Anthropology Team (EAAF), which is still active today.

The EAAF team developed working principles that are still applied to humanitarian and human rights exhumations around the world (Moon, 2012). The bodies or remains were to be analysed with a dual purpose: the cause of death was to be investigated in order to provide evidence for trials against the perpetrators, and the remains were to be identified and returned to families for dignified burial. Although the EAAF cooperated closely with the transitional government and contributed evidence to the court cases against the perpetrators, it has retained its position as an independent NGO.

As is well known and widely discussed by scholars, the Madres movement was divided into two competing factions, Asociación Madres de Plaza de Mayo and Madres de Plaza de Mayo – Línea Fundadora (e.g. Robben, 2005: 328–31; Rosenblatt, 2015: 83–119). The disagreement that led to the split was specifically about the acceptability of the exhumations, and it was to have a profound impact on the practical forensic work on the disappeared, and also on the ways in which the disappeared have actually reappeared – as bodies and bones, or as political fervour and demands for accountability in the public sphere. While the Línea Fundadora has been supportive of the exhumations and identifications, the Asociación is against them; the inconsistency shown in the politics towards the perpetrators after the return to democracy, going back and forth between amnesty laws and the pursuit of responsibility, has fed into the latter group's persistent argument that exhumations are an attempt to bring the political process to an end and suppress the demands for accountability (Robben, 2005: 330–40; Moon, 2012: 163–5; Rosenblatt, 2015: 83–122).

The EAAF's efforts to identify the remains has continued over the years since the fall of the junta. The methods have been multiple and innovative, including archival work, fingerprint analysis, interviews with family members of the missing and people involved with the repressive machinery, anthropometric measurements and dental analysis, combining available AM and PM data and DNA-based genetic analysis. EAAF annual reports (e.g. EAAF, 2003) show the detailed, time-consuming work of combining such multiple sources of data in ways that echo detective work. The 'modernity' of the Argentinian politics of enforced disappearance, discussed in Chapter 1, became visible in the almost schizophrenic operation of the state under the junta: on the one hand, the state kidnapped, detained and clandestinely killed its citizens and, on the other, the police meticulously recorded the unidentified bodies left behind by the killing machine, including taking the fingerprints of those to be buried in 'N.N.' graves (EAAF, 2003: 22–6). As a consequence, fingerprints have been an important tool in the process of identification: the fact that all Argentinians give their fingerprints to state agencies to obtain mandatory identity cards has enabled the EAAF to compare prints from mortuary records with those in the national registers (EAFF, 2003: 24).

Those remains that have been identified have been returned to their families for dignified burial, and the funerals have been important moments for the families, and sometimes also politically charged occasions that have attracted people beyond the close family and friendship circles (Robben, 2005: 338–40). However, the reburials of the remains have not developed into large-scale spectacles or moments of visibly re-inserting the disappeared into the political community to the same extent as in Bosnia, especially in Srebrenica (discussed below).

In Argentina, DNA has not gained as prominent a place in the identification of the disappeared as in Bosnia, even though its importance has grown over the years (see EAAF, 2003). However, DNA has been crucial in giving rise to another kind of reappearance: some of the women who were abducted by the junta were pregnant and gave birth in captivity, and their children were raised by adoptive parents without their knowing their biological origin. The 'grandparenting index' was created to trace these children, and this was a successful moment of applying genetics in a human rights context, predating the 'DNA revolution' in Bosnia discussed below (Schwartz-Marín and Cruz-Santiago, 2016b: 486). This practice successfully brought some of these children and their biological grandparents together, giving rise to yet another pair of social identities and groups challenging the legacy of the junta: the Abuelas de Plaza de Mayo and Hijos de los Desaparecidos, that is, the grandmothers of the Plaza de Mayo and the children of the disappeared (e.g. Taylor, 2003: 161–89).[7]

The search for remains in Argentina has witnessed the strong involvement of both the transitional and later governments, and also civil society organisations, especially the Madres and the EAAF. Moreover, a high level of international support for the human rights organisations in the country has been crucial (see e.g. Robben, 2005: 306–17; Rosenblatt, 2015: 3; Schwartz-Marín and Cruz-Santiago, 2016b: 486). The project has been contested and controversial, but it has certainly affected political life and changed public discourses and interpretations of history in Argentina. Even though the international support has been important, and the involvement of certain international experts crucial, the process has been in the hands of Argentinians – unlike in Bosnia, where the role of international actors has been prominent.

The controversies around the exhumations and the outright opposition to them have probably meant that fewer bodies have been identified than would otherwise have been possible. The identification work continues today, decades after the original disappearances. Crossland (2000) argues that the discourse that emphasises 'bodies as evidence', put forward by the EAAF and its supporters after the collapse of the junta, in an uncanny way continued the perpetrators' practice of objectifying the detained-disappeared; the opposition to exhumations grew at least partly out of this disturbing continuity. However, the members of the EAAF team in the early period stressed their intent to 'return the names and histories to those from whom they had been stolen' (Crossland, 2000: 151). Many, if not most, of these members were (and are) Argentinians themselves, with a strong commitment to working for the democratisation of Argentinian society. Many of them were personally affected by the disappearances, and they emphasised the significance of proper burial and sought to work closely with families. Crossland's analysis of the contestation around the exhumations ends by noting that those who have voiced their opposition have actually themselves appropriated and propagated the disjunction initiated by the perpetrators between the remains and individuals, or the remains and identities and, finally, between the individuals and their communities (Crossland, 2000: 150).

The disappeared have reappeared in Argentina as identified remains, often bones, that have been returned to families and buried with dignity. More prominently, however, they have reappeared in the continued public visibility of the Madres and their demands for political change and the accountability of the perpetrators. They have also reappeared in discursive forms, in the widely-sold *Nunca Más* report and a multitude of other literary work, and in the proliferation of artistic, therapeutic and commemorative practices to be discussed in the next chapter.

Bosnia-Herzegovina

'I believe in DNA', said Esad, a man of Bosnian origin whose three brothers disappeared in Srebrenica in 1995, and whom I introduce in Chapter 1. I spoke with him in Finland in 2014 about his brothers' disappearance, and about their reappearance during the process of locating and identifying the Srebrenica victims. His formulation of 'believing in DNA' reflects the profound changes in the ways in which Bosnians have learned to think and talk about identity, identification and kinship connections in the post-war years, when DNA-based methods have come to dominate the scene of identification (Wagner, 2008; ICMP, 2014). The search for the missing has touched the lives of numerous Bosnians and, at the same time, has been the subject of fervent public debate.

As discussed in Chapter 1, disappearances in Bosnia took place during an acute armed conflict; consequently, the first attempts to uncover the fate of the missing took on a different form from those in Argentina. While Argentinians went to the police and to state offices and courts to demand answers, the Bosnians reported their missing both to the local Red Cross, which had been registering and working with missing person cases in the area since the Second World War, and to its International Committee (ICRC), which had established itself in the area as early as 1991, when the disturbances connected with the dissolution of Yugoslavia began, starting in Slovenia (ICMP, 2014: 27). During the conflict, there were also attempts by the warring parties to account for their own dead and missing (ICMP, 2014: 27–8; Jugo and Škulj, 2015: 41–2, 46–7), and by 1992 the UN Working Group on Enforced or Involuntary Disappearances was already turning its attention to the worrying situation in the country (ICMP, 2014: 26).

The Dayton peace agreement, brokered by the USA, ended the fighting in 1995 and set in motion the intensive work of locating and identifying the missing, as finding and identifying the missing was included in the Peace Agreement itself.[8] As the country emerged from a protracted armed conflict, the situation was closely monitored by various interventionist forces, including NATO and peace-keeping military forces. The search for the missing was tied from the beginning to this tense geopolitical situation, and initiatives did not come from civil society but rather from the international interventionist actors present in the country – even though families of the missing had started to form their own networks and had been actively registering their missing with the Red Cross. The outside forces having this key role was perhaps the only viable possibility in a situation where ethnicised violence had tormented the population and created an atmosphere of profound mistrust between ethno-national groups. Yet this top-down model gives the process a particular flavour, affecting local people's relationship to it in many ways.

The disappeared reappeared first as upturned soil in aerial photographs, provided by military intelligence in the area, indicating places where earth had recently been disturbed and thus hinting at the possibility of a mass grave (Wagner, 2008: 55; Jugo and Wastell, 2015: 150–1). Consequently, the first mass graves containing bodies of the Srebrenica disappeared were located in July 1996, setting in motion the search for further graves in the area. There were competing agendas for the excavations from the very beginning. The very first excavations were carried out under the authority of the Office of the High Representative (OHR), the institution overseeing the implementation of the peace agreement in Bosnia, in the context of the so-called Joint Exhumation Process (JEP), an agreement between local governments and the international community. The first efforts were scantly resourced, and did not bring significant results. The situation was commented on by Elisabeth Rehn,[9] the UN Special Rapporteur of the Commission on Human Rights, who appealed for resources to investigate crimes in the area. As a consequence, a mission of Finnish experts was sent to carry out excavations; they managed to unearth some remains before the local authorities in the *Republika Srpska* entity interfered and stopped their work (Jugo and Škulj, 2015: 42–3).

The Finnish group's focus was a humanitarian one, emphasising the identification of individuals and their return to families for dignified burials. The focus changed when the ICTY[10] took over the responsibility for the excavation. Now, the dominant motivation was to find evidence of crimes for court proceedings against war criminals. At this point, the identification of individual remains was left to the local governments of the two entities of the divided Bosnia-Herzegovina (Jugo and Škulj, 2015: 42–3).

When the ICTY ended its excavations, the ICMP, which was set up specifically to address the fate of those disappeared during the war, took over the responsibility for both excavation and identification. The initiative that led to the establishment of the ICMP is attributed to US President Bill Clinton, and to the blatant failure of the UN and the Western forces in the country to protect the eight thousand boys and men who went missing from the Srebrenica enclave in July 1995, as discussed in Chapter 1.

In this tense situation, the ICMP emerged as the actor coordinating the search. It operated with external funding, mainly donor money from the Western states, which was one of the key factors behind its success.[11] The ways in which the ICMP has worked with the issue have evolved over the years. It gradually adopted a 'holistic' approach to disappearances, combining humanitarian and human rights approaches; beyond search and identification efforts, it has worked with legal issues, namely the legislation concerning missing persons in Bosnia, and social issues such as working with civil society organisations and commemoration. The ICMP hired many local Bosnians to work in various positions in the commission, and it was active in the creation of the Missing Persons Institute, the Bosnian state-level institution with responsibility for the issue. Moreover, although they never achieved as powerful a position as the Madres in Argentina, a range of family associations and other civil society groups emerged in the post-war period to address the fate of the missing and other victims (e.g. Huttunen, 2016a: 208–9). Thus, local people, the Bosnian state, international interventionist forces and international organisations – the ICRC, Physicians for Human Rights (PHR) and ICMP – were intertwined in the processes of making the disappeared reappear in Bosnia. This particular mix of local and international actors and projects has continued to mark the reappearance of the Bosnian missing.

Both the huge numbers of bodies and the condition of the gravesites in Bosnia have made the task of identification extremely challenging and time-consuming (Stover and Peress, 1998; Jugo and Wastell, 2015). International forensic experts were involved in the projects from the beginning, including the EAAF, the PHR and the ICRC. Institutionally, the presence of the EAAF represents an interesting continuum from the Argentinians' search for their disappeared.

The missing often emerged from the mass graves, and also the surface graves, as bodies and remains in an advanced state of decomposition, many of them already skeletonised. As discussed in Chapter 1, many bodies had been moved in a heavy-handed way from a primary gravesite to a second or even third site with bulldozers and other unrefined technical equipment. Bodies were often torn to pieces and bones fragmented and, consequently, sometimes only a solitary bone of a missing person has been located.

Maja Petrović-Šteger (2009: 52–9) shows how in the post-conflict political atmosphere, marked by attempts by all sides of the conflict to manipulate the search and identification work, the forensic specialists were instructed to restrain themselves from interacting with the locals (see also Stover and Peress, 1998; Koff, 2004). This made the process rather different from that in Argentina, where co-operation with families of the disappeared, at least with those supportive of the exhumations, was at the heart of the work of the forensic team.

In the early stages, the so-called traditional methods of identification, including comparison between AM and PM data and visual recognition of clothes worn by the victims, were applied when working with the Srebrenica victims (Wagner, 2008; Jugo and Škulj, 2015). However, these turned out to be unreliable and extremely difficult to use, for many reasons. In most cases, the condition of the mass graves made it impossible for family members to visually identify the remains. In general, the sheer number of mortal remains in an advanced stage of decomposition made it difficult to compare AM and PM data, and this issue was exacerbated by the lack of AM dental records and other useful medical data among populations originating from rural areas. In the early days of the search, the ICRC compiled 'The Book of the Missing' or 'Book of Belongings', two volumes cataloguing images of clothes worn by the bodies in the mass graves and personal items found there, but the practice of sharing clothing and other belongings in the besieged enclave of Srebrenica before the assault made such items a rather unreliable basis for identification (Wagner, 2008: 123–50; Jugo, 2017: 31–2).

The introduction of a new DNA-based technology brought about a real breakthrough in the identification process. Experts at the ICMP introduced two innovations: first, a method for extracting DNA from bone samples that had been in the earth for some considerable time; and second, a system of comparing this DNA with that from blood samples given by family members of those reported missing.[12] Computer software translated these calculations into the probability of a kin relation between the bone and blood samples. DNA had never before been applied as a tool for identification on such a mass scale (Wagner, 2008: 82–122; ICMP, 2014: 52).

To be successful, the new DNA method required reference samples to be gathered from family members of the missing. Between 2000 and 2014, the ICMP ran a family outreach programme to collect blood samples both in Bosnia and in the diaspora created by the war, reaching from Western European states to the USA and Australia. The ample resourcing of the ICMP by Western states enabled this ambitious programme to be run and completed successfully. Identification of the mortal remains accelerated significantly after the first successful DNA-based identification in 2001 and, by 2023, close to 80 per cent of the remains had been identified.

Even though the search and identification project in Bosnia has been more successful in numerical terms than such projects anywhere else in the world where violently disappeared people have been searched for, the process has been long and strenuous; the search continues today, more than twenty-seven years after the peace agreement. Many of the perpetrators of

114 *Missing persons, political landscapes and cultural practices*

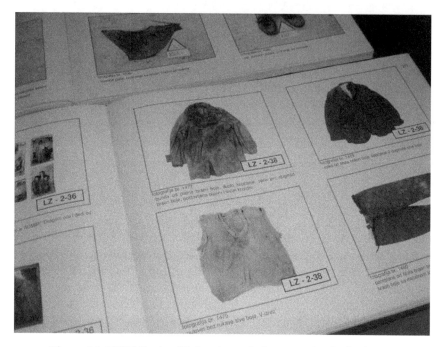

Figure 4.1 ICRC Book of Belongings; clothes worn by the bodies in the mass graves in Srebrenica, here on display in the ICMP premises. Credit: Laura Huttunen.

the Yugoslavian wars have been sentenced at the Hague war tribunal, partly on the basis of evidence from the mass graves, but locally in Bosnia the issue is still contested and politically disputed (e.g. Wagner, 2008; Petrović-Šteger, 2009; Halilovich, 2013; Jugo and Škulj, 2015; Jugo and Wastell, 2015; Huttunen, 2016a; Huttunen, 2016b; Huttunen, 2014).

For my interlocutors of Bosnian origin living in Finland, the long process of search and identification has meant several things. First of all, many have lived for years in a state of ambiguity, swinging between fear and hope: the fear of never finding out the truth about the fate of their family member; the fear that they have suffered the same horrific fate as those found in the mass graves; hope for a miracle, of finding the missing person alive; and, finally, simply hope that they will learn the truth and be able to bring an end to the search and the waiting. Graphic images of bodies in the mass graves have circulated in the public domain, giving rise to anxious and agitated anticipation of the fate of the missing. Many people have given blood samples in the family outreach programme, thus integrating their personal search with the institutional process. Many have travelled to Bosnia for the funerals of identified family members, neighbours and friends. For those who spend their summer holidays in Bosnia, this time of year has been marked

Material reappearances 115

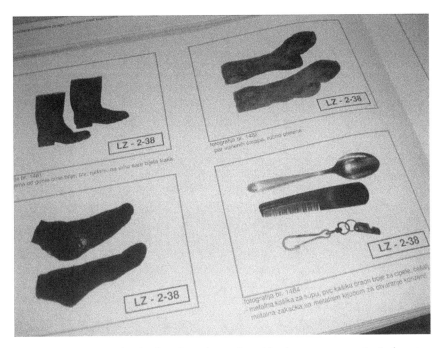

Figure 4.2 ICRC Book of Belongings; items found in the mass graves in Srebrenica, here on display in the ICMP premises. Credit: Laura Huttunen.

by reappearances of the missing because it is when funerals for the identified disappeared, especially in the Srebrenica and Prijedor/Banja Luka areas, tend to be organised (Wagner, 2008: 185–212; Halilovich, 2013: 81–4).

The high identification rate has also fed expectations of closure among families of the missing. For those whose family member has not been located or identified, the successfully proceeding search and identification process has created an anxious atmosphere of expectation that has stretched over years or even decades; under such conditions, it has been very difficult to negotiate any alternative ways of coming to terms with the absence of the missing (Huttunen, 2024).

In Bosnia, there has not been the same kind of objection to excavation as in Argentina, but the processes of search and identification have been marked by multiple tensions and controversies. Maja Petrović-Šteger (2009) argues against simplified understandings of the excavations and identifications in ex-Yugoslavia as leading easily to societal and political reconciliation (see also Jugo and Škulj, 2015; Jugo and Wastell, 2015). She points to the ways in which the numbers of victims and the remains of the missing have been manipulated by all sides in post-war Bosnia's bitter political climate. The 'scientific' evidentiary power of DNA testing has at times been

Figure 4.3 Blood samples by family members of the missing in the fridge in the ICMP premises in Bosnia-Herzegovina in 2013. Credit: Laura Huttunen.

interpreted by the locals in surprising ways, including as indicating victimhood or culpability (Petrović-Šteger, 2009: 68).

Petrović-Šteger's example of the various ways of understanding DNA testing resonates interestingly with Esad's statement about 'believing in DNA' quoted above. Both Esad's comment and those of Petrović-Šteger's interlocutors show that biomedical knowledge is not readily understandable by everybody, nor credible as evidence, without processes of interpretation. ICMP employees working closely with families confirm this; one of them told me that sometimes the possibility of recognising a T-shirt or another familiar item made the identification more credible for family members for whom it was a challenge to comprehend the logic of DNA identification (cf. Jugo, 2017: 21–2, 34).

Moreover, Petrović-Šteger argues that search and identification are often valuable for people in the private realm because they enable them to reconnect with their missing loved ones, while in the public and political realms, these practices often feed into continuous tensions (Petrović-Šteger, 2009: 67–9). Resonating with this argument, Esad hesitated when contemplating how to signify the re-emergence of his brothers' bones. For Esad, this reappearance was both consoling and agitating; he was relieved at being able to

Material reappearances

Figure 4.4 Decoded and transcribed DNA-information in the ICMP archive room, Bosnia-Herzegovina 2013. Credit: Laura Huttunen.

give the bones a dignified burial, while being deeply troubled by the brutality of his brothers' fate and the intentionality of the necropolitical violence. The burial did not resolve his political resentment, even though it brought to a close the period of agitated search.

While funerals of the identified missing in Argentina have mostly been those of individuals, the located and identified missing in Bosnia are often buried together. Lejla's husband, discussed at the beginning of this chapter, was buried with several other identified bodies from the same village, and Lejla's daughter's description of the event revealed how the particular nature of their death reverberated in the funeral ceremony (cf. Halilovich, 2013: 81–4).

Especially in the Srebrenica area, the funerals of the identified missing have grown into large-scale events with a performative nature and political overtones. Every year since 1999, those identified during the previous year have been buried in the cemetery in in Potočari, at the site where the Srebrenica-Potočari memorial centre has been built. The event takes place on 11 July, the date of the beginning of the assault on Srebrenica in 1995. During the peak years of identification, the number of bodies rose to around five hundred annually. These events are heavily ritualised, involving music, prayer and public addresses. Similar procedures are repeated year after year, some of them breaking with previous burial traditions in the area and improvising new ones (Wagner, 2008: 229–32; also Jugo and Wastell, 2015: 162–3). The international attention paid to Bosnia and the prominence of international interventionalist forces is reflected in the speeches given. For example, during one of the commemoration ceremonies in 2013, an address by US Secretary of State, John Kerry, defining the Srebrenica executions as a crime against humanity, was read out by US Ambassador Patrick S. Moon.[13]

The event has grown from being a funeral ceremony for families into a large annual occasion, attended by thousands of Bosniaks from the area and beyond, most of them travelling from the Federation side of Bosnia as well as from the global diaspora. Some people go there to bury their relatives, while others travel to meet living friends and relatives and to participate in the event.

Esad's brothers' bones were also buried in Potočari in 2011, at the same time as several hundreds of others. Esad and his wife Jasminka showed me pictures from the funeral, depicting a large crowd of people and rows of coffins being carried towards the graves. For them, this ritual seemed to carry many meanings. It gave a proper dignified burial to the brothers and, simultaneously, it was an event that brought them back into the realm of the social or, as Jasminka put it, 'back to existence among us'. 'Now we know where they are', said Esad. While showing me the photographs, Esad and his wife pointed out several friends and acquaintances among the crowd attending the event; it was clearly also a moment of recreating a community dispersed by the war, at least momentarily.

I suggest that the Potočari funerals are spectacles that transfer the disappeared-dead from the horrific liminality of mass graves into dead-and-properly-buried members of the political community. While the genocidal violence of the 1990s, including enforced disappearances, was a project of eliminating the targeted group from the political structure, in these reburial rites, the identified bodies are returned as rightful members of that structure.

The event is, however, increasingly being taken over by the Bosniak leadership, immersed in nationalistic discourses and struggles over the 'numbers' and 'degrees' of suffering (cf. Verdery, 1999: 95–127; Jansen, 2005), to the extent that some anti-nationalistic Bosniaks distance themselves from it. 'I hate July the 11th!' exclaimed my interlocutor, a Sarajevo-based Bosniak man in his thirties who took me to visit the memorial centre there in April 2013. He explained to me how, for him, the event represents a hijacking of the tragedy by the nationalist leadership (cf. Halilovich, 2013: 93–8).

Moreover, the Potočari funerals have a life of their own on the internet. On YouTube alone, there are hundreds of video clips of the event from over the years. Some of them show the whole ceremony from beginning to end, while others are short clips of just a couple of minutes that depict a particular person's coffin being carried towards the graves. Some of the videos are framed with political commentary, while others simply document a specific moment. Elsewhere (Huttunen, 2016b), I suggest that these clips work in different registers: on the one hand, they announce to the dispersed diasporic Bosnian community the end of the liminality of a particular person, now that they have been identified and buried and, on the other hand, they make political claims and frame individual burials within a history that has a heavy political legacy.

The disappeared have reappeared in Bosnia as mortal remains that have been identified and returned to families more often perhaps than anywhere else and, consequently, they are now present as gravesites in the landscape. This has ended the period of liminality for families of the identified missing, but it has not resolved political tensions. The legacy of death and disappearance in the area is still debated both within the country and in international forums.

Reappearing migrant bodies

The reappearance of the migrant missing takes place in profoundly different circumstances from reappearances in Argentina and Bosnia – institutionally, politically and geographically. In Argentina and Bosnia, the remains of the disappeared have, with a few exceptions, rarely reappeared spontaneously; rather, it has been as a result of great effort and investment in the search. The situation is quite different with the remains of dead migrants, as they often do turn up unexpectedly. Of course, migrants' families do search for their missing members but often in situations in which they still hope to find them alive – in the Mediterranean area by seeking information via informal channels (Kobelinsky, 2020a: 710–11; Kobelinsky, 2020b; Kivilahti and Huttunen, 2023) and in the US–Mexico border area also by organising search teams in the desert (Reineke, 2019: 153–4).

Dead migrants often reappear along migratory routes as bodily remains affected by both time and the elements – sea water or desert heat. The reappearing remains exercise an ambiguous power over individuals and communities who come face to face with them. Gerhild Perl, while analysing the effects of the deadly shipwreck of a migrant boat near the Spanish coastal town of Rota in 2013, quotes one of the town's residents:

> In the entire bay of Cádiz one corpse after another appeared, day after day. People were devastated. Ruined. Do you know what a human body looks like

after being in the water for a couple of days? [...] I couldn't imagine that this had been a human being!

(Perl, 2018: 88; cf. Kovras and Robins, 2016: 41)

Robin Reineke, academic and co-founder of the NGO Colibrí, which works with migrant deaths and disappearances in the US–Mexico desert area, describes her encounters with migrants' remains:

What I have seen is blackened skin stretched thinly around bone. I have seen bodies without faces, without arms, without feet. I have seen mummified remains where the skin is as hard as leather. I have seen the teeth marks of animals. I have seen bones that are bleached, gnawed on, dismembered, or crumbling.

(Reineke, 2019: 154)

Both these quotes indicate that human remains are powerful, and that they affect those who encounter them in many ways. In the Mediterranean area, fishermen come across dead bodies on the shore or floating in the water, and bodies, body parts and personal belongings end up in their nets; images of the remains often haunt them long afterwards (Perl, 2018: 89; see also Zagaria, 2020). In the coastal town of Zarzis in Tunisia, bodies and remains of dead migrants are often washed up on the shore and their presence has become a normalised but nonetheless disturbing phenomenon, as described by Valentina Zagaria. Many locals, including doctors, police officers and undertakers, are forced to interact with the dead. The remains are present as a cemetery of unnamed graves, created on a former dumpsite, but also, more intrusively, as an odour emanating from the van that transports them across town; locals readily recognise both the van and the smell (see also M'charek, 2018: 95). As Zarzis is both a place from which undocumented migrants depart on a dangerous journey and a place where the unidentified remains of migrants from further south in Africa end up, a moral discussion surrounds both the remains and their treatment (Zagaria, 2020).

In Zarzis, at least in the period described by Zagaria, no efforts were made to identify the remains when they were considered non-local, and for a long time now a similar lack of effort has characterised encounters with dead migrants on the European side of the Mediterranean.[14] On the Greek islands and in the Evros-river area in Greece, on the Italian island of Lampedusa and in the coastal areas of Italy and Spain, in all these places, one can find cemeteries with unnamed graves, marked with inscriptions such as 'N.N.' or 'Inmigrante de Marruecos' (Perl, 2016: 199–202), or something similar indicating an unidentified body (also Laakkonen, 2023a). In the USA, as well as being buried in unmarked graves (Reineke, 2022: 27), unidentified remains are sometimes cremated (Reineke, 2019: 164–5).

However, in this millennium, efforts to identify migrant remains have gradually gained momentum, and new practices for achieving this have emerged and become more established. Taking fingerprints from the bodies and documenting personal items found on them, along with jewellery and tattoos, are among the clues that help with efforts to trace the identity of the deceased even in such demanding circumstances (Perl, 2016; Perl, 2019a; Reineke, 2019; Reineke, 2022). Nowadays in Europe, DNA samples are taken, at least in many cases, from unidentified remains before burial, to enable future identification. Carolina Kobelinsky (2020b: 527) describes the routine measures taken by the Spanish police and the Guardia Civil when they come across a dead migrant body, including fingerprinting and DNA sampling. But, as Kobelinsky's analysis shows, these measures lead to identification in the case she discusses only because of the intervention of a local NGO, as the authorities lack protocols for proceeding with identification beyond these preliminary measures (see also M'charek, 2018). In Lesvos, Kovras and Robins (2016: 41–2) describe a 'grey zone' round the management of migrant bodies, characterised by ill-defined responsibilities, unclear procedures, indifference and under-resourced key actors, resulting in non-identification as the prevailing condition.

In the USA, the Pima County Office of the Medical Examiner in Tucson, Arizona has developed successful methods for working with remains, and also for reaching out to families via NGOs (Reineke, 2016; Reineke, 2022). As a consequence, the numbers of identified remains in this area are much higher than in some other states of the US border region. Yet, even here, few migrant dead are identified and returned to their families. There is a whole range of challenges for identification when working with migrants' remains, both in the USA and the Mediterranean and beyond: migrants originate from a vast, indeterminate area, and it is often sheer guesswork to start to map their communities of origin; the bodies seldom carry ID documentation or, if they do, it is often false; there are difficulties with fingerprinting, either because the bodies have been in the sea for so long or because they have become desiccated in the desert heat. Moreover, passport and visa regimes restrict families' possibilities to travel to search for information, carry out visual identification or give blood samples for DNA identification. And without contact with families, there are no DNA reference samples, no access to AM data and scant possibilities of visual identification (Kovras and Robins, 2016; Olivieri *et al.*, 2018; M'charek and Casartelli, 2019; Reineke, 2022).

In structures imbued with indifference, dedicated individuals can make a difference. Robin Reineke (2022) argues that within the US medico-legal apparatus that deals with migrant remains, dedicated individuals in official positions can significantly affect the success of identifications. Martin Zamorra, a Spanish undertaker who has worked with migrant communities and the repatriation of migrant bodies in the Mediterranean, stands out as an individual with a 're-civilising' agenda to make identifications happen: he has become famous for his success in finding families for unidentified migrant remains in Spain. He has put a great deal of effort into the process: he has built relationships with the Moroccan community in Spain and has found phone numbers sewn into the clothes of dead migrants and used them to trace relatives. He has also taken dead people's clothes and personal objects over the border to Morocco and shown them to people in order to obtain information about the deceased. With this detective work, he has succeeded in identifying and repatriating dozens of bodies. At the same time, he has become ambiguously famous, because he as an undertaker has benefitted from this work. However, his work has shown that dedicated effort, detailed research and the right contacts can enable identification even in demanding circumstances (Perl, 2016: 202–6).

There are only a few projects that invest in searching for the unretrieved remains of dead migrants on a large scale, and there is nothing comparable to the search projects in Argentina and Bosnia. This fact reflects these migrants' disappearability and their politically marginalised position, as discussed in Chapter 2. However, there have been some pioneering projects, initiated by the Italian Government, to retrieve and identify the bodies of migrants who died in the shipwrecks off Lampedusa in 2013 and 2015 (see Olivieri *et al.*, 2018; M'charek and Casartelli, 2019). The scale and visibility of these disasters challenged the prevailing atmosphere of indifference and gave rise to action.

In both Argentina and Bosnia, existing established forensic methods needed to be significantly adapted and developed to enable mass-scale identification in demanding circumstances. When working with migrant bodies and remains, further innovations and new applications of previous methods and protocols are needed. M'charek and Casartelli (2019: 739) quote Cristina Cattaneo, a leading forensic specialist in Italy, who spoke at the launch of the Melilli5[15] identification project in Lampedusa: 'we have to reinvent forensics anew. Nothing seems to work.'

These projects to identify the victims of the Lampedusa shipwrecks have been remarkable exceptions to the general lack of investment in the identification of migrant remains. The 2013 project was the first tentative attempt in Italy to collect the necessary AM and PM data and design procedures for comparing them; relatives were contacted through NGOs and embassies, thus creating a version of a family outreach programme. Interestingly, visual means, that is recognition by way of facial features and bodily marks, became important again, after the hype of DNA in Bosnia: often the only available AM data was photographs and videos of the missing, provided by those family members who had European residence permits and were willing to work with the authorities. Although photographs are usually regarded as unreliable tools for identification, Lara Olivieri and her colleagues, all forensic specialists, propose a method for reading distinctive marks from them to enable identification (Olivieri *et al.*, 2018; see also Kobelinsky, 2020b: 529).

In 2015, as part of the Melilli5 project, the shipwrecked boat was lifted out of the sea, bodies were retrieved with care and dignity, and more new practices of working with the remains were developed, to enable identification. Special attention was paid to protocols and procedures but also to many small mundane acts of care during the identification process (M'charek and Casartelli, 2019). Yet the scale of the challenges that exist for identification under such circumstances is illustrated by the fact that only 31 out of the 360 retrieved victims were actually identified and returned to their families (M'charek and Casartelli, 2019: 217) Unfortunately, at the time of writing, these efforts have not been renewed; they remain exceptions in the prevailing political climate of indifference towards migrant deaths and disappearances.

As a result of the low proportion of identifications, for ordinary people in the Mediterranean region, disappeared migrants often reappear as graves without names in local cemeteries. In 2018, according to Olivieri and her colleagues (Olivieri *et al.*, 2018) over 60 per cent of dead migrants in the Mediterranean area were buried unidentified. This is, of course, only an estimate, but it indicates how the majority of the dead remain unidentified, and missing or disappeared for their families in the countries of origin. The 're-civilising' work of forensic anthropology remains ineffective if not totally paralysed by the conditions in the area; by the same token, family members' search efforts continue.

In both Argentina and Bosnia, a particular configuration of actors emerged in the course of searching for and identifying the disappeared, which combined the state, civil society, international organisations and other actors in certain ways. The configuration of actors who work with disappeared migrants is even more complicated; this should not come as a surprise, given that migrants move within large geographical areas and across the jurisdiction of various states.

The institutional framing of the search for and identification of migrants' remains is different, to some extent, in the Mediterranean and US–Mexico border areas; in other geographical areas where migrants disappear, other kinds of institutional arrangement still prevail. What is similar, however, is the plurality of actors and the inconsistency of protocols and bureaucratic processes dealing with the remains. States are, at least in principle, responsible for the treatment of the dead within their territory. However, in these two particular locations, the area in which missing migrants move is split into different states – along the US–Mexico border, into the various federal states of the USA and Mexico and, in Europe, into different nation-states. Each state has its own jurisdiction and bureaucracy, and cooperation and pooling of information between states is underdeveloped. The inefficiency of states in identifying migrant remains has created space for a whole assortment of other actors to address the issue, ranging from large international organisations such as the ICRC, IOM and ICMP to small family organisations and local NGOs.

It is impossible to give an exhaustive account of the actors working to make missing migrants reappear, both because the field is so large and fragmented and because it is constantly changing. It could be characterised as a global architecture of agents in the process of making (cf. M'charek, 2018). I will make some observations here about this field, while acknowledging that a full analytical description is beyond the possibilities of this book.

The large international organisations, the ICRC and ICMP, have undertaken initiatives on identification practices and have offered their expertise in the actual work with the remains.[16] Their approach is humanitarian; they do not explicitly challenge the political order that exposes migrants to deadly routes; rather, their focus is family-centred, foregrounding the need to know what has happened, to identify bodies and return them to families for funerals.[17]

Smaller NGOs can be very effective locally or regionally; for instance, the Colibrí Center for Human Rights[18] in the southern states of the USA cooperates closely with the state institution responsible for the dead in the area, the Pima County Office of the Medical Examiner. By building networks between families and state officials, the centre has significantly contributed to identification rates (see Reineke, 2022). In addition to Colibrí, several other search and rescue teams work in the US–Mexico border area (Reineke, forthcoming), contributing to the emergence of 'lay forensics' or 'community forensics', which is discussed further towards the end of this chapter.

In Europe also, some local NGOs have contributed to the identification of dead migrants in various ways, or have helped families to detect traces of their missing loved ones: for instance, Stichting: Platform for Transnational Forensic Assistance[19] in Greece, Ca-minando Fronteras[20] and CIPMID[21] in Spain, and Boats 4 People[22] in the Mediterranean area, to name just a few, seek to work in the vacuums left by inefficient and/or under-resourced state agencies.

Several family organisations have emerged to demand answers regarding the fate of relatives who have disappeared while en route. For instance, in Tunisia, another family movement has arisen; wives and parents of the missing 'harraga', that is, migrants travelling along irregular routes, have organised demonstrations, sit-ins and other actions in which they demand that the Tunisian and Italian states acknowledge their responsibility – they demand both knowledge of the whereabouts of their missing family members and the acceptance of political responsibility for their deaths by both states (Stimmatini and De Gourcy, 2022).

Many NGOs, such as Missing at the Borders, discussed in Chapter 2, also have goals other than just helping with search and identification; they often challenge the border regimes that produce such large numbers of missing persons. Sometimes the significance of these organisations lies more in the ways in which they make the whole issue of migrant disappearances visible in the public arena than in their actually making the disappeared reappear in a concrete sense. These more symbolic reappearances will be discussed in the next chapter.

Because the official identification practices are so ineffective, an intense exchange of knowledge about the fate of migrants takes place via unofficial and informal channels. Information and witness accounts from co-travellers and other eyewitnesses are often the only chance for families and others left behind to gain an understanding of what has happened to their absent loved one (Lucht, 2012: 216–58; Kobelinsky, 2020a: 710–11; Kivilahti and Huttunen, 2023). As a consequence, the eventual reappearance of disappeared migrants often remains ambiguous and uncertain. All this points to the utterly unprotected position of undocumented migrants within global regimes of power. At the same time, if we accept Finn Stepputat's (2014) claim that governing the transition from life to death is an important moment for claiming sovereignty, the governance of migrants' remains raises disturbing questions concerning the nature of sovereignty within these transnational spaces.

Reappearances across the globe: institutionalisation, competing projects and the rise of citizen-led forensics

The three contexts discussed in this chapter reveal significant variation in the ways in which a state or states, civil society actors, local NGOs and large international organisations come together in search and identification projects. On a global scale, the variety is even wider. There is endless variation in the ways in which search and identification are arranged, ranging from heavily state-driven projects to those led by non-governmental, humanitarian actors.

Sometimes, even within one state, projects focused on making the missing reappear are run by different actors and with differing goals. For example, in Zimbabwe, there is a complicated history of violence stretching from colonial times to post-independence struggles, and the forcibly disappeared and the not-properly-buried have reappeared in different, differently run projects. There are the UNESCO-sponsored 'liberation heritage' projects and the state-driven projects of exhuming the liberation war dead (Fontein, 2018: 341–2) but also localised NGO-run projects involved in excavating local victims of violence perpetrated by the postcolonial state, the so-called 'Gukurahundi' violence (Eppel, 2014).

Cambodia, Rwanda and Burundi – also sites with complicated histories of violence – have been particular sites of reappearance. Cambodia under the Khmer Rouge regime (1975–79) and Rwanda and Burundi during the 1994 genocidal violence campaigns were all marked by excessive violence and death, to the extent that a 'breakdown of cultural worlds' ensued (Bennett, 2018). Cultural scripts lost their significance in the face of the ubiquitousness of death, and established ways of dealing with the dead broke down. In all these places, attempts to identify individual remains and return them to families are scant or non-existent, and forensic attention to these remains has been sporadic and small scale, to paraphrase Caroline Bennett's words (2019: 577–9). What has happened instead is that bones and skulls of the dead have been gathered to be exhibited in museums and at memorial sites, not as identified individuals but as representatives of a collective group of victims (e.g. Lesley, 2015; Bennett, 2018; Bennett, 2019; Jamar and Major, 2022).

The forensic turn means that new cases and new sites, with their social and political idiosyncrasies, have come to be addressed with techniques and concepts developed within the field of humanitarian and human rights forensics. For instance, Iraq is a place where long, complicated histories of violence have produced large numbers of disappeared people from various time periods, and this has attracted the attention of the actors within the field; this layered history of disappearances has resulted in complicated, politically tense projects of making reappear.[23] Similarly in South and Southeast Asia, the decades-long history of armed conflicts and state violence has produced layered histories of disappearance and reappearance in Vietnam (Ngô, 2021), Sri Lanka (de Alwis, 2009; Kodikara, 2023) and Timor-Leste (Kent, 2020; Kent 2024). In all these places, again, the configurations of actors who come together to make the disappeared reappear have each been unique.

For some scholars, this ever-enlarging field of humanitarian or human rights forensics, with their emphasis on reclaiming the mortal remains, indicates a promise of 'truth and justice' (e.g. Rosenblatt, 2015), while others are suspicious of its depoliticising effect, which foregrounds legal and technical issues and overshadows political ones (Smith, 2016). The institutionalisation of the field has certainly led to standardisation and professionalisation, and to also the emergence of a new 'industry' and a new professional field, each with their own agendas and interests, including commercial ones (Smith, 2016).

However, a counter-movement seems to be developing alongside this professionalisation. Several writers, such as Schwartz-Marín and Cruz-Santiago (2016a; 2016b), Robledo Silvestre and Ramírez González (2022); Castillo Hernández (2023) and Reineke (forthcoming), argue that something revolutionary is, again, taking place in Latin America. In Mexico and Colombia, the active engagement of ordinary people in the search for mass graves, and in exhumations and actual forensic work, has seriously challenged the state-centred and expert-centred paradigm of forensic work. In Mexico in particular, a profound mistrust of the state and the absence of the rule of law have given rise to what Schwartz-Marín and Cruz-Santiago call 'forensic civism' (2016a) or 'lay forensic research'[24] (2016b: 489), that is, groups of activists who have trained themselves in forensic techniques. More recently, Cruz-Santiago (2020) has referred to these practices as 'citizen-led forensics', and has observed their gradual development and also their surprising efficacy in some cases. These groups have developed skills in searching for mass graves and, by marking their findings with flags and supervising them until the authorities arrive, they force the law-enforcement bodies to take them seriously; they have set up a citizen-led DNA database to enable the identification of the remains, have taught themselves to use GPS, have developed skills in analysing potential crime scenes and keep detailed records of their observations (Schwarz-Marín and Cruz-Santiago, 2016a; Schwarz-Marín and Cruz-Santiago, 2016b).

Such practices lead to the remains reappearing in the public sphere, even if they are not always successfully identified (Schwartz-Marín and Cruz-Santiago, 2016b: 496). In areas where thousands of disappeared people would probably otherwise remain in mass graves, because of the 'forensic crisis' (Mandolessi, 2022) discussed in Chapter 1, these citizen-led reappearances of remains are significant in many ways. The practices blur the boundaries between families and experts, and question the idea that the family's role is one of passively waiting (see also Reineke, 2022). Finally, the relationship with the state is necessarily renegotiated in the process, in ways that some scholars have conceptualised as 'forensic citizenship' and 'relational citizenship' (e.g. M'charek and Casartelli, 2019; Reineke, 2022).

In many places outside Latin America, there are also local understandings of how to treat the remains and make reliable identifications that go against the scientific DNA-led approach. For instance, according to Fontein (2018:

341–6), many local actors in Zimbabwe argue for traditional 'African' practices of identifying remains through divination. Similarly in Timor-Leste, commissions working on identifying and honouring those who died during the Indonesian occupation often rely on a variety of methods that are classified as traditional (Kent, 2020: 293–5). What is different in the Latin American citizen-led forensics initiatives, when compared with these 'traditional' approaches, is that in Latin America, non-professional citizens seek to appropriate expert scientific knowledge for their own use, rather than arguing for a competing epistemology. They (in most cases) are fighting a battle for truth within the scientific paradigm – they are not challenging the paradigm as such but rather questioning who has the right to use it and simultaneously also stretching its boundaries (Cruz-Santiago, 2020).

Yet, in many places, the disappeared still remain unsearched for. Anstett (2011: 8) calls for a mapping of the cemeteries of the Gulag victims in the former Soviet space and a systematic identification of the remains in these cemeteries with DNA-based techniques. Sadly, human history has created several other places where there have been no attempts, so far, to find or identify the disappeared or to address questions of accountability. This suggests that we can anticipate the emergence of more new projects of making reappear in the future, along with contestations over the right way to go about them.

Conclusion: care for the dead

All the search and identification projects analysed in this chapter point to the enormous productive force of human disappearances, as discussed in the introduction to this book. The disappearance of a loved one is an unbearable condition for family members and friends, but socially and culturally, it is also an unbearable condition more generally. This productive force pushes individuals, both family members and professionals, to dedicate time, energy and resources to search and identification, but it also gives rise to new social relations, new structures and processes, new institutions, and new professional fields and scientific innovations, as described above. The productive force both makes the physical remains reappear and reconnects them with names and identities, thus making them reappear as identified individuals to family members and communities.

The cases analysed in this chapter show that reappearances always take place in specific historical, political and cultural circumstances – reappearance, including identification of the mortal remains, is never just a technical question but always also a cultural, political and ethical one. Idiosyncratic configurations of actors come together and enable (or obstruct and hamper) the processes that might reconnect the disappeared with their families and communities. Likewise, scientific and technical developments take place in specific historic circumstances – the development, from Argentina via Bosnia to current migrant disappearances, of DNA-based methodologies in human rights and humanitarian work shows this clearly.

Several scholars, including Adam Rosenblatt (2015) and Amade M'charek and Julia Black (2020), have framed exhumation and identification work as a mode of care for the dead. Likewise, in the professional field of human rights forensics, many proponents of the scientific mode of approaching the disappeared-dead through exhumations and science-based identifications present these practices as care work. This interestingly ties in with the ways in which the relationship between the dead and the living in Southeast Asian and many African cultures is depicted by anthropologists specialising in these areas: they emphasise how the reciprocity between the dead and the living is a crucial feature of the cultural worlds they study (e.g. Langford, 2009; Langford, 2013; Eppel, 2014). In the discourse of human rights forensics, care for the dead re-emerges as a fundamental, universal value across cultural differences, this time within the scientific frame.

Claire Moon (2019) poses the question of whether the dead have human rights (see also Rosenblatt, 2015: 153–65) and ties this in with questions regarding the treatment of human remains. Moon argues that the dead are often seen as having at least two rights: the residual right to be treated with dignity (Moon, 2019: 54), and the posthumous and rehabilitative right to identity and to be returned to their families. This latter right is understood to compensate for rights that were stripped away when they were still alive (Moon, 2019: 55).

These discussions show that the reappearance of the disappeared as mortal remains forces individuals, communities and states to face not only technical questions of identification but also fundamental moral and ethical questions about human life and death. Moreover, as the examples discussed in this chapter reveal, large-scale disappearance always leaves behind difficult political legacies that are not resolved merely by the returning of bodies to families for reburial, however important this is for the individuals concerned.

Notes

1 According to the Balkan Investigative Reporting Network's website *Bitter Land: Interactive map of mass graves from the wars in the Former Yugoslavia,* remains of the missing in ex-Yugoslavia have been found in some 1,600 locations; sixty-eight of these are classified as mass graves, and the majority of them are in Bosnia. Mass Graves Database (https://massgravesmap.balkaninsight.com/) (accessed 14 February 2024).

130 *Missing persons, political landscapes and cultural practices*

2 Estimates of the number of bodies vary across news articles and policy reports. According to BIRN's website (see previous note), 435 people were found in this site and, of these, 274 have been identified. Tomasica – Mass Graves Database (https://massgravesmap.balkaninsight.com/tomasica-2/) (accessed 14 February 2024).

3 'Human rights forensics' refers to the idea that the main purpose of exhumations is to find evidence of crimes and seek justice in legal terms, see e.g. https://humanrightshistory.umich.edu/research-and-advocacy/forensic-evidence-and-human-rights-reporting/ (accessed 14 February 2024); in contrast, the 'humanitarian' approach emphasises families' need to know the fate of their loved ones and give them a proper burial, see e.g. 'How does ICRC use forensic science for humanitarian purposes?', ICRC (https://www.icrc.org/en/document/how-does-icrc-use-forensic-science-humanitarian-purposes) (accessed 14 February 2024). In practice, the line between these approaches often becomes blurred, and for this reason I make reference to them both throughout my discussion. For an interesting discussion and critique of the terms, see Reineke (forthcoming).

4 See Chapter 3 for interviews with the Finnish police.

5 The estimation was produced by Carlos Somigliana, one of the EAAF's leading figures, and quoted in a newspaper article on the ongoing identification work in Argentina – see 'Argentina sends out DNA kits in drive to identify thousands "disappeared" under dictatorship', EAAF (https://eaaf.org/argentina-sends-out-dna-kits-in-drive-to-identify-thousands-disappeared-under-dictatorship/) (accessed 6 July 2023). Originally published in *The Guardian* on 28 May 2021. Other figures have also been presented, but more exact numbers of the identified Argentinian victims are rather hard to come by. Special thanks to Anthony Robben for helping me to uncover information on this matter.

6 Scholars report on this period in slightly differing ways. According to Adam Rosenblatt (2015: 3–4), some members of the Madres travelled to the USA and made contact with the Argentinian emigre, paediatrician and geneticist Victor Penchaszadeh, and this was the starting point for the genetic testing; later the role of Eric Stover, the then director of the American Association for the Advancement of Science's Science and Human Rights Program, became crucial, and it was he who brought Clyde Snow, an already well-known forensic anthropologist, to work in Argentina. Other writers emphasise CONADEP's role in officially inviting Snow to work in Argentina (e.g. Robben, 2005: 326–31; Moon, 2012). See Smith (2016) for a further version of the birth of the EAAF.

7 The process of re-attaching the abducted children to their biological grandparents was not always smooth, as the children had grown attached to their new families, see e.g. Robben (2005: 354–5). For a critical discussion on the Abuelas' naturalising discourse on identity, see Gatti (2014: 77–95).

8 Article V of Annex 7 of the Dayton peace agreement states: 'The Parties shall provide information through the tracing mechanism of the ICRC on all persons unaccounted for. The Parties shall also cooperate fully with the ICRC in

Material reappearances 131

its efforts to determine the identities, whereabouts and fate of the uncounted for.' Annex 7, Office of the High Representative (http://www.ohr.int/dayton-peace-agreement/annex-7-2/) (accessed 7 July 2023). Interestingly, the ICRC is named here as the key institution for gathering information and working with disappearances but, within the year, the ICMP would occupy this role and become that key institution.

9 Elisabeth Rehn is a Finnish politician, a former Minister of Defence and a visible advocate for human rights, who served between 1995 and 1999 as the UN Special Rapporteur on the situation in the former Yugoslavia. For the Bosnian community in Finland, she became a significant figure, someone who talked about Bosnia to local audiences, and many of my interlocutors referred to her as one of the very few persons there who 'really' understood the circumstances that led to their fleeing to Finland.

10 The ICTY had been established by the UN Security Council in 1993, reflecting a deep concern among the international community about the human rights situation in the area. See e.g. ICMP 2014: 49).

11 For a detailed history of the establishment of the ICMP and its connections with other institutions, see Jennings (2013) and ICMP (2014).

12 This method was based on the innovative technique of extracting short tandem repeat (STR) DNA from bones in graves that was also developed by the ICMP experts. See ICMP 2014: 52–5).

13 My understanding of the Potočari funerals is based on the accounts of my Bosnian interlocutors and on the extensive visual material, including film footage, that is available on the internet and which I have been watching together with these interlocutors (see also Huttunen, 2016b). These sources have been complemented by literature, e.g. Wagner (2008).

14 For example, Sarah Green describes practices of burying bodies on Lesvos in the early years of this millennium, with no attempt to identify them. Green has published this material in Greek ('Absent details: the transnational lives of undocumented dead bodies in the Aegean'). I do not read Greek, but I have heard her speaking about the subject several times.

15 Melilli is the name of a village on the Sicilian coast. There had been four earlier missions to retrieve the bodies from the wreck before Melilli5 was launched. See M'charek and Casartelli (2019: 738–9).

16 See, for example, the ICMP Missing Migrants and Refugees Program (https://www.icmp.int/wp-content/uploads/2020/12/Missing-Migrants-Program-Factsheet-English.pdf) (accessed 27 June 2023). See M'charek (2018) for other initiatives, including those by ICRC.

17 Both organisations describe their activities in detail on their websites, see 'Missing migrants', ICRC (https://www.icrc.org/en/missing-migrants) and ICMP (https://www.icmp.int/) (both accessed 27 June 2023).

18 Colibrí Center – Colibrí Center for Human Rights (https://colibricenter.org/) (accessed 4 April 2023).

19 MissingInMigration, Forensic Missing Migrant Initiative, Greece (https://forensicmigration.wixsite.com/missingmigrants) (accessed 12 April 2023).

20 Ca-minando Fronteras (https://caminandofronteras.org/en/) (accessed 12 April 2023).
21 Centro Internacional Para La Identificación De Migrantes Desaparecidos (https://cipimigrantesdesaparecidos.org/) (accessed 1 April 2023).
22 Boats 4 People – English version (https://boats4people.org/guide/en/#Home) (accessed 14 April 2023).
23 See the ICMP website for various projects in Iraq focused on excavating mass graves and identifying people ICMP Iraq (https://www.icmp.int/where-we-work/middle-east-and-north-africa/iraq/) (accessed 7 July 2023). See Bennett (2014) for one of the few academic papers discussing forensic work in Iraq; see also Rosenblatt (2015: 35–6).
24 Practices that challenge the hierarchy between forensic professionals and self-educated citizens are discussed using several different terms, e.g. 'counter-forensics' and 'community forensics' (Reineke, forthcoming), and 'vernacular forensics', coined by Marina Alamo-Bryan, see Vernacular Forensics: Searching for the Disappeared, Bureaucratic Violence and Communal Exhumations of Clandestine Burials in Contemporary Mexico, Academic Commons (https://academiccommons.columbia.edu/doi/10.7916/gf1x-x935) (accessed 29 June 2023).

5

Symbolic reappearances: photographs, memorials and ghosts

One afternoon in December 2022, while I was queuing at a supermarket check-out in Tampere, Finland, and absent-mindedly glancing at the magazines on a nearby rack, something interesting suddenly caught my eye. One of the publications was titled *Löydetyt* ('Those found' in English) and had the subtitle 'Those who fell in the war between 1939 and 1945 are still being returned to Finland'. On the cover, a woman who was maybe in her 60s was holding a black-and-white photograph of a young couple, the man dressed in the uniform of the Finnish army during the Second World War. The text next to the woman's face said, 'I got my father home.' At that time, I was deep in the process of writing this book, and it felt like the cover was speaking directly to the thoughts that were preoccupying me.

I snatched the magazine from the rack, paid for it and took it home. It turned out to be a special edition of the Finnish newspaper *Ilta-lehti*.[1] Its 98 pages were packed with stories about Finnish soldiers who went missing on the frontline within the Soviet Union during the Second World War, and about the identification of some of them in this millennium: several accounts of soldiers whose remains had been identified and who had been returned to their relatives and given a burial ceremony; an article describing the modern DNA-based identification technique; a couple of stories about people who had been active in the search for these missing soldiers; and, finally, a list of the 416 Finnish men who had been found, identified and returned to their remaining kin since 1992, when searching for missing soldiers in the former Soviet space became possible.

This magazine is an example of the ways in which the disappeared keep on reappearing, if not alive or as mortal remains then in symbolic form – in this case, Finnish soldiers who went missing more than seventy years ago reappeared to me in the midst of the comings and goings of a late-afternoon supermarket crowd, busy with their everyday chores. Even though the magazine refers to the material reappearance of human remains, it is in itself a symbolic form that announces the insistent reappearance of this particular group of missing persons; for me, they marked a mundane December afternoon with their presence. This example also points to the fact that the material and the symbolic are often intertwined in complex ways, feeding into each other's emergence.

In this chapter, I explore the ways in which the missing and the disappeared reappear in symbolic form in the social and cultural space. I call these reappearances 'symbolic' so as to differentiate them from cases in which actual mortal remains are found and identified, as discussed in the previous chapter. I am interested in material objects, but also in practices and discourses that refer to the missing, that stand for them in their absence in one way or another. Some of these symbolic forms are ephemeral and imaginary, while others are solid and material; some are discursive, while others are better understood as performative and emergent. A number of the phenomena discussed here, such as ghosts and spirits, sit rather awkwardly within this categorisation; in many places, people do not see ghosts as symbols but rather as real presences with power and agency. Yet, as their presence usually emerges most strongly in situations where the actual mortal remains are not found, I consider it pertinent to discuss them under the notion of the symbolic, together with other things that come to stand for the missing in their material absence.

I am interested in moments in which a particular disappeared person reappears in symbolic form, even though they or their remains have not been found, but I am also interested in discursive and performative forms that more generally make the disappeared as a category present in the social and cultural spheres, such as political projects that bring particular disappearances into focus and demand information about the whereabouts of these missing.

Before going any further, I want to present a conceptual note about the idea of 'reappearance'. Especially when analysing symbolic reappearances in the private realm, it is useful to ask whether the phenomena being discussed should be conceptualised as continuities rather than as reappearances. Missing persons' family members often have objects and photographs that help them to retain a sense of connection to the absent one in times of searching and waiting, and they sometimes talk about seesawing between a harrowing sense of unaccounted-for absence and a sense of connection-in the-absence with the disappeared person. Constant thoughts about the absent one make them symbolically present for some interlocutors. I will probe this tension between continuity and reappearance in what follows.

In this chapter, I relinquish the logic of structuring the text into sections addressing Argentina, Bosnia, migratory contexts and the Global North. Instead, I make observations about symbolic reappearances across various sites, times and contexts, including but going beyond the four above, to produce an understanding of the great variety of ways in which the disappeared reappear in the social and cultural spheres, even if not always materially as bodies or remains. I am fully aware of the fact that my exploration of this vast field remains necessarily cursory; every section of this chapter merits a fuller treatment of its own. Thus, rather than being an in-depth study of photographs, clothes and mementoes, museums and memorials, artwork and media spectacles or ghosts and spirits, this chapter both explores the various ways in which the disappeared can reappear in symbolic form and makes suggestions for further research in these areas. Again, my thinking about reappearances takes place along the axes of intimate versus political and private versus public, and in their complicated intersections.

Private memories: photographs and other mementoes

The most common, most obvious way in which the missing are present in the lives of those left behind is through photographs. Although pictures make an absent person present in a powerful way,[2] in the case of a missing person, this presence is fraught with tension and ambiguity.

This ambiguity is reflected in the way in which Sabiha – the Bosnian woman I introduce in Chapter 1 and whose disappeared husband has not been found to date – talks about the subject: 'It is too painful to have his [her disappeared husband's] photograph in sight all the time. Sometimes I take it out and hang it on the wall, but mostly I keep it away, somewhere hidden.' Another Bosnian woman, Elma, whose son went missing in the Srebrenica area in 1995, said: 'I cannot put his picture among the pictures of the dead.' Elma is a Bosnian woman in her 60s who has lived in Finland since the mid-1990s. She has pictures of dead family members on a shelf, but none of the missing son. The liminality and ambiguity of the category of the missing are translated into daily struggles over the ways in which the missing may be remembered and made present in their absence.

Fiona Parrot (2010) argues that we should always understand the relationship between photographs, death and mourning as a dynamic one; remembering and mourning the dead are evolving practices rather than fixed and established ones, even when there is nothing as dramatic as disappearance connected with the death. According to her, the ways in which photographs of deceased family members are displayed, or not displayed, and where and when, are connected to ongoing negotiations over loss and absence, and over the relationship with the deceased person. When a family member is missing and their fate is unresolved, these negotiations are even more fraught with tension. But even if photographs of the missing are not necessarily on show at home, or not placed with images of those who are known to be dead, they are still very important for family members. My

Bosnian interlocutors' accounts prove that even if they are kept in a drawer or a cupboard, photographs are valued artefacts that symbolically re-install the absent one into the world of those left behind (cf. Blejmar, 2017: 119). Photographs can produce a sense of the continual presence of the absent person, albeit a sense of presence that is repeatedly interrupted by the material, bodily absence.

The importance of photographs has been recognised by regimes carrying out enforced disappearance. Several scholars discuss the ways in which, in the 1970s and 1980s, representatives of Argentina's military regime, when forcing their way into the private homes of those they were to abduct, confiscated or destroyed photographs and other personal belongings, often while the family were watching (e.g. Robben, 2005: 210; Gordon, 2008: 103). In this way, they sought to create a total void by also making the disappeared person symbolically non-existent in their social worlds.

In social worlds wounded by such purposive violence, photographs can have peculiar afterlives. Gabriel Gatti (2014) points out a surprising way of using photographs in post-dictatorship Argentina. He relates the story of a family he visited, the son of which was abducted by the military regime when he was only a few months old and decades later identified via DNA. At that time, he was an adult who had grown up in another family. In the family album of his original, biological family, a photo of him as a baby is followed by pictures of his biological father at various ages, from childhood up to the age when the boy, now a grown man, was reconnected with the family. The gap, the absence, is filled with an imaginary series of pictures of how he could, or should, have been, in this family; through these photographs, the time spent apart is reimagined as shared life (Gatti, 2014: 79–80; cf. Blejmar, 2017: 115–43).

However, it is not only photographs that have the potential to be turned into an embodiment of the missing person, or a carrier of their presence. Sabiha, who could not bear to have her missing husband's photograph on the wall, told me that she had kept his coat and a key to his workplace – she found the key in the coat pocket years ago. 'I cannot throw them away!' she said. The clothes of the disappeared often hold a particular significance for those left behind, as they have intimately touched the body of the absent person (cf. de Alwis, 2009). Sabiha carried her husband's belongings, the coat and the key, all the way from Bosnia to her new exiled life in Finland. It could be asked whether it would be better to conceptualise this as continuity, rather than as reappearance, as Sabiha has had the objects since the time when she still lived with her husband. However, I suggest that although there is an element of continuity in her relationship with these artefacts, the meanings of the coat and the key have changed over the years, in a negotiation similar to that involving photographs, suggested by Parrot (2010).

Over time, the coat and the key have become specific artefacts that stand for the disappeared husband, substitutes for his presence due to their 'immediate associability with their owner' (Jugo, 2017: 22; see also Renshaw, 2011: 27–8). In this way, they have the capacity to make the disappeared person reappear symbolically.

Some clothes and personal belongings of the missing do concretely reappear to family members during the search period. Amir Jugo (2017) discusses the significance of clothes and artefacts that have reappeared along with remains when mass graves have been excavated in Bosnia. He argues that the artefacts have both 'social and forensic lives' (Jugo, 2017: 35): they have been used as evidence in court proceedings against the perpetrators, but for family members they have become mementoes that connect them with the missing. The objects are not just mementoes, however; they hold a deeper significance, with family members often seeing them as forming a physical connection with the missing loved one, as something that has touched their body. Via this connection, they become signifiers standing for the disappeared one, sometimes the only things family members have left of them. Jugo argues that these objects become 'relics' (Jugo, 2017: 35–6), reminiscent of their medieval Christian counterparts in their ability to connect with the benevolent presence of the deceased person.

Another kind of intimate presence of the missing loved one is articulated by Selma's mother, the Bosniak woman discussed in Chapter 1. She moved back to the Srebrenica area after the peace agreement, to a house built by her disappeared husband, insisting that she could feel his presence in its structures. This presence is perhaps made more significant in a landscape where thousands of Bosniak homes were destroyed in the course of ethnic cleansing (Huttunen, 2009; Halilovich, 2013). For Selma's mother, the house probably stands for continuity, or a sustained connection with her missing husband. From another point of view, the house itself made Selma's mother return, made her reappear, in a way, in a landscape from which Bosniaks had been violently ejected. Continuities and reappearances are intertwined in complex ways, and with complex consequences in both the lives of those left behind and the social worlds wounded by large-scale disappearance.

Photographs in the public sphere: political movements

In the private realm, photographs, clothes and other mementoes have the potential to create a presence of the disappeared person, or a connection to them that may be both consoling and disturbing. Their significance is intimate and is tied to the particular personal relationship with the absent person. But when photographs and other such artefacts enter the public realm, they acquire new meanings and functions.

On the Missing at the Borders website discussed in Chapter 2, everybody giving a witness account of the disappearance of a family member is holding their photograph. These pictures are their personal mementoes, discussed explicitly as such in some of the accounts, and some of the witnesses also reflect on the ambiguities of displaying photographs of the missing at home. By holding the photographs in these video clips, however, family members bring them into the public sphere and make the disappeared reappear as public figures. In the same move, the photographs become politically laden; they become framed within a discourse that demands dignity and protection for the missing loved ones and changes to border regimes that expose people to deadly circumstances.

The Madres de Plaza de Mayo in Argentina was the first human rights movement – or at least the first to gain global visibility for this action – to bring photographs of missing loved ones into the public sphere, thus investing them with political significance. Nowadays, the image of the Madres, parading enlarged black-and-white ID photographs of their disappeared children and grandchildren around Plaza de Mayo, has become widely known and celebrated. In these demonstrations, forcibly disappeared Argentinians have reappeared in the public sphere with their names and faces, and the media have enlarged the public space from the Plaza de Mayo to global audiences. The disappeared have entered the social and cultural worlds through this insistence on the existence-in-absence of the people the regime tried to erase (Blejmar, 2017: 119–21). At the same time, the fact that those carrying the pictures were, and are, the mothers of the disappeared creates a powerful argument that has effectively translated the pain of absence in the private sphere into a demand for accountability and political change in the public realm (see e.g. Bouvard, 1994; Taylor, 1997; Robben, 2005: 299–317).

Since the early years of the Madres, photographs of the missing have been flooding public spaces in different places around the world. In Bosnia, the Majke Srebrenice (the Mothers of Srebrenica, or the Mothers of the Srebrenica and Zepa Enclaves, as the group is also known) have, since early in this millennium, organised demonstrations in which they carry photographs of the disappeared and also pillowcases embroidered with their names and years of birth.[3] The movement has not restricted its activity to demonstrations; it has brought court cases against the Dutch Government regarding the 1995 Srebrenica massacre, as the Dutch battalion, under the United Nations, was in a prominent position in the town at the time. Moreover, the Mothers have initiated civil action against the UN regarding the same tragedy.[4] They are still parading in public spaces with the photographs, gathering in Tuzla's central square on the eleventh of every month[5] to demand both accountability for the violence and clarity regarding the fate of those still missing. The movement has made individual missing persons reappear as photographs and names in the public sphere while simultaneously keeping alive and visible the missing as a category.

Similar modes of political mobilisation are repeated across the globe, in places where political projects target people and make them disappear. To give just a few examples, in Sri Lanka, mothers of the disappeared have carried both photographs of their missing children and items of their clothing in public spaces in Colombo (de Alwis, 2009) and, in Guatemala, photographs of the missing have entered the public space in both demonstrations and artistic performances (Hoelscher, 2008). These movements all demand political accountability, and often also political change. At the same time, they make the disappeared reappear as photographs traversing public spaces, and also in discursive forms that act as a reminder of the disappeared as a category. Both the pictures of the individuals and the political assertions of their rights as the disappeared serve as reminders of their absence and, by the same token, of their disrupted and liminal existence.

While political movements that address the violence of authoritarian governments make claims against local regimes, migration activists often target a larger spectrum of actors, because the governance of migration is transnational in character, as discussed in Chapters 2 and 4. Besides Missing at the Borders, there are numerous other civil society groups and NGOs in Europe and the Americas that work with different aspects of undocumented migration; they often demand political recognition for migrant deaths and disappearances and, simultaneously, radical change in border politics and migration regulation. The public activities of these groups often bring disappeared individuals into the public realm as photographs and names, to demand clarification of their fate. At the same time, they make disappeared migrants, as a group or collectivity, reappear symbolically in the public sphere, by insisting on their existence-in-absence. Sometimes this activity is small-scale and built around individual cases (e.g. Kobelinsky, 2020b: 533–5), while at other times, more generalised demands regarding the rights of dead and disappeared migrants are made. Sometimes these movements grow into activities that produce new relationships and affect the lives of the families of the missing in concrete ways; for example, in southern Spain, a solidarity organisation was founded to work with the village of origin of a number of migrants who drowned off the Spanish coast (Perl, 2018).

Photographs of missing persons have also entered the public space in political contexts that differ radically from those discussed above. After the 9/11 terrorist attacks in New York in 2001, the city was flooded with missing person posters, often showing a photograph of somebody disappeared in the attack, with their name, personal details and some contact information for the person searching for them (see e.g. Jones, Zagacki and Lewis, 2007; Edkins, 2011: 15–37). These photographs were in the public sphere not to make demands for political change but rather as search tools, especially during the first days after the tragedy. Later, they gained other meanings as well, including as criticism of the ways in which the incident was handled and narrativised by the authorities (Edkins, 2011: 33–7; see also Colwell-Chanthaphohn, 2011 and Greenwald, 2011). Moreover, according to some scholars, they served other, perhaps ritual and performative purposes (Jones, Zagacki and Lewis, 2007), which again made the disappeared forcefully present-in-absence for people moving about in New York.

There are also NGOs and movements that do not bring photographs of individual missing persons into the public realm but nevertheless insist on making the missing and disappeared present as a group in the social and political spheres. For instance, the Platform for Transnational Forensic Assistance is a charity that works in Greece, through its Forensic Missing Migrant Initiative, to improve forensic work with migrants' remains; in its own words, it aims 'to enhance the procedures, practices and protocols for registration, medico-legal identification and tracing of missing migrants in Europe at local, national and transnational level through networking, knowledge exchange, research, trainings and operational fieldwork'.[6] In other words, it speaks directly to the inefficacy of the efforts, discussed in Chapter 4, to search for and identify missing and dead undocumented migrants. Instead of pictures of missing persons, the initiative's webpage shows images of artefacts found on unidentified dead migrants, such as jewellery, prayer books and eyeglasses. These artefacts work in two registers: on the one hand, they invite anybody who might recognise an object to engage with the organisation's identification work; and, on the other, they speak to larger audiences metonymically about the missing persons and their existence-in-absence.

Another actor that does not parade photographs is Last Rights,[7] a movement that focuses on migrant deaths and disappearances in the Mediterranean; departing from a legal perspective, it insists on the rights of both the dead and disappeared individuals and their family members. The right to safe passage, the right to know, the right to identity and the right to be buried with dignity are among the claims put forward by the movement. Last Rights makes the category of the disappeared, closely intertwined with the category of the (often-unidentified) dead in the Mediterranean, strongly present in the public sphere, but it does not display any pictures of individual missing persons on its website. Rather, the missing and their family members emerge in the movement's discourse as legal subjects endowed with human rights.

Museums and memorials

Museums and memorials,[8] conceptualised as 'hard memory' by Alexander Etkind (2009), insert interpretations of history into the public space with the authority of institutions. In the case of the disappeared, monumentalising them makes them reappear powerfully in this space. Simultaneously, monuments embed disappearances in narratives and discourses that (almost) inevitably make political claims. Memorialising past atrocities is always a politically fraught practice, and the various ways in which the disappeared are memorialised in different places is affected by fluctuating contestations over interpretations of the past.

The establishment of museums and public memorials is mostly initiated and controlled by the state and, consequently, they produce historical narratives that are approved by the prevailing regimes of power. However, sometimes smaller memorials flourish in the shadow of official monuments, of the official 'narratives set in stone'; for example, numerous monuments have been installed by private individuals, local communities and NGOs in Russia (Etkind, 2009: 194–5), Guatemala (Hoelscher, 2008: 206–7), Nepal (Robins, 2014) and Timor-Leste (Kent, 2011: 434–5), to name just a few. In post-conflict situations and after major political change, competing memorials often emerge in the public realm, and existing memorials are contested and debated. Transitional justice endeavours are often elite-led and capital-city-centred processes (Robins, 2012), and local memorialisation practices challenge, or at least nuance, them in many ways.

In Argentina, the culture of remembrance around disappearances is particularly rich. Its roots are in the period of the junta regime, especially in the activities of the Madres, but it has intensified during the years following the transition to democracy. The back and forth between amnesty laws and insistent demands for accountability has deeply affected both state-sponsored and popular modes of remembrance. From these debates, a sprawling landscape of practices and discourses has emerged, including the fervent reconstruction of sites of memory by people Gatti (2014: 33–55) calls 'activists of meaning', that is, archaeologists and archivists[9] who work to reconstruct the 'truth' of the events and to memorialise sites where the violence of the junta took place. Several locations connected with enforced disappearances have been converted into memorial sites and museum spaces.

In Buenos Aires, in addition to several smaller places of memory,[10] there are two major sites that bring the disappeared to the public: ESMA, a museum and site of memory,[11] and the Parque de la Memoria,[12] or Memorial Park. ESMA, like several other memorial sites, is a former locus of terror: the Escuela Superior de Mecánica de la Armada (naval college), which became a detention centre under the junta. Both ESMA and the Memorial

Park exhibit photographs of the dead and the disappeared; they document the perpetrators' practices and build a political narrative around the disappearances. In both places, the individual missing reappear symbolically as names and photographs and, simultaneously, as a category. In the exhibiting practices of both locations, the dead and the disappeared as categories leak into each other, which makes sense in a way, as the process of searching for and identifying the victims still continues. The dead and the disappeared emerge together as a category of victims that is translated into a powerful argument against the military regime of the 1970s and 1980s.

Post-war Bosnia has been affected by a boom in memorial building by the three main ethno-national groups, all of them with competing narrativisations of the conflict (e.g. Sokol, 2014). As the Bosnian state is still divided into two entities, and the political landscape torn apart by competing forms of nationalism and the continued denial of past atrocities by many, museums and memorials have emerged in a highly contested political terrain, in which it is impossible to name a prevailing narrative that would be accepted by all sides.

There are several sites where the disappeared victims of the violence of 1990s' Bosnia reappear in various ways. The memorialisation of the tragedy of Srebrenica has gained most visibility; two major sites address the 1995 events, one in Potočari, the other in Sarajevo.[13] Within the severely divided and politically tense post-war atmosphere, and given the prominence of the 'international community' (or the 'international interventionist forces') in Bosnia, as discussed in the previous chapter, it should come as no surprise that the establishment of both these major sites has been supported by outside donors.

Located in a prominent position in Sarajevo's historic centre, Galerija 11/07/95[14] is a museum space dedicated to the history of the Srebrenica genocide. On the front wall of the building hangs a huge poster with the text 'Srebrenica Genocide Memorial Exhibition, Gallery 11/07/95' (in English) and a picture of a doll with no arms lying on muddy ground captures the attention of passers-by. The museum space includes several elements; first, there is 'The Wall of Death', inscribed with the names and ages of all 8,372 people killed in Srebrenica. Then there is a collection of 640 black-and-white photographs of the victims of the genocide, compiled in cooperation with the Mothers of Srebrenica: row after row of images of individuals, mostly men, looking out at the viewer. Several rooms are occupied by beautiful large black-and-white pictures taken by the photographer Tarik Samarah. They include landscapes of the Srebrenica area, views of the everyday lives of survivors of the massacre and intimate portraits of them and snapshots of the excavations of the mass graves and of the burials in Potočari. A room called 'Srebrenica – Mapping genocide' contains maps, texts, photographs, drawings and film clips, including clips of the judicial proceedings at the Hague war tribunal (ICTY); together these elements build a compelling historical narrative for the other sections. Within this whole, the disappeared reappear symbolically, both as individuals and as a collective. Like in Argentina, the line between the dead and the disappeared as categories becomes blurred; as in Argentina, the process of identifying the victims and transferring them from the latter category into the former continues in Bosnia, even though the peak years of identification are over.

In Potočari, located between Srebrenica and Bratunac in eastern Bosnia, stands the Srebrenica-Potočari Memorial and Cemetery for the Victims of the 1995 Genocide.[15] Like ESMA in Buenos Aires, it is a former site of terror; it is the place where, before the assault on the town, civilians sought refuge and the protection of the UN troops but were notoriously turned down. It consists of a cemetery where the identified victims of the 1995 assault have been buried since 1999, and a memorial site. The latter comprises an exhibition called 'Memorial Room – Personal Stories', located in a former factory that served as the UN battalion's headquarters during the assault on Srebrenica; a small room for temporary exhibitions; an open-air mosque; and an imposing, powerful stone installation displaying the names of all 8,372 victims of the genocide, both those found and identified and those still missing. In the permanent Memorial Room exhibition, there are videos of the events, filmed and transcribed testimonies of survivors and also artefacts exhumed from the mass graves (see also Figures 4.1 and 4.2); those who have donated these artefacts have thus transformed their personal mementoes into public indexes of past violence. However, as not all family members were willing to donate their only material reminders of their loved ones to the public exhibition, some artefacts are represented only as photographs (Jugo, 2017: 37).

The disappeared reappear symbolically in this space as names on the memorial stone and as photographs and artefacts in the Memorial Room. At the same time, the identified missing persons reappear materially in the graveyard, where gravestones with their individual names symbolically mark the site of their material remains. The site comes alive every year on 11 July, during the annual anniversary-cum-burial ceremony discussed in the previous chapter. This vivid interaction with the materiality of the memory space imbues it with a significance (cf. Etkind, 2009: 194–5) that is recognised well beyond Bosnia, as the global media frequently report on the Potočari funerals.

There is a growing number of museums and memorials dedicated to enforced disappearance in different parts of the world; most often they address the dead and the disappeared side by side. Like the Argentinian and Bosnian examples, they are often built around a narrative that shows

144 *Missing persons, political landscapes and cultural practices*

Figure 5.1 The memorial stone in Srebrenica-Potočari Memorial displaying the names of all the 8,372 victims of the genocide. Credit: Laura Huttunen.

the events that led to the excessive violence, and they document the practices of the perpetrators. In this way, the museums make disappeared individuals present in the public, cultural sphere, even if their remains have not been located and identified. In addition, the museums make the disappeared as a collectivity present in the political narrative of the state. Often their presence-in-absence is turned into a powerful argument against previous regimes.

In Potočari, the burial site is separate from the memorial exhibition but other memorial sites or museums combine symbolic memorialisation with actual mortal remains; in Rwanda, Burundi and Cambodia, unidentified bones and skulls of genocide victims are exhibited at several locations (see e.g. Korman, 2015; Lesley, 2015; Bennett, 2019). Even though, at some of these memorial sites, names of victims are listed alongside photographs of the disappeared, the actual bones that are on display remain unidentified and unlabelled. The bones are not returned to families for individual mortuary rituals but are exhibited together with other victims' remains. Instead of recreating individual identities and family ties, these practices of making reappear produce collective identities for the remains. While some scholars have interpreted these exhibiting practices as manipulating the remains

Symbolic reappearances

Figure 5.2 Gravestones in Srebrenica-Potočari Memorial and Cemetery for the Victims of the 1995 Genocide. Credit: Laura Huttunen.

for political gain (Lesley, 2015; Jamar and Major, 2022), others have suggested that in such extreme circumstances, when most of the relatives of the remains are dead or in exile, the memorial sites enable the remains to be cared for, even if this is within a politically orchestrated exhibit (Bennett, 2019: 579).

Likewise, in the 9/11 Memorial Museum in New York, unidentified remains of victims of the attacks on the World Trade Center are placed in a specific construction, a 'sacred bedrock' (Greenwald, 2011) – 'human remains' in this case refers to debris from the attack site containing minute traces of human remains that cannot be separated out. The exhibition practices in such places intertwine symbolic and material reappearances and, according to some critics, confuse conventional understandings of museum space and burial space. Ongoing debates, both scholarly and popular (e.g. Colwell-Chanthaphohn, 2011; Greenwald, 2011; Auchter, 2014; Korman, 2015; Lesley, 2015; Jamar and Major, 2022), point to the salience of these issues. Beyond disagreements over the political narratives of the events that made some people disappear, there are keen debates on the proper ways to combine the material and symbolic and make the disappeared reappear with dignity.

Artistic and media presences: literary work, visual arts and media spectacles

Art in different forms and genres is fertile ground for artists, touched by the disappearance of their loved ones or co-citizens in various ways, to address the issue. Such artworks can be interpreted from different angles, for instance by focusing on the ways in which they depict the void of the unaccounted-for absence or the experience of living with protracted uncertainty. At the same time, these artworks also make the disappeared reappear symbolically by serving as a reminder of their existence-in-absence.

The graphic novel *Isä* by Hanneriina Moisseinen, which I discuss in detail in Chapter 3, is an excellent example of the reappearance of a disappeared person in artistic work. In that novel, Moisseinen's disappeared father reappears as a real-life character up to the point of his disappearance, and he then has alternative, possible ghostly, lives, imagined by his daughter. Even though his eventual fate in real life, and in the book, remains a mystery, this father, disappeared decades ago, re-enters the public space and the cultural sphere in symbolic form through his compelling presence in this artwork.

In Argentina, there is a flourishing genre of memoirs written by survivors of enforced disappearance, those who were disappeared from their families and communities and lived through the horror of detainment but managed to survive and reappear to those left behind as flesh-and-blood (albeit sometimes barely living) persons. According to Gatti (2014; 121–2), they reappeared also to themselves, as the systematic violence and unimaginable forms of torture they suffered at the hands of the agents of enforced disappearance broke their psychic integrity and made them, in a way, disappear from themselves. Their memoirs can be read as a form of travel literature, depicting a trip to hell, darkness and disintegration and then a gradual return to light, normalcy and existence, culminating in their reappearance to both themselves and their surroundings (Gatti, 2014: 121–2). The literary work in this genre makes an individual reappear in the public sphere, by announcing their survival, and simultaneously renders the 'reappeared-disappeared' (Gatti, 2014: 123) as a category present in the social world – a political move against the objectives of enforced disappearance.

In Bosnia, Rezak Hukanović's memoir *The Tenth Circle of Hell* (1998; original in 1993) falls into this genre. The book depicts Hukanović's experience of being abducted by Serb forces in Prijedor at around the same time that Sabiha's husband went missing. Hukanović was taken to prison camps run by the invading forces, from which he was freed by International Red Cross representatives who were able to enter the camps in 1992. These camps, discussed also in Chapter 1 of this book, were notorious for their systematic use of lethal violence. Interestingly, the memoir is written in the third person. Hukanović has explained this choice by saying that it felt as though all the horror happened to somebody else. This resonates with Gatti's idea of the victims of enforced disappearance disappearing also from themselves. Like its Argentinian counterparts, Hukanović's book is a depiction of a trip into darkness and back into the 'normal' world and, at the same time, it makes the once-disappeared individual reappear as a public person.

Other artistic genres have also flourished in places marked by large-scale disappearance. Both Gabriel Gatti (2014: 129–54) and Jordana Blejmar (2017) look at novels, films and photography produced by the generation of children of the disappeared in Argentina – or simply 'children of', as Gatti puts it, in an ironic reference to the institutionalisation of discourses and victim positions around the history of disappearances in post-dictatorship Argentina. Artistic works are analysed by these two researchers as sites of renegotiation of this generation's identities, and both scholars pay attention to the ways in which the identities and memories of the children's generation differ from those of the previous one. These younger people's experiences are often articulated, perhaps surprisingly, in parody, collage and other playful and experimental modes.

While these artworks deal with the multitude of ways in which the disappearance of a loved one affects the lives of those left behind, I am particularly interested in how they make disappeared persons themselves reappear in symbolic form and give them a presence in the social and cultural spheres. Like the father in Moisseinen's *Isä*, the disappeared reappear in different forms in this artistic work; for example, in Albertina Carri's famous film *Los Rubios* (2003), which addresses enforced disappearances in Argentina, Carri's disappeared parents reappear as Playmobil figures in a scene depicting their abduction, and in their daughter's memory of the event (see Blejmar, 2017: 45–68). Even though the main focus of these artworks is often to explore the social world of the next generation, they simultaneously remind us that the disappeared used to exist in this world, and still do through the traces they have left in the lives of those left behind.

Reappearance in art can, however, be more ephemeral, and sometimes the disappeared person is present in artwork as a void, a hint or a gesture. In Argentina – and in other Latin-American countries with a history of enforced disappearance – there is a flourishing visual arts scene, especially photography, that addresses the violent history. Jordana Blejmar argues that the post-dictatorship generation in Argentina, or the generation of the children of the disappeared, has developed alternative ways of visualising violence and absence through means such as collage, montage and the juxtaposition of incongruous elements, thus creating a particular visual language with which to bring the disappeared into the cultural sphere of the present, not as direct representations but as embodiments of complex histories and multivocal afterlives (Blejmar, 2017: 121–69; see also Hoelscher, 2008; Fortuny, 2014).

Another kind of visual language that points to the disappeared while not actually presenting them can be found in contemporary photographic work on migrant deaths and disappearances. For instance, the photography series *Migrant Bodies/Corpi Migranti* (2015–17) by Max Hinzel, which was exhibited at the P21 Gallery in London in 2019 and later published as a book,[16] focuses on the aftermath of the shipwreck off the coast of the island of Lampedusa in 2015, and 'provides a series of scenes, objects, forensic tools and practices, including photographs depicting fragmentary human remains and a photo of the victims' relatives at the burial sites' (Dziuban, 2023: 259). Moreover, these pictures of death are juxtaposed with images of living migrants being monitored at the European borders. Thus, instead of bringing the disappeared themselves into the public sphere as photographs (with the exception of some pictures of unidentified human remains), the series makes them reappear symbolically via a detour, by showing the conditions in which they disappeared. A similar visual language, verging on documentary, is applied by the Finnish photographer Anna Autio, who, together with journalist Taina Tervonen, published a book on deaths in the Mediterranean called *Hukkuneet* (Tervonen and Autio, 2019), which translates as 'The drowned'. In the book, text by Tervonen and photography by Autio depict the vastness of the sea, piles of discarded life-vests, personal belongings of the drowned sealed in plastic bags by forensic pathologists and graves without names in Spain. In both this and Hinzel's series, various objects, for example a water-damaged ID card and a discarded life-jacket, stand metonymically for the disappeared persons themselves; at the same time, both series bring the issue of migrant disappearances, and the category of the missing, into the public sphere.

Besides such artistically tuned representations of the missing, there are other genres that make particular missing persons reappear in the public sphere. The liminal and anomalous nature of human disappearances has given rise to media spectacles and commodified media productions, ranging from the flourishing genre of true crime to fictitious TV series, from books and newspaper articles addressing unsolved real-life disappearances to podcasts doing the same. For instance, while I have been working with this topic, a book titled *Ei jälkeäkään* (Saari and Majamaa, 2020) – 'Without a trace' in English – has been published in Finland. The book reports, in a journalistic style, on eleven cases of unsolved disappearance in Finland. It brings into focus one missing person at a time, gives their full name and the circumstances of their disappearance and then presents interviews with family members and an overview of the related police work. A sense of mystery, of not-properly-investigated events is created. Like the artwork discussed above, the book makes these eleven disappeared persons reappear in the public sphere as figures to be seen, remembered and still searched for.

In the USA, the true-crime series *Disappeared* ran for six seasons between 2009 and 2013, with an additional season in 2016 and a podcast in 2021. The programmes were made in documentary format, following individual disappearance cases. Similar national TV series have been broadcast in many countries, in more or less documentary format. In recent years, podcasts focusing on true crime, including disappearance cases, have flourished alongside TV and film, and books focusing on real-life cases are being published across the globe.

While the missing are not seen as forming a social category of victims in these productions, their disturbing absence and unresolved fate resonate with profound questions of safety and protection, of personhood, life course and human condition, that appeal to the general public. Can somebody just vanish without a trace? Whatever the circumstances, disappearance is always disturbing and culturally anomalous and, as such, fertile material for such commodified productions.

While it can be argued that many of these books and media productions simply capitalise on the power of the liminality of disappearance, Anna Matyska (2024) argues that some of this output genuinely seeks to contribute to the search for the missing. In the Polish TV series *Has anybody seen, does anybody know*, which has been running since 1996, the audience are actively invited to provide information, should they have any, on the cases presented, and some of this has proved useful in ongoing searches. I suggest that programmes like this can be seen simultaneously as tools in the search for the missing and forums that make the missing present and visible as a category. The individual missing persons presented also, of course, reappear as public figures. Such programmes are another example of the complex ways in which symbolic and material reappearances feed into each other.

Ghosts and restless spirits

> Whenever I go to V. [her village of origin], I get frightened at some point. It is okay in daytime, but when night falls, I get frightened. I keep on listening to noises, to something, I do not know what. And I hear noises and I cannot sleep. I think about all the dead and the missing. I think about all the violence that took place there. And I cannot sleep.

This quotation is from Lejla, the Bosnian woman discussed in Chapter 4. Like numerous other Bosnians, after the war she reclaimed the family home in her village in north-western Bosnia. She now lives in Finland but almost every summer she travels to Bosnia to stay in the house, usually with her children and their spouses. However, the visits are marked by a sense of her being troubled and frightened by the violent history of the place (cf. Schindel, 2014: 253–5). Lejla does not explicitly mention ghosts, but a sense of being haunted colours her description of these visits.

Ghosts, spirits and spectres have become popular in the humanities and social sciences since Jacques Derrida's introduction of the idea of 'hauntology' in his *Specters of Marx* in 1994 (the original French version appeared in 1993); the popularity of ghostly apparitions has become so widespread that some scholars argue that a 'spectral turn' has taken place in these fields of study (e.g. Blanco and Peeren, 2013a). Within this line of scholarship, ghosts and haunting are often understood metaphorically, as 'conceptual metaphors' that 'perform theoretical work' (Blanco and Peeren, 2013b: 1–2, see also Auchter, 2014). My initial inspiration for my treatment of ghosts and spirits in this book, however, comes from another direction. I have been inspired by many anthropologists' attempts to take seriously the prevailing alternative ontologies and epistemologies in the communities they study; according to these ontologies, ghosts and spirits are often real actors in the social and cultural worlds they inhabit (e.g. Langford, 2013; Kent, 2024). Nevertheless, the various forms of haunting that I analyse below are in some cases easier to interpret metaphorically, as traces of the past or as the resurfacing of traumatic events (cf. Gordon, 2008; Blanco and Peeren, 2013b: 11–15). However, at the same time, I want to remain faithful to anthropological sensibilities, and to the idea of taking seriously the epistemologies of the people we study. Resonating with this, Blanco and Peeren (2013b: 9) suggest that Derrida's hauntology, or the idea of taking ghosts seriously, is an openness to 'the specter as possibility' or, in other words, to taking other ontologies seriously, and giving space to the indeterminacy and uncertainty of life (see also Kent, 2024).

Many scholars who have worked in contexts marked by extensive violence in different places around the globe describe the presence of ghosts and restless spirits in the local cultural worlds. In particular, places affected by enforced disappearances, or by a large number of otherwise missing persons, are densely populated by ghosts and restless spirits, in a metaphorical or a more literal sense (e.g. Kwon, 2008; Langford, 2013; Eppel, 2014; Meinert and Whyte, 2017; Bennett, 2018; Fontein 2018; Kent, 2024; Kent, 2020). This also applies to those who die as victims of violence but are not buried properly – they are not actually missing in the strict sense of the word, as their families know where their grave is. These situations violate cultural understandings so brutally that the not-properly-buried return to haunt the living, just like the disappeared do.

Ghostly presences can take different forms. Some family members seek contact with missing loved ones via clairvoyants, sorcerers or telepathic means (e.g. Robben, 2005: 291; Matyska, 2023b). In Moisseinen's novel, the daughter imagines that she sees her disappeared father's face time and again in different places, only to be disappointed when she realises that the person is somebody else. Likewise, in the narratives on the Missing at the Borders website, many family members describe seeing their disappeared loved one's face everywhere, for instance on walls and on their plate at mealtimes (and then not being able to eat any more). Similar experiences are reported by my Bosnian interlocutors; they talk about seeing their missing family member's face in crowds, in dreams, in unexpected spaces. Again, I interpret these experiences as people seesawing between a harrowing sense of the disappeared one's absence and a sense of their continuous presence-in-absence.

My Bosnian interlocutors never told me that they had witnessed the appearance of actual ghosts or spirits. Instead, the idea of a missing family member somehow being restless in (putative) death is often repeated. Sabiha, whom I introduce in Chapter 1, insists that even though she understands that her husband must be dead, without a proper burial 'there is no peace for him', as she puts it. But this restlessness also engulfs her as a mode of haunting: 'there is no peace, not for him, not for me', she says. A similar idea of the missing, or of those who are presumably in the mass graves, as restless beings is repeated by my other interlocutors as well.

I read another kind of ghostly presence in an account related by Emina, a young woman of Bosnian origin whose father went missing in Bosnia's Prijedor area in the early days of the war. Emina was around seven years old when her father disappeared, so her memories of him are scant, albeit affectionate. When I talked with her in Finland – where she had moved with her mother and siblings – she told me about her visits to her village of origin. She said, with pride in her voice, 'When I go there, people say to me: "We do not need to ask whose daughter you are! You look exactly like your father!"' While Emina clearly found some comfort in this physical resemblance, this account disturbed me. What kind of legacy is it for a young person, to enter the space of violence as the embodiment of her forcibly disappeared father? While this legacy connects Emina with her absent father, it simultaneously embeds her within a brutal history of genocide; moreover, I cannot help but detect in this sentence a lingering obligation for Emina to represent her father, to re-enter the 'ethnically cleansed' space as the politically burdened re-embodiment of him.

Estela Schindel (2014) describes stories of haunting and ghostly presences at ESMA, the former site of detention and torture discussed above, that has been turned into a museum. Construction workers and museum employees report strange noises and other signs of ghostly presence, albeit often based on hearsay rather than on their own experience. In the contexts discussed by Schindel, stories of haunting are often fragmentary and inconsistent and are told not by those who actually witnessed the incidents but second-hand; such ghostly rumours proliferate rhizomatically, that is, underground and horizontally, and they have neither concrete authors nor clear beginnings and endings (Schindel, 2014: 249). Schindel suggests that ghosts and haunting should be regarded as symptoms of unease: they draw attention to the latent legacy of the past that appears in the margins of rational discourses; they hint at aspects of the past that are difficult to address within the official discourses; and they point to the unfathomable nature of the violence carried out during the Argentinian dictatorship. This understanding resonates with Gabriel Gatti's (2014) argument that enforced disappearances are marked by the breakdown of meaning and the impotence of rational accounts. Referring to historian Louise White's account of vampire stories in postcolonial Africa, Schindel argues that what such supernatural stories may reveal 'is not information about external facts but knowledge about the deep conflicts that trouble society' (Schindel, 2014: 250).

In other cultural contexts, for example in Southeast Asia, Uganda and Zimbabwe, researchers argue that ghosts and restless spirits are concrete, individual beings that demand action from people, most often from their own families. In these contexts, it is not hard to find informants who will talk openly about ghosts and the ways in which they affect the lives and fortunes of their family members. Often, informants feel that it is only successful burial and fitting ceremonies that can calm down these restless beings (Kwon, 2008; Langford, 2013; Eppel, 2014; Bennett, 2018; Fontein, 2018; Kent, 2020).

However, Meinert and Whyte (2017), writing about the legacies of violence in Uganda, remind their readers that such 'traditional' ontologies live side by side with other understandings, including modern 'scientific' explanations. Moreover, 'traditional' and animistic ontologies are in most places intertwined with other religious cosmologies, such as the Christian, Islamic or Buddhist ones. Within such layered cosmologies, ghosts of the disappeared are often insistent reminders of the importance of taking care of the dead and of dealing with death in culturally appropriate ways. They remind family members of their obligations and, through ghost stories circulating in local society, they evoke larger moral concerns.

Fenella Cannell (2013) argues that ghosts (and ancestors) also exist in different forms in the cultural worlds of the 'Modern West'; interestingly, even there, the most compelling ghosts seem to be those of the disappeared or not properly buried, such as those of First World War soldiers whose remains were never returned to their homeland (Cannell, 2013: 217). Cannell's argument resonates with that of Meinert and Whyte in insisting that rational and 'scientific' modes live side by side with 'traditional', irrational and imaginative ways of making sense of the complexities of human life, including human disappearances, all around the world.

Yet another account of ghostly existence emerging from the violence of disappearance is related by Esad, whom I introduce in Chapter 1. 'My life after 1995 is a miracle! It is extra time; I am living on borrowed time!' he exclaimed when I interviewed him about his three brothers who died in the assault on Srebrenica in July 1995. His own narrow escape from the besieged town, and the violent fate of his brothers and of many friends and neighbours just a couple of days later, left him tormented by a guilty conscience: why did he survive when so many others died? Why did he survive, when most of his closest male friends and his brothers were murdered or disappeared? According to his wife, Jasminka, Esad often finds it hard to sleep as he ruminates on the events and these tormenting questions. His identity as a survivor is inescapably tied to that of the dead and missing, those annihilated by the brutal necropolitical power exercised by the wartime leadership in the area. Such a sense of living on 'borrowed time' points to the ways in which excessive violence shakes the very foundation of life for those who survive, and imbues their life with a ghostly quality.

Conclusion: insistent reappearances

In this chapter, I argue that if the disappeared are found neither alive nor as dead bodies or identifiable remains they keep on returning in symbolic forms – that is, forms that stand for them and make them present in the absence, forms that refer to them either as individuals or as a category of victims. This symbolic return can occur in different modes, ranging from personal mementoes to political activism, from state-run museums to small NGO-sponsored memorials, from nuanced artwork to media spectacles, from dreams to ghosts and restless spirits. The disappeared reappear in the private realm, to their family members and others who knew them personally, but also in the public and political arena. In the latter case, they are often brought into the public space by family members, political activists or NGOs who demand certainty about their fate, and often also political responsibility for their disappearance. In the private and intimate sphere, the disappeared reappear as individuals, as photographs or mementoes that make the absent one present symbolically, or as ghosts or restless spirits demanding attention and care. In the public space, they reappear both as individuals and as the category of the missing or disappeared, often framed within political narratives that invest the reappearance with political significance.

The concrete reappearance of the missing as bodies or remains and the symbolic reappearances feed into each other, often in complex ways. While my key argument in this chapter is that the failure to find a missing person or their mortal remains gives rise to this variety of symbolic reappearances, the relationship in most cases is more complex. In many instances, the symbolic reappearance of the missing in public places contributes to their material reappearance as well; the Madres, their protests in Argentina and their contribution to the actual search and identification work, are a good example of this. On the other hand, the missing and disappeared who have been found, identified and buried with dignity still often figure in symbolic places, such as museums and memorials to the missing, long after their material reappearance. Moreover, the reappearance of some mortal remains may give rise to the symbolic reappearance of others – the publication mentioned at the start of this chapter, about Finnish soldiers who disappeared during the Second World War but have been found and identified in this millennium, is a symbolic reminder of those still missing while also a commemoration of the reappeared and reburied. This list of the complex entanglements of material and symbolic reappearances could certainly be continued, but these examples suffice to make the point.

I end this chapter with an intriguing example of a form of symbolic reappearance that fed into the actual reappearance of mortal remains. Leyla Renshaw (2010: 56–7) describes children's ritualised play in a Spanish village where several of the residents had been killed and buried clandestinely during the civil war. Children who had heard 'half-understood fragments from adults' (Renshaw, 2010: 56) about the clandestine burial sites developed games and rhymes, and invented rituals such as taking longer routes to avoid certain places or speeding up when passing them 'in an atmosphere of fear and excitement' (Renshaw, 2010: 56). In Renshaw's account, children's bodily practices in the form of play rituals, marked by both fear and curiosity, kept the memory of the burial locations alive, and this helped to locate them decades later, when exhumation became possible after a regime change. I read Renshaw's account as an intriguing example of the multiple ways in which the disappeared keep on reappearing in social and cultural worlds, or, if conceptualised as continuity, of the disappeared's insistent ghostly presence in children's folklore contributing to their later exhumation and reburial. I read this as yet another example of the insistent return or reappearance of the missing and disappeared, and of the surprising variety of ways in which reappearance takes place.

Notes

1 *Löydetyt, Ilta-sanomien erikoislehti*. The electronic version can be found at Löydetyt-erikoislehti kertoo talvi- ja jatkosodan sotavainajien pitkästä matkasta kotiin – Kotimaa – Ilta-Sanomat (https://www.is.fi/kotimaa/art-2000009223160.html) (accessed 18 April 2023).
2 There is an extensive theoretical and philosophical discussion on the ways in which photographs represent and signify (see e.g. Barthes, 1981; Batchen, 1997; Batchen, 2004; Blejmar, 2017: 115–43). Within the scope of this book, however, it is impossible to go deeper into this discussion, however interesting this would be in relation to missing and disappeared persons.
3 On the early years of the movement, including public displays of photographs of the missing, see Wagner (2008: 66–81).
4 ICD – Mothers of Srebrenica v. the Netherlands and the UN – Asser Institute (https://www.internationalcrimesdatabase.org/Case/769/Mothers-of-Srebrenica-v-the-Netherlands-and-the-UN/) (accessed 24 May 2023).
5 Mothers of Srebrenica Still on Streets Demanding Justice, Balkan Insight (https://balkaninsight.com/2022/08/11/mothers-of-srebrenica-still-on-streets-demanding-justice/) (accessed 25 April 2023).
6 The Initiative, Forensic Missing Migrant Initiative, Greece (https://forensicmigration.wixsite.com/missingmigrants/missingmigrants) (accessed 5 June 2023).
7 Last Rights (http://www.lastrights.net/) (accessed 25 May 2023).
8 I have not conducted systematic research on museums or memorial practices, and I am aware that there is a flourishing literature on historical and cultural memory, memorial practices and museum work in changing times. Due to lack of space, I am unable to go further into this discussion here.
9 Gatti also includes psychologists in the group of 'activists of meaning', but their engagement in meaning-making takes place in therapeutic sessions with individuals rather than in public memorial-building.
10 See for example Route of Remembrance, Official English Website for the City of Buenos Aires (https://turismo.buenosaires.gob.ar/en/article/route-remembrance) (accessed 12 May 2023).
11 Museo Sitio de Memoria Esma (http://www.museositioesma.gob.ar/en/) (accessed 3 May 2023).
12 Park – Parque de la Memoria (https://parquedelamemoria.org.ar/en/park/) (accessed 3 May 2023).
13 I have visited these sites myself, but not the Argentinian locations and the other memorial sites discussed in this section. My first visit to the Potočari site was in 2001, when it was marked only by a small memorial stone. I returned in 2014 with a Bosnian guide, with whom I had interesting discussions about

memory practices in post-war Bosnia. In that year I also visited Galerija 11 July 1995.
14 Frontpage – Galerija, 11 July 1995 (https://galerija110795.ba/) (accessed 2 May 2023).
15 Srebrenica Memorial Center (https://srebrenicamemorial.org/en) (accessed 12 May 2023).
16 For the book publication, see Migrant bodies – Borderline Sicilia (https://www.borderlinesicilia.it/en/news-en/migrant-bodies/) (accessed 10 May 2023).

Conclusion: violent absences, haunting presences

In this volume's subtitle, I claim that absences created by human disappearances are always violent, in one way or another. Sometimes they are violent in a literal sense: they are produced by intentional acts of violence, perpetrated by the state or by other actors striving for power. In other cases, the violence is of a different kind: sometimes disappearance takes place in conditions that expose people to dangerous circumstances and make them susceptible to violence; in yet other instances, something in the disappeared person's life propels them to leave without informing those around them. With my choice of title, I also argue that, whatever the reason behind disappearance, from the point of view of those left behind, there is always something violent in the unaccounted-for absence. It creates voids in social relations, with practical, emotional, social and sometimes also political consequences, and it disturbs deep-rooted cultural practices around the transition from life to death. The empirical material that I have discussed in this book, both my own ethnographic material and other researchers' data, shows the diversity that exists in the violence of absence in different locations and contexts. The quality, intensity and political significance of violence varies hugely, but in the experience of those left behind, there is always something disruptive in the unaccounted-for absence of a loved one.

At the same time, the title claims that human disappearances create presences that often have a haunting quality. People cannot just vanish, or cease to exist – those left behind need explanations, rituals, bureaucratic procedures and personal processes of making sense, and those who disappear leave behind both powerful voids and traces of their existence. This haunting, or insistent presence-in-absence, takes many forms, as Chapters 4 and 5 of this book argue. First, it gives rise to a great variety of projects that focus on searching for the missing and invest in identifying them, if found dead, and reconnecting them with their families and communities. Secondly, it gives rise to a plethora of symbolic reappearances, ranging from private mementoes to state-run museums, from artwork and media spectacles to ghosts and restless spirits haunting both places and individuals.

Juxtaposing absence and presence in this way urges us to think about human disappearances in dynamic terms and to pay attention to processes that connect disappearances and reappearances with each other. At the heart of my understanding of the violent force of disappearances is Gabriel Gatti's (2014) argument that disappearance cuts individuals off from their social worlds, from their families, kinship connections and communities, and from their histories. It creates bodies without identities and voids in social worlds. Both investment in the search for and identification of the missing and symbolic forms of reappearance emerge to fill these voids and to repair and restore the relationships that have been so violently severed.

I have emphasised throughout this book the importance of embedding every case of human disappearance, and reappearance, within its social, cultural and political context through careful ethnographic work. Beyond this, I suggest in the introduction that we need to place both disappearance and reappearance within a historical frame; the significance of presence and absence, personhood and the individual, the role of the state and of the state-based international system, ways of memorialising, and ways of identifying both living and dead individuals have all changed significantly over the course of human history, some of them over just a couple of decades. All this suggests that human disappearance is a phenomenon that varies across time and location. Analytically, this urges us to both map variation and simultaneously ask questions about similarities and continuities across this diversity.

Anthropology of disappearance, or towards theorising disappearances in social sciences

In this book, I have suggested ways to develop anthropological, or more generally social-scientific, approaches to human disappearances across political and cultural differences and geographical contexts. The key axes along which I have approached the issue are disappearance and reappearance, life and death, state and kinship, and intimate and political. My focus is on anthropology, but I believe that my suggestions make sense for a variety of humanities and social sciences.

Throughout, I argue that the missing are liminal figures between life and death. Even though in many places the probability is that missing persons are dead, without a body there is no certainty, and the indeterminate state continues, often becoming a chronic condition that affects the lives of the families and communities left behind. Moreover, in many places there are people who are violently killed and buried in undignified ways, and the families or other community members know where these unproper graves are situated. These dead are not missing in the strict sense of the word, as their whereabouts are known by their families, but the state of not being properly buried assigns these remains to the category of the liminal, and in this sense akin to the disappeared. Such liminality is an unresolved state of being that reverberates through communities and societies in countless ways.

One of the book's key arguments is that, in order to understand the dynamics of human disappearance and reappearance in today's world, we need to look at both the politics that make some people disappear (Chapters 1 and 2) and the politics that allow some of the disappeared to reappear either alive, or as dead bodies or mortal remains (Chapter 4). There is a dynamic relationship between the two: the circumstances of disappearance affect the form that reappearance takes. Both disappearance and reappearance take place in historically unique circumstances; Argentina, Bosnia and the Mediterranean have served as key comparative points for analysing such dynamics and I have brought in other places and contexts as well, to illuminate the complexity of the phenomena being discussed.

Moreover, I argue that understanding the varied role of the state, or states, in relation to disappearances is crucial. In Chapter 1, I provide examples of contexts where the state has purposefully targeted its citizens or residents within its territory, often killing them and simultaneously hiding the act to create a political landscape of fear and submission. The practice of enforced disappearance is often an individuating strategy that targets individuals because of their political allegiances, their ethnic, racial or religious background, or a combination of these. In Chapter 2, I argue that, in the contemporary world, people forced to migrate without proper documentation, along irregular routes, are exposed to circumstances in which they are highly disappearable, that is, they are positioned outside state protection, in circumstances in which they are exposed either to being individually targeted or to the forces of the natural environment, such as the sea or the desert. In this context, states along migratory routes emerge as imbued with indifference, abandoning people within their territory or jurisdiction to an unprotected state of being. In many cases, this practice is not individuating in the same way as 'classical' modes of enforced disappearance, and who ends up dead or disappeared is a more random matter. However, there are also examples of state complicity in targeting individual migrants, which makes the picture more complicated and alerts us to the need to critically examine the role of the state in each case.

In Chapter 3, I suggest that in (more or less) stable democracies based on the rule of law, the state recognises its role as the protector of missing citizens and others (legally) within its jurisdiction. Emotionally strained situations often give rise to criticism about the shortcomings of police work in missing person cases, and about the indifference of authorities when faced with families' pain. However, it is crucial to understand the difference between such rule-of-law societies and the cases discussed above: in rule-of-law–based democracies, the protocols and structures of search are there, and people expect the state to apply the protocols and invest in finding the missing person, while other contexts are often characterised by a profound mistrust of the state and/or a lack of adequate channels via which to report a missing person or to initiate the search process. However, more research is needed to explore the limits of the guardianship of the state in places that are, in principle, governed by democratic standards: how do gender, social class, ethnicity, racial profiling and other forms of distinction affect a state's commitment to finding the missing and to effectively investing in search and identification?

States are often involved in various ways in projects aimed at making the disappeared reappear as living persons, dead bodies or mortal remains – even though in some cases, they persistently try to hamper search efforts. In today's world, however, especially after mass atrocities and natural disasters, the local state is just one actor, and various supra-national, international and non-state actors participate in the processes. Moreover, the language and terminology with which the events – both disappearances and projects of making reappear – are talked about are circulating globally. The anthropology of disappearance, or the social-scientific approach to disappearances, should be attentive to the range of configurations of actors and discourses, local and global, that come together in various ethnographic sites, and to their significance for local communities and for the ways in which these projects are carried out.

The projects of making reappear take place in constantly changing circumstances, as technologies, both those enabling the search for human beings and biomedical identification techniques, are developing rapidly. These developments give rise to many challenging questions: where and when should expensive techniques be applied? Who should be in charge of the projects? Who should invest in them? How should local understandings of death, corporeality, cosmology and the transition from life to death be taken into account? How are Western 'scientific' techniques understood and signified by local actors? Are there local ways of approaching questions of identification, exhumation and reburial? The anthropological approach to human disappearance and reappearance should be sensitive to such challenges, and should also serve as a reminder that in most cases there is no single 'local' view – in fact, there are often several competing ones – regarding how the search, exhumation and identification should proceed.

While states – embedded in complex geopolitical situations and global networks of state, supra-state and non-state actors – have a key role in creating the politics around disappearances and reappearances, intimate relations and everyday communities are the sites where the void of disappearance is most acutely encountered, with all its consequences. The anthropology of disappearance should be attentive to the ways in which disappearances and reappearances are signified locally, and how they disrupt, and often create new, social relations and cultural practices.

The productive power of disappearances becomes tangible in the variety of ways in which the disappeared reappear symbolically when they are found neither dead nor alive. As discussed in Chapter 5, symbolic reappearances (and continuities) often take place in the private and intimate spheres, in the cherishing of photographs or artefacts that have belonged to the disappeared and have touched their body, or in ghost-like encounters and experiences of haunting. These private agonies are often translated into public projects, demonstrations and movements, and also into memorials and museums. Anthropological analyses of disappearance and reappearance could further develop our understanding of the ways in which the intimate and public dimensions on the one hand and the material and symbolic ones on the other are intertwined, how they feed into each other and what their significance is in local social and cultural worlds.

Finally, I suggest that anthropology of disappearance is a fruitful project in many ways. It challenges ways of thinking about the state, citizenship and exclusion, life and death, personhood and community, knowledge and knowledge production, protection and vulnerability, presence and absence, and rupture and continuity. As such, anthropological studies of the missing and disappeared can enrich the discipline, and social sciences more generally, in significant ways.

Human disappearances represent a heavy research topic that has taken me into deep waters, in many cases to face extremes of human suffering and human cruelty – and this is certainly the case for anybody working with the subject matter. However, within this landscape of violence, loss and uncertainty, inequality and abandonment, I want to end by placing the spotlight on the insistent emergence of modes of care. The myriad search and identification projects, the private and public acts of engaging with the disappeared and reconnecting them with their social worlds, remembering and commemorating the absent and the acts of concretely redignifying violated bodies all suggest that compassion and care stubbornly emerge in places of death and violation, and that hope and compassion are persistent human capacities with a productive force of their own.

Bibliography

Agamben, Giorgio (2005) *State of Exception*. Translated by Kevin Attell. Chicago, IL: University of Chicago Press.

Agosin, Marjorie (1990) *Mothers de Plaza de Mayo (Linea Fundadora): The Story of Renee Eppelbaum 1976–1985*. Trenton, NJ: Red Sea Press.

Andersson, Ruben (2014a) *Illegality Inc: Clandestine Migration and the Business of Bordering Europe*. Oakland, CA: University of California Press.

Andersson, Ruben (2014b) 'Hunter and prey: Patrolling clandestine migration in the Euro-African borderlands', *Anthropological Quarterly* 87:1, 119–50.

Andersson, Ruben (2019) *No Go World: How Fear Is Redrawing Our Maps and Infecting Our Politics*. Oakland, CA: University of California Press.

Anstett, Élisabeth (2011) 'Memory of political repression in post-Soviet Russia: The example of the Gulag', *SciencePo: Online Encyclopedia of Mass Violence*. Available at: www.massviolence.org./Article?id_article=562 (accessed 9 August 2024).

Anstett, Élisabeth (2014) 'An anthropological approach to human remains from the Gulags' in Élisabeth Anstett and Jean-Marc Dreyfus (eds) *Destruction and Human Remains*. Manchester: Manchester University Press.

Anstett, Élisabeth and Dreyfus, Jean-Marc (eds) (2014a) *Destruction and Human Remains*. Manchester: Manchester University Press.

Anstett, Élisabeth and Dreyfus, Jean-Marc (2014b) 'Introduction: The tales destruction tells' in Élisabeth Anstett and Jean-Marc Dreyfus (eds) *Destruction and Human Remains*. Manchester: Manchester University Press.

Anstett, Élisabeth and Dreyfus, Jean-Marc (2015) 'Introduction: Why exhume? Why identify' in Élisabeth Anstett and Jean-Marc Dreyfus (eds) *Human Remains and Identification: Mass Violence, Genocide, and the 'Forensic Turn'*. Manchester: Manchester University Press.

Apps, Joe (2017) 'Missing abroad' in Lilian Alys and Karen Shalev Greene (eds) *Missing Persons: A Handbook of Research*. London: Routledge.

Aragüete-Toribio, Zahira (2022) 'Introduction: Anthropologies of forensic expertise in the aftermath of mass violence', *Social Anthropology/ Anthropologie Sociale* 30:3, 1–18.

Auchter, Jessica (2014) *The Politics of Haunting and Memory in International Relations*. London: Routledge.

Auchter, Jessica (2019) 'Imag(in)ing the severed head: ISIS beheadings and the absent spectacle' in Daniel Bertrand Monk (ed.) *Who's Afraid of ISIS: Towards a Doxology of War*. London: Routledge.

Bal, Mieke (2002) *Travelling Concepts in the Humanities: A Rough Guide*. Toronto, ON: University of Toronto Press.

Barthes, Roland (1981) *Camera Lucida*. New York: Hill and Wang.

Batchen, Geoffrey (1997) *Photography's Objects*. Albuquerque, NM: University of New Mexico Press.

Batchen, Geoffrey (2004) *Forget Me Not: Photography and Remembrance*. New York: Princeton Architectural Press.

Bennett, Caroline (2014) 'Who knows who we are?: Questioning DNA analysis in disaster victim identification', *New Genetics and Society: Critical Studies of Contemporary Biosciences* 33:3, 239–56.

Bennett, Caroline (2018) 'Living with the dead in the killing fields of Cambodia', *Journal of Southeast Asian Studies* 49:2, 184–203.

Bennett, Caroline (2019) 'Human remains from the Khmer Rouge regime, Cambodia' in David Errickson, Nicholas Márques-Grant and Kirsty Squires (eds) *Ethical Approaches to Human Remains*. Cham: Springer.

Berg, Ulla D. and Tamagno, Carla (2013) 'Migration brokers and document fixers: The making of migrant subjects in urban Peru' in Thomas Gammeltoft-Hansen and Ninna Nyberg Sørensen (eds) *The Migration Industry and the Commercialization of International Migration*. London: Routledge.

Bille, Mikkel, Hastrup, Frida and Flor Sorensen, Tim (2010) 'Introduction: An anthropology of absence' in Mikkel Bille, Tim Flor Sorensen and Frida Hastrup (eds) *An Anthropology of Absence: Materializations of Transcendence and Loss*. New York: Springer.

Black, Julia, Dearden, Kate, Singleton, Ann and Laczko, Frank (2017) 'Global overview of the available data on migrant detahs and disappearances' in *Fatal Journeys 3, Part 1*. International Organization of Migration IOM's Global Migration Data Analysis Centre GMDAC, pp. 1–21.

Blanco, María del Pilar and Peeren, Esther (2013a) (eds) *The Spectralities Reader: Ghosts and Haunting in Contemporary Cultural Theory*. London: Bloomsbury.

Blanco, María del Pilar and Peeren, Esther (2013b) 'Introduction: Conceptualizing spectralities' in María del Pilar Blanco and Esther Peeren (eds) *The Spectralities Reader: Ghosts and Haunting in Contemporary Cultural Theory*. London: Bloomsbury.

Blejmar, Jordana (2017) *Playful Memories: The Autofictional Turn in Post-Dictatorship Argentina*. Cham: Palgrave Macmillan.

Boss, Pauline (2007) 'Ambiguous loss theory: Challenges for scholars and practitioners', *Family Relations* 56:2, 105–11.

Bouvard, Marguerite G. (1994) *Revolutionizing Motherhood: The Mothers of the Plaza de Mayo*. Wilmington, DE: Scholarly Resources Inc.

Burchianti, Margaret (2004) 'Building bridges of memory: The Mothers of Plaza de Mayo and the cultural politics of maternal memories', *History and Anthropology* 15:2, 133–50.

Butler, Judith (2009) *Frames of War: When Is Life Grievable?* London: Verso.
Callon, Michel and Law, John (1995) 'Agency and the hybrid collectif', *South Atlantic Quarterly* 94:2, 481–507.
Cannell, Fenella (2013) 'Ghosts and ancestors in the modern West' in Janice Boddy and Michael Lambeck (eds) *A Companion to the Anthropology of Religion*. Oxford: John Wiley & Sons.
Caplan, Jane and Torpey, John (2001) 'Introduction' in Jane Caplan and John Torpey (eds) *Documenting Individual Identity: The Development of State Practices in the Modern World*. Princeton, NJ: Princeton University Press.
Castillo Hernández, Aída (2023) 'Chronicles of violence in contemporary Mexico: Feminist reflections on memory and disappearance' in Laura Huttunen and Gerhild Perl (eds) *An Anthropology of Disappearance: Politics, Intimacies and the Troubling Question of Knowing*. New York: Berghahn Books.
Chaure, Trupti and Hicks, Daniel (2021) 'The right to work and to live: The implications of India's NREGS Program for Missing Women', *Social Science Quarterly* 102:6, 2528–51.
Citroni, Gabriella (2017) 'The first Attempt in Mexico and Central America to address the phenomenon of missing and disappeared migrants', *International Review of the Red Cross* 99:2, 735–57.
Cohen, Erik (2009) 'Death in paradise: Tourist fatalities in the tsunami disaster in Thailand', *Current Issues in Tourism* 12:2, 183–99.
Colwell-Chanthaphohn, Chip (2011) '"The disappeared": Power over the dead in the aftermath of 9/11', *Anthropology Today* 27:3, 5–11.
Comaroff, Jean and Comaroff, John (2016) *The Truth about Crime: Sovereignty, Knowledge, Social Order*. Chicago, IL: University of Chicago Press.
Comaty, Lyna (2019) *Post-Conflict Transition in Lebanon: The Disappeared of the Civil War*. London: Routledge.
CONADEP (Comisión Nacional sobre la Desaparición de Personas) (1984) *Nunca Más: The Report of the Argentine National Commission on the Disappeared*. New York: Farrar, Straus and Giroux.
Crenzell, Emilio (2011) 'Between the voices of the state and the human rights movement: Never again and the memories of the disappeared in Argentina', *Journal of Social History* 44:4, 163–76.
Crossland, Zoë (2000) 'Buried lives: Forensic archaeology and the disappeared in Argentina', *Archeological Dialogues* 7:2, 146–59.
Cruz-Santiago, Arely (2020) 'Lists, maps and bones: the untold journeys if citizen-led forensics in Mexico', *Victims and Offenders: An International Journal of Evidence-based Research, Policy and Practice* 15:3, 350–69.
Cuttitta, Paolo and Last, Tamara (eds) (2019) *Border Deaths: Causes, Dynamics and Consequences of Migration-Related Mortality*. Amsterdam: Amsterdam University Press.
de Alwis, Malathi (2009) '"Disappearance" and "displacement" in Sri Lanka', *Journal of Refugee Studies* 22:3, 378–91.
Dean, Amber (2015) *Remembering Vancouver's Disappeared Women: Settler Colonialism and the Difficulty of Inheritance*. Toronto, ON: University of Toronto Press.

Dearden, Kate, Last, Tamara, Spencer, Craig and Cuttitta, Paolo (2020) 'Mortality and borders deaths data: Key challenges and ways forward' in Paolo Cuttitta and Tamara Last (eds) *Border Deaths: Causes and Consequences of Migration-Related Mortality*. Amsterdam: Amsterdam University Press.

Debrix, Francois (2017) *Global Powers of Horror: Security, Politics, and the Body in Pieces*. London: Routledge.

De Genova, Nicholas (2002) 'Migrant "illegality" and deportability in everyday life', *Annual Review of Anthropology* 31:1, 419–47.

De Genova, Nicholas (ed.) (2017) *The Borders of 'Europe': Autonomy of Migration, Tactics of Bordering*. Durham, NC: Duke University Press.

De León, Jason (2015) *The Land of Open Graves: Living and Dying on the Migrant Trail*. Oakland, CA: University of California Press.

Derrida, Jacques (1994) *Specters of Marx: The State of the Debt, the Work of Mourning, and the New International*; trans. Peggy Kamuf. London: Routledge.

de Vecchi Gerli, Maria (2022) 'Memorializing absence: Memorials to the disappeared in Mexico' in Silvana Mandolessi and Katia Olalde Rico (eds) *Disappearances in Mexico: From the 'Dirty War' to the 'War on Drugs'*. London: Routledge.

Dirkmaat, Dennis C. and Cabo, Luis L. (2012) 'Forensic anthropology: Embracing the new paradigm' in Dennis C. Dirkmaat (ed.) *A Companion to Forensic Anthropology*. Chichester: Blackwell Publishing.

Douglas, Mary (1966) *Purity and Danger: An Analysis of the Concepts of Pollution and Taboo*. London: Routledge.

Drotbohm, Heike (2023) 'On the slow silencing of absences: Sensing social disappearances in Cape Verde' in Laura Huttunen and Gerhild Perl (eds) *An Anthropology of Disappearance: Politics, Intimacies and the Troubling Question of Knowing*. New York: Berghahn Books.

D'Souza, Paul (2015) 'Conflict of Kashmir and the problem of disappearance', *Economic and Political Weekly* 50:5, 78–81.

Duhaime, Bernard and Thibault, Andreanne (2017) 'Protection of migrants from enforced disappearance: A human rights perspective', *International Review of the Red Cross* 99:2, 569–87.

Dyer, Geoff (1994) *The Missing of the Somme*. Edinburgh: Canongate.

Dziuban, Zuzanna (2020) 'Disappearance as a travelling concept: The politics and aesthetics of a transregional exchange' in Gabriel Gatti and Estela Schindel (eds) *Social Disappearance: Explorations between Latin America and Eastern Europe*. Berlin: Dossiers, Forum Transregionale Studien.

Dziuban, Zuzanna (2023) 'The Mediterranean as a forensic archive', in Laura Huttunen and Gerhild Perl (eds) *An Anthropology of Disappearance: Politics, Intimacies and the Troubling Question of Knowing*. New York: Berghahn Books.

EAAF (Equipo Argentino de Antropología Forense) (2003) Annual Report. Available at: https://eaaf.org/wp-content/uploads/2018/08/argentina2003.pdf (accessed 9 August 2024).

Edkins, Jenny (2011) *Missing: Persons and Politics*. Ithaca, NY: Cornell University Press.

Eppel, Shari (2009) 'A tale of three dinner plates: Truth and the challenge of human rights research in Zimbabwe', *Journal of Southern African Studies* 35:4, 967–76.

Bibliography

Eppel, Shari (2014) '"Bones in the forest" in Matabeland, Zimbabwe: Exhumations as a tool for transformation', *The International Journal of Transitional Justice* 8, 404–25.

Etkind, Alexander (2009) 'Post-Soviet hauntology: Cultural memory of the Soviet terror', *Constellations* 16:1, 182–200.

Ferrándiz, Francisco (2015) 'Mass graves, landscapes of terror: A Spanish tale' in Francisco Ferrándiz and Antonius C.G.M. Robben (eds) *Necropolitics: Mass Graves and Exhumations in the Age of Human Rights*. Philadelphia, PA: University of Pennsylvania Press.

Ferrándiz, Francisco and Robben, Antonius C.G.M. (eds) (2015a) *Necropolitics: Mass Graves and Exhumations in the Age of Human Rights*. Philadelphia, PA: University of Pennsylvania Press.

Ferrándiz, Francisco and Robben, Antonius C.G.M. (2015b) 'Introduction: The ethnography of exhumations' in Francisco Ferrandiz and Antonius C.G.M. Robben (eds) *Necropolitics: Mass Graves and Exhumations in the Age of Human Rights*. Philadelphia, PA: University of Pennsylvania Press.

Fforde, Cressida (2013) 'In search for others: The history and legacy of "race" collections' in Liv Nilsson Stutz and Sarah Tarlow (eds) *The Oxford Handbook of the Archeology of Death and Burial*. Oxford: Oxford Academic, online edition.

Fisher, Jo (1989) *Mothers of the Disappeared*. Boston, MA: South End Press.

Fletcher, Laurel E. (2014) 'The right to a remedy for enforced disappearances in India: A legal analysis of international and domestic law relating to victims of enforced disappearances', *SSRN Electronic Journal. International Human Rights Law Clinic, Working Paper Series No. 1*.

Follis, Karolina S. (2015) 'Responsibility, emergency, blame: Reporting on migrant deaths on the Mediterranean in the Council of Europe', *Journal of Human Rights* 14:1, 41–62.

Fontein, Joost (2010) 'Between tortured bodies and resurfacing bones: The politics of the dead in Zimbabwe', *Journal of Material Culture* 15:4, 423–48.

Fontein, Joost (2018) 'Death, corporeality and uncertainty in Zimbabwe' in Antonius C.G.M. Robben (ed.) *A Companion to the Anthropology of Death*. Chichester: John Wiley & Sons.

Forde, Maarit and Hume, Yanique (eds) (2018) *Passages and Afterworlds: Anthropological Perspectives on Death in the Caribbean*. Durham, NC: Duke University Press.

Fortuny, Natalia (2014) *Memorias Fotográficas: Imagen e Dictatura en la Argentina Contemporánea*. Buenos Aires: La luminosa.

Foucault, Michel (1977) *Discipline and Punish: The Birth of the Prison*. New York: Random House.

Frey, Barbara A. (2009) 'Los Desaparecidos: The Latin American experience as a narrative framework for the international norm against enforced disappearances', *Human Rights in Latin American and Iberian Cultures. Hispanic Issues Online* 5:1, 52–71. Available at: https://conservancy.umn.edu/bitstream/handle/11299 /182852/hiol_05_04_frey_los_desaparecidos_1.pdf?sequence=1 (accessed 9 August 2024).

Gammeltoft-Hansen, Thomas and Nyberg Sørensen, Ninna (eds) (2013) *The Migration Industry and the Commercialization of International Migration.* London: Routledge.

Gatti, Gabriel (2014) *Surviving Forced Disappearance in Argentina and Uruguay: Identity and Meaning.* New York: Palgrave Macmillan.

Gatti, Gabriel (2020) 'The Social disappeared: Genealogy, global circulation and (possible) uses of a category for bad life', *Public Culture* 32:1, 25–43.

Gatti, Gabriel, Irazuzta, Ignacio and Martínez, María (2021) 'Inverted exception: Ideas for thinking about the new disappearances through two case studies', *Journal of Latin American Cultural Studies: Travesía* 29:4, 581–604.

Gilchrist, Kristen (2010) '"Newsworthy" victims?', *Feminist Media Studies* 10:4, 373–90.

Gordon, Avery F. (2008) *Ghostly Matters: Haunting and the Sociological Imagination.* Minneapolis, MN: University of Minnesota Press.

Gorman, Robert F. (1992) 'Citizenship, obligation and exile in the Greek and Roman exile', *Public Affairs Quaterly* 6:1, 5–22.

Green, Sarah (2013) 'Borders and the relocation of Europe', *Annual Review of Anthropology* 42:1, 345–61.

Greenwald, Alice M. (2011) 'Reply to Colwell-Chanthaphohn', *Anthropology Today* 27:3, 11.

Grünenberg, Kristina (2020) 'Wearing someone else's face: Biometric technologies, anti-spoofing and the fear of the unknown', *Ethnos* 87:2, 223–40.

Grünenberg, Kristina, Møhl, Perle, Fog Olwig, Karen and Simonsen, Anja (2020) 'Issue introduction: Identites and identity: Biometric technologies, borders and migration', *Ethnos* 87:2, 211–22.

Gutman, Roy (1993) *A Witness to Genocide: The First Inside Account of the Horrors of Ethnic Cleansing in Bosnia.* Shaftesbury: Element.

Hage, Ghassan (2009) 'Waiting out the crisis: On stuckedness and governmentality' in Ghassa Hage (ed.) *Waiting.* Melbourne: Melbourne University Press.

Halilovich, Hariz (2013) *Places of Pain: Forced Displacement, Popular Memory and Trans-Local Identities in Bosnian War-Torn Communities.* New York: Berghahn Books.

Hansen, Saana (2023) *Economies of Care and Politics of Return: Sustaining Life among Injivas and Their Families in Bulawyao, Zimbabwe.* PhD dissertation, University of Helsinki. Available at: https://helda.helsinki.fi/items/acf59d34-074f-4986-b26c-a23c7e1fcab1

Hertz, Robert (1960) *Death and the Right Hand.* London: Routledge.

Hiam, Lucinda, Steele, Sarah and McKee, Martin (2018) 'Creating a "hostile environment" for migrants: The British Government's use of health service data to restrict immigration is a very bad idea', *Health Economics, Policy and Law* 13:2, 107–17.

Hinton, Alexander Laban (1998) 'A head for an eye: Revenge in the Cambodian genocide', *American Ethnologist* 25:3, 352–77.

Hoelscher, Steven (2008) 'Angels of memory: Photography and haunting in Guatemala City', *GeoJournal* 73:3, 195–217.

Hoerder, Dirk (2019) 'Migrations and macro-regions in times of crises: Long-term historiographic perspectives' in Cecilia Menjivar, Immanuel Ness and Marie Ruiz (eds) *The Oxford Handbook of Migration Crises*. Oxford: Oxford University Press.

Holmes, Lucy (2017) 'Intentionality and missing adults' in Lilian Alys and Karen Shalev Greene (eds) *Missing Persons: A Handbook of Research*. London: Routledge.

Hukanović, Rezak (1998) *The Tenth Circle of Hell: A Memoir of Life in the Death Camps of Bosnia*, trans. Colleen London and Midhat Ridjanović. London: Abacus.

Huttunen, Laura (2002) *Kotona, maanpaossa, matkalla: Kodin merkitykset maahanmuuttajien omaelämäkerroissa* [At Home, in Exile, en Route: The Meanings of Home in Autobiographies by People with Migrant Background]. Helsinki: Suomalaisen Kirjallisuuden Seura.

Huttunen, Laura (2009) 'Undoing and redoing homes: The Bosnian war and diasporic home-making' in Hanna Johansson and Kirsi Saarikangas (eds) *Homes in Transformation: Dwelling, Moving, Belonging*. Helsinki: Suomalaisen Kirjallisuuden Seura.

Huttunen, Laura (2014) 'From individual grief to a shared history of the Bosnian war: Voice, audience and the political in psychotherapeutic practices with refugees', *Focaal* 68, 91–104.

Huttunen, Laura (2016a) 'Liminality and contested communitas: The missing persons in Bosnia-Herzegovina', *Conflict and Society* 2:1, 201–18.

Huttunen, Laura (2016b) 'Remembering, witnessing, bringing closure: Srebrenica burial ceremonies on YouTube' in Andrea Hajek, Christine Lohmeier and Christian Pentzold (eds) *Memory in a Mediated World: Remembrance and Reconstruction*. London: Palgrave Macmillan.

Huttunen, Laura (2024) 'Narratives of absence: Making sense of loss and liminality in the post-war Bosnian diaspora' in Brigitte Bonisch-Brednich, Anastasia Christou, Silke Meyer, Marie Johanna Karner and Anton Jakob Escher (eds) *Migrant Narratives – Moving Stories: Modalities of Agency, Collectivity and Performativity*. London: Routledge.

Huttunen, Laura and Perl, Gerhild (2023) 'Why an anthropology of disappearance? A tentative introduction' in Laura Huttunen and Gerhild Perl (eds) *An Anthropology of Disappearance: Politics, Intimacies and the Troubling Question of Knowing*. New York: Berghahn Books.

ICMP (International Commission in Missing Persons) (2014) *Missing Persons from the Armed Conflicts of the 1990s: A Stocktaking*. Available at: https://www.icmp.int/wp-content/uploads/2014/12/StocktakingReport_ENG_web.pdf (accessed 9 August 2024).

ICRC (International Committee of the Red Cross) (2013) *Accompanying the Families of Missing persons: A Practical Handbook*. Geneva: ICRC. Available at: https://www.icrc.org/en/publication/4110-accompanying-families-missing-persons-practical-handbook (accessed 9 August 2024).

ICRC (International Committee of the Red Cross) (2019) *Humanitarian Consequences of Family Separation and People Going Missing*. Geneva: ICRC.

Available at: https://redcross.eu/uploads/files/Positions/Migration/Family%20Separation/rapport-2019-humanitarian-consequences-of-family-separation-and-people-going-missing.pdf (accessed 9 August 2024).

IOM (International Organization for Migration) (2021) *Families of Missing Migrants: Their Search for Answers and the Impact of Loss. Lessons across Four Countries*. Report by the International Organization for Migration. Genova: International Organization for Migration. Available at: https://publications.iom.int/books/families-missing-migrants-their-search-answers-and-impacts-loss (accessed 9 August 2024).

Irazuzta, Ignazio (2020) 'Social disappearance: Notes from the experience from migration in transit through Mexico' in Gabriel Gatti and Estela Schindel (eds) *Social Disappearance: Exploration between Latin America and Eastern Europe*. Berlin: Forum Transregionale Studien.

Jamar, Astrid and Major, Laura (2022) 'Managing mass graves in Rwanda and Burundi: Vernaculars of the right to truth', *Social Anthropology/ Anthropologie Social* 30:3, 56–78.

Jansen, Stef (2005) 'National numbers in context: Maps and stats in representations of the post-Yugoslav wars', *Identities: Studies in Culture and Power* 12:1, 45–68.

Jansen, Stef (2015) *Yearning in the Meantime: 'Normal Lives' and the State in a Sarajevo Apartment Complex*. Oxford: Berghahn Books.

Jennings, Christian (2013) *Bosnia's Million Bones: Solving the World's Greatest Forensic Puzzle*. New York: Palgrave Macmillan.

Jessee, Erin (2012) 'Promoting reconciliation through exhuming and identifying vistims in the 1994 Rwandan genocide', *Cigi African Initiative, Discussion paper series no. 4*.

Jones, Kevin T., Zagacki, Kenneth S. and Lewis, Todd V. (2007) 'Communication, liminality and hope: The September 11th missing person posters', *Communication Studies* 58:1, 101–21.

Jugo, Admir (2017) 'Artefacts and personal effects from mass graves in Bosnia and Herzegovina: Symbols of persons, forensic evidence or public relics?', *Les Cahiers Sirice* 19:2, 21–40.

Jugo, Admir and Škulj, Senem (2015) 'Ghosts of the past: The competing agendas of forensic work in identifying the missing across Bosnia and Herzegovina', *Human Remains and Violence* 1:1, 39–56.

Jugo, Admir and Wastell, Sari (2015) 'Disassembling the pieces, reassembling the social: The forensic and political lives of secondary mass graves in Bosnia and Herzegovina', in Élisabeth Anstett and Jean-Marc Dreyfus (eds) *Human Remains and Identification: Mass Violence, Genocide and the 'Forensic Turn'*. Manchester: Manchester University Press.

Kalir, Barak and Wissink, Lieke (2015) 'The deportation continuum: Convergences between state agents and NGO workers in the Dutch deportation field', *Citizenship Studies* 20:1, 34–49.

Katz, Ori (2023) '"What to do?": Searching for missing persons in Israel', in Laura Huttunen and Gerhild Perl (eds) *An Anthropology of Disappearance: Politics, Intimacies and Alternative Ways of Knowing*. New York: Berghahn Books.

Bibliography

Kent, Lia (2011) 'Local memory practices in East Timor: Disrupting transitional justice narratives', *International Journal of Transitional Justice* 3:1, 434–55.

Kent, Lia (2020) 'Gathering the dead, imagining the state?' in Lia Kent and Rui Garça Fedjó (eds) *The Dead as Ancestors, Martyrs and Heroes in Timor-Leste*. Amsterdam: Amsterdam University Press.

Kent, Lia (2024) *The Unruly Dead: Spirits, Memory and State Formation in Timor-Leste*. Madison, WI: University of Wisconsin Press.

Kent, Lia and Garça Fedjó, Rui (2020) 'Introduction. Martyrs, ancestors and heroes: The multiple lives of dead bodies in independent Timor-Leste' in Lia Kent and Rui Garça Fedjó (eds) *The Dead as Ancestors, Martyrs and Heroes in Timor-Leste*. Amsterdam: Amsterdam University Press.

Kivilahti, Saila (2016) *'Jos ei voi kuvitella matkan päätä, ei tarinaa voi päättää': Suomalaisten kadonneiden henkilöiden elämän ja kuoleman välisen liminaalisen tilan tarkastelua hyvän ja huonon kuoleman näkökulmasta*. MA thesis, University of Helsinki.

Kivilahti, Saila and Huttunen, Laura (2023) 'Negotiating epistemic uncertainties: Coming to terms with migrant disappearances in the Western Mediterranean' in Laura Huttunen and Gerhild Perl (eds) *An Anthropology of Disappearance: Politics, Intimacies and Alternative Ways of Knowing*. New York: Berghahn Books.

Kobelinsky, Carolina (2017) 'Exister au risc du disparaitre: Récrits sur la morte pendant la traversée vers l'Europe' [Existing at risk of disappearing: Narratives on death during travel to Europe], *Revue Européenne des Migrations Internationales* 33, 115–31.

Kobelinsky, Carolina (2020a) 'Border beings: Present absences among migrants in the Spanish enclave of Melilla', *Death Studies* 44:11, 709–17.

Kobelinsky, Carolina (2020b) 'Who cares about Ouancil?: The postmortem itinerary of a young border crosser', *American Behavioral Scientist* 64:4, 525–39.

Kodikara, Chulani (2023) 'The office of missing persons in Sri Lanka: Why truth is a radical proposition', *The International Journal of Transitional Justice* 17, 157–72.

Koff, Clea (2004) *The Bone Woman: Among the Dead in Rwanda, Bosnia, Croatia and Kosovo*. London: Atlantic Books.

Korman, Rémi (2015) 'Bury or display? The politics of exhumation in post-genocide Rwanda' in Élisabeth Anstett and Jean-Marc Dreyfus (eds) *Human Remains and Identification: Mass Violence, Genocide and the 'Forensic Turn'*. Manchester: Manchester University Press.

Kovras, Iosif and Robins, Simon (2016) 'Death as the border: Managing missing migrants and unidentified bodies at the EU's Mediterranean frontier', *Political Geography* 55: 40–9.

Kwon, Heonik (2006) *After the Massacre: Commemoration and Consolation in Ha My and My Lai*. Berkeley, CA: University of California Press.

Kwon, Heonik (2008) *Ghosts of War in Vietnam*. Cambridge: Cambridge University Press.

Laakkonen, Ville (2022) 'Deaths, disappearances, borders: Migrant disappearability as a technology of deterrence', *Political Geography* 99, Article 102767.

Laakkonen, Ville (2023a) 'Ágnostoi: Greece and the forensic bordering of fortress Europe', *Suomen Antropologi: Journal of the Finnish Anthropological Society* 47:2, 7–28.

Laakkonen, Ville (2023b) 'Being there in the presence of absence: Researching the remains of migrant disappearances' in Laura Huttunen and Gerhild Perl (eds) *An Anthropology of Disappearance: Politics, Intimacies and Alternative Ways of Knowing*. New York: Berghahn Books.

Laczko, Frank, Singleton, Ann and Black, Julia (2017) 'Introduction' in *Fatal Journeys 3, Part 2*. International Organization of Migration IOM's Global Migration Data Analysis Centre GMDAC, xv–xx. Available in fatal_journeys _3_part2.pdf (iom.int) (accessed 16 August 2024).

Lampe, John R. (2000) *Yugoslavia as History: Twice There Was a Country*. Cambridge: Cambridge University Press, 2nd edn.

Langford, Jean M. (2009) 'Gifts intercepted: Biopolitics and spirit debt', *Cultural Anthropology* 24:4, 681–711.

Langford, Jean M. (2013) *Consoling Ghosts: Stories of Medicine and Mourning from Southeast Asians in Exile*. Minneapolis. MN: University of Minnesota Press.

Laqueur, Thomas W. (2015) *The Work of the Dead: A Cultural History of Mortal Remains*. Princeton, NJ: Princeton University Press.

Last, Tamara, Mirto, Giorgia, Ulusoy Orçun, Urquijo, Ignazio, Harte, Joke and Bami, Nefeli (2017) 'Deaths at the borders database: Evidence of deceased migrants' bodies found along the southern external borders of the European Union', *Journal of Ethnic and Migrant Studies* 43:5, 693–712.

Lazar, Sian (2013) 'Introduction' in Sian Lazar (ed.) *Anthropology of Citizenship: A Reader*. Oxford: Wiley Blackwell.

Le Courant, Stefan (2019) 'Imposture at the border: Law and the construction of identities among undocumented migrants', *Social Anthropology/ Anthropologie Sociale* 27:3, 472–85.

Leppäkorpi, Mervi (2022) *In Search of a Normal Life: An Ethnography of Migrant Irregularity in Northern Europe*. Joensuu: University of Eastern Finland Press.

Lesley, Elena (2015) 'Death on display: Bones and bodies in Cambodia and Rwanda' in Francisco Ferrándiz and Antonius C.G.M. Robben (eds) *Necropolitics: Mass Graves and Exhumations in the Age of Human Rights*. Philadelphia, PA: University of Pennsylvania Press.

Lewicki, Pawel (2020) 'The social disappearance of HIV-positive marginalized Polish migrants in Berlin' in Gabriel Gatti and Estela Schindel (eds) *Social Disappearance: Explorations between Latin America and Eastern Europe*. Berlin: Forum Transregionale Studien.

Lock, Margaret (2002) 'Inventing a new death and making it believable', *Anthropology & Medicine* 9:2, 97–115.

Lowenkron, Laura and Ferreira, Leticia (2014) 'Anthropological perspectives on documents: Ethnographic dialogues on the trail of papers', *Vibrant: Virtual Brazilian Anthropology* 11:2, 76–112.

Bibliography

Lucht, Hans (2012) *Darkness Before Daybreak: African Migrants Living on the Margins in Southern Italy Today*. Berkeley, CA: University of California Press.

Lucht, Hans (2013) 'Pusher stories: Ghanaian connection men and the expansion of the EU's border regimes in Africa' in Thomas Gammeltoft-Hansen and Ninna Nyberg Sørensen (eds) *The Migration Industry and the Commercialization of International Migration*. London: Routledge.

Maass, Peter (1996) *Love Thy Neighbour. A Story of War*. London: Macmillan.

Mainwaring, Cetta and DeBono, Daniela (2021) 'Criminalizing solidarity: Search and rescue in a neo-colonial sea', *Environment and Planning C: Politics and Space* 39:5, 1030–48.

Malcolm, Noel (1996) *Bosnia: A Short History*. London: Macmillan.

Malkki, Liisa (1995) *Purity and Exile: Violence, Memory and National Cosmology among Hutu Refugees in Tanzania*. Chicago, IL: University of Chicago Press.

Mandolessi, Silvana (2022) 'Introduction – disappearances in Mexico' in Silvana Mandolessi and Katia Olalde Rico (eds) *Disappearances in Mexico: From the 'Dirty War' to the 'War on Drugs'*. Abingdon: Routledge.

Mandolessi, Silvana and Olalde Rico, Katia (2022) *Disappearances in Mexico: From the 'Dirty War' to the 'War on Drugs'*. Abingdon: Routledge.

Matyska, Anna (2020) 'Keeping the transnational search alive: The missing, social presences and disappearances' in Gabriel Gatti and Estela Schindel (eds) *Social Disappearance: Explorations between Latin America and Eastern Europe*. Berlin: Dossiers, Forum Transregionale Studien.

Matyska, Anna (2023a) 'Conceptualizing transnational disappearances: Polish missing abroad and the governance of the search', *Global Networks: A Journal of Transnational Affairs* 00, 1–15.

Matyska, Anna (2023b) 'A right to disappear? State, regulatory politics and the entitlements of kinship' in Laura Huttunen and Gerhild Perl (eds) *An Anthropology of Disappearance: Politics, Intimacies and Alternative Ways of Knowing*. New York: Berghahn Books.

Matyska, Anna (2024a) 'Marginalized disappearances: Shaping power relations of the search for the missing', *European Journal of Cultural Studies*.

Matyska, Anna (2024b) 'Tracing infrastructure and its evolution in the search for the missing in Poland', *Suomen Antropologi: Journal of the Finnish Anthropological Society* 4:2, 127–31.

Mbembe, Achille (2003) 'Necropolitics', trans. Libby Meitjes, *Public Culture* 15:1, 11–40.

M'charek, Amade (2018) '"Dead-bodies-at-the-border": Distributed evidence and emerging forensic infrastructure for identification' in Mark Maguire, Ursula Rao and Niels Zurawski (eds) *Bodies as Evidence: Security, Knowledge, and Power*. Durham, NC: Duke University Press.

M'charek, Amade and Black, Julia (2020) 'Engaging bodies as matter of care: Counting and accounting for death during migration' in Paolo Cuttitta and Tamara Last (eds) *Border Deaths: Causes, Dynamics and Consequences of Migration-related Mortality*. Amsterdam: Amsterdam University Press.

M'charek, Amade and Casartelli, Sara (2019) 'Identifying dead migrants: Forensic care work and relational citizenship', *Citizenship Studies* 23:7, 738–75.

Meinert, Lotte and Whyte, Susan Reynolds (2017) '"These things continue": Violence as contamination in everyday life after war in northern Uganda', *Ethos* 45:2, 271–86.

Metcalf, Peter and Huntington, Richard (1991) *Celebrations of Death: The Anthropology of Mortuary Ritual.* Cambridge: Cambridge University Press.

Millar, Stefan (2023) 'Enforced disappearances, colonial legacies and political affect in Kakuma refugee camp, Kenya' in Laura Huttunen and Gerhild Perl (eds) *An Anthropology of Disappearance: Politics, Intimacies and Alternative Ways of Knowing.* New York: Berghahn Books.

Møhl, Perle (2020) 'Biometric technologies, data and the sensory work of border control', *Ethnos* 87:2, 241–56.

Moisseinen, Hanneriina (2013) *Isä/Father.* Helsinki: Huuda Huuda.

Moon, Claire (2012) 'Interpreters of the dead: Forensic knowledge, human remains and the politics of the past', *Social and Legal Studies* 22:2, 149–69.

Moon, Claire (2019) 'What remains?: Human rights after death' in Kirsty Squires, David Erickson and Nicolas Márquez-Grant (eds) *Ethical Approaches to Human Remains: A Global Challenge in Bioarcheology and Forensic Anthropology.* Cham: Springer.

Ngô, Tâm T.T. (2021) 'Bones of contention: Situating the dead the 1979 Sino-Vietnamese border war', *American Ethnologist* 48:2, 192–205.

Nyberg Sørensen, Ninna (2013) 'Migration between social and criminal networks: Jumping the remains of the Honduran migration train' in Thomas Gammeltoft-Hansen and Ninna Nyberg Sørensen (eds) *The Migration Industry and the Commercialization of International Migration.* London: Routledge.

Nyberg Sørensen, Ninna (2014) 'Governing through the mutilated female body: Corpse, body politics and contestation in contemporary Guatemala' in Finn Stepputat (ed.) *Governing the Dead: Sovereignty and the Politics of Dead Bodies.* Manchester: Manchester University Press.

Nyberg Sørensen, Ninna (2018) 'Wars and migration crises in central America: On missing persons during armed conflict and international migration' in Cecilia Menjívar, Immanuel Ness and Marie Ruiz (eds) *The Oxford Handbook of Migration Crises.* Oxford: Oxford University Press.

Nyberg Sørensen, Ninna and Huttunen, Laura (2020) 'Missing migrants and the politics of disappearance in armed conflicts and migratory contexts', *Ethnos* 87:2, 321–37.

Olivieri, Lara, Mazzarelli, Debora, Bertoglio, Barbara, De Angelis, Danilo, Previdere, Carlo, Grignani, Pierargela, Cappella, Annalisa, Presciuttini, Silvano, Bertuglia, Caterina, Di Simone, Paola, Polizzi, Nicolo, Iadicicco, Agata, Piscitelli, Vittorio and Cattaneo, Christina (2018) 'Challenges in the identification of dead migrants in the Mediterranean: The case study of the Lampedusa shipwreck of October 3rd 2013', *Forensic Science International* 258, 121–8.

Parr, Hester and Fyfe, Nicholas (2012) 'Missing geographies', *Progress in Human Geography* 37:5, 615–38.

Parr, Hester and Stevenson, Olivia (2015) '"No news today": Talk of witnessing with families of missing people', *Cultural Geographies* 22:2, 297–315.

Parr, Hester, Stevenson, Olivia and Woolnough, Penny (2016) 'Search/ing for missing people: Families living with ambiguous absence', *Emotion, Space and Society* 19, 66–75.

Parrot, Fiona R. (2010) 'Bringing home the dead: Photographs, family imaginaries and moral remains' in Mikke Bille, Tim Flor Sorensen and Frida Hastrup (eds) *An Anthropology of Absence: Materializations of Transcendence and Loss*. New York: Springer.

Passaro, Sari (2022) *Reino Savukoski: Suomen tunnetuin kadonneiden etsijä* [Reino Savukoski: The Most Famous Searcher of the Missing Persons in Finland]. Helsinki: Minerva.

Perl, Gerhild (2016) 'Uncertain belongings: Absent mourning, burial and post-mortem repatriation at the external border of the EU and Spain', *Journal of Intercultural Studies* 37:2, 195–209.

Perl, Gerhild (2018) 'Lethal borders and the translocal politics of "ordinary people"', *Anthropological Journal of European Cultures* 27:2, 85–104.

Perl, Gerhild (2019a) *Traces of Death: Exploring Affective Responsiveness Across the Spanish-Moroccan Sea*. PhD Thesis, University of Bern.

Perl, Gerhild (2019b) 'Migration as survival: Withheld stories and the limits of ethnographic knowability', *Migration and Society: Advances in Research* 2, 12–25.

Perl, Gerhild and Strasser, Sabina (2018) 'Transnational moralities: The politics of ir/responsibility of and against the EU border regime', *Identities: Global Studies in Culture and Power* 25:5, 507–23.

Petrović-Šteger, Maja (2009) 'Anatomizing conflict – Accommodating human remains' in Helen Lambert and Maryon McDonald (eds) *Social Bodies*. New York: Berghahn Books.

Petryna, Adirana and Follis, Karolina (2015) 'Risks of citizenship and fault lines of survival', *Annual Review of Anthropology* 44:1, 401–17.

Reeves, Madeleine (2013) 'Clean fake: Authenticating documents and persons in migrant Moscow', *American Ethnologist* 40:3, 508–24.

Reineke, Robin (2016) 'Migrant deaths in the Americas (United States and Mexico)' in *Fatal Journeys: Tracking Lives Lost during Migration*. International Organization of Migration IOM's Global Migration Data Analysis Centre GMDAC.

Reineke, Robin (2019) 'Necroviolence and postmortem care along the US–México border' in Randall H. McGuire and Thomas E. Sheridan (eds) *The Border and Its Bodies: The Embodiment of Risk along the U.S.–México Line*. Amerind Studies. Tucson, AZ: University of Arizona Press.

Reineke, Robin (2022) 'Forensic citizenship among families of missing migrants along the U.S.–Mexico border', *Citizenship Studies* 26:1, 21–37.

Reineke, Robin (forthcoming) 'Community forensics along the U.S.–Mexico border', *Annals of Anthropological Practice*.

Renshaw, Layla (2010) 'Missing bodies near-at-hand: The dissonant memory and dormant graves of the Spanish Civil War' in Mikke Bille, Tim Flor Sorensen

and Frida Hastrup (eds) *An Anthropology of Absence: Materializations of Transcendence and Loss*. New York: Springer.
Renshaw, Layla (2011) *Exhuming Loss: Memory, Materiality and Mass Graves of the Spanish Civil War*. London: Routledge.
Robben, Antonius C.G.M. (ed.) (2004a) *Death, Mourning and Burial: A Cross-Cultural Reader*. London: Blackwell.
Robben, Antonius C.G.M. (2004b) 'State terror in the netherworld: Disappearance and reburial in Argentina' in Antonius C.G.M. Robben (ed.) *Death, Mourning and Burial: A Cross-Cultural Reader*. London: Blackwell.
Robben, Antonius C.G.M. (2005) *Political Violence and Trauma in Argentina*. Philadelphia, PA: University of Pennsylvania Press.
Robben, Antonius C.G.M. (2018) *Argentina Betrayed: Memory, Mourning and Accountability*. Philadelphia, PA: University of Pennsylvania Press.
Robins, Simon (2012) 'Transitional justice as an elite discourse: Human rights practice where the global meets the local in post-conflict Nepal', *Critical Asian Studies* 44:1, 3–30.
Robins, Simon (2014) 'Constructing meaning from disappearance: Local memorialization of disappearance in Nepal', *International Journal of Conflict and Violence* 8:1, 104–18.
Robins, Simon (2019) 'The affective border: Missing migrants and the governance of migrant bodies at the EU's southern frontier', *Journal of Refugee Studies* 35:2, 948–67.
Robledo Silvestre, Carolina and Ramírez González, Paola Alejandra (2022) 'Situating the investigation on clandestine graves in Mexico', *Social Anthropology* 30:3, 79–95.
Rojas-Perez, Isaias (2015) 'Death in transition: The truth commission and the politics of reburial in postconflict Peru' in Francisco Ferrándiz and Antonius C.G.M. Robben (eds) *Necropolitics: Mass Graves and Exhumations in the Age of Human Rights*. Philadelphia, PA: University of Pennsylvania Press.
Rojas-Perez, Isaias (2017) *Mourning Remains: State Atrocity, Exhumation and Governing the Dead in Peru's Postwar Andes*. Stanford, CA: Stanford University Press.
Rosenblatt, Adam (2015) *Digging for the Disappeared: Forensic Science after Atrocity*. Stanford, CA: Stanford University Press.
Rozema, Ralph (2011) 'Forced disappearance in an era of globalization: Biopolitics, shadow networks and imagined worlds', *American Anthropologist* 113:4, 582–93.
Saari, Tiina and Majamaa, Maiju (2020) *Ei Jälkeäkään: 11 Suomalaista Kadonnutta ja Kaivattua* [Not a Trace: 11 Finnish Disappeared and Missed Persons]. Helsinki: Into.
Sanchez, Gabriella E. (2014) *Human Smuggling and Border Crossings*. London: Routledge.
Sanford, Victoria (2003) *Buried Secrets: Truth and Human Rights in Guatemala*. New York: Palgrave Macmillan.
Sant Cassia, Paul (2005) *Bodies of Evidence: Burial, Memory and the Recovery of Missing Persons in Cyprus*. Oxford: Berghahn Books.

Schielke, Samuli (2015) *Egypt in the Future Tense: Hope, Frustration and Ambivalence before and after 2011*. Bloomington, IN: Indiana University Press.

Schielke, Samuli (2019) 'A bigger prison: Egyptian migrations and the experience of limited movement', *Suomen Antropologi: Journal of the Finnish Anthropological Society* 44:2, 40–58.

Schindel, Estela (2014) 'Ghosts and companeros: Haunting stories and the quest for justice around Argentina's former terror sites', *Rethinking History* 18:2, 244–64.

Schindel, Estela (2020a) 'Mobility and disappearance: Transregional threads, historical resonances' in Gabriel Gatti and Estela Schindel (eds) *Social Disappearance: Exploration between Latin America and Eastern Europe*. Berlin: Forum Transregionale Studien.

Schindel, Estela (2020b) 'Death and disappearances in migration to Europe: Exploring the uses of a transnational category', *American Behavioral Scientists* 64:4, 389–407.

Schmoll, Camille (2014) 'Gendered spatialities of power in "border-land" Europe: An approach through mobile and immobile bodies', *International Journal of Migration and Border Studies* 1:2, 139–53.

Schwartz-Marín, Ernesto and Cruz-Santiago, Arely (2016a) 'Forensic civism: Articulating science, DNA and kinship in contemporary Mexico and Colombia', *Human Remains and Violence* 2:1, 58–74.

Schwartz-Marín, Ernesto and Cruz-Santiago, Arely (2016b) 'Pure corpses, dangerous citizens: Transgressing the boundaries between experts and mourners in the search for the disappeared in Mexico', *Social Research* 83:2, 483–510.

Sen, Atreyee (2023) '"Who has taken my son (Amar cheleke ke nilo)?": Pervasive missingness, custodial disappearances and revolutionary violence in urban India' in Laura Huttunen and Gerhild Perl (eds) *An Anthropology of Disappearance: Politics, Intimacies and Alternative Ways of Knowing*. New York: Berghahn Books.

Shalev Greene, Karen and Alys, Lilian (eds) (2017) *Missing Persons: A Handbook of Research*. London: Routledge.

Sharma, Aradhana and Gupta, Akhil (2006) 'Introduction: Rethinking theories of the state in the age of globalization' in Aradhana Sharma and Akhil Gupta (eds) *The Anthropology of the State: A Reader*. Malden, MA: Blackwell Publishing.

Silber, Laura and Little, Allan (1996) *Yugoslavia: Death of a Nation*. London: Penguin.

Smith, Lindsay (2016) 'The missing, the martyred and the disappeared: Global networks, technical intensification and the end of human rights genetics', *Social Studies of Science* 47:3, 398–416.

Sokol, Anida (2014) 'War monuments: Instruments of nation-building in Bosnia and Herzegovina', *Croatian Political Science Review* 5, 105–26.

Stepputat, Finn (2014) 'Introduction' in Finn Stepputat (ed.) *Governing the Dead: Sovereignty and the Politics of Dead Bodies*. Manchester: Manchester University Press.

Stewart, David J. (2011) *The Sea Their Graves: An Archeology of Death and Remembrance in Maritime Culture*. Gainesville, FL: University Press of Florida.

Stierl, Maurice (2021) 'The Mediterranean as a carceral seascape', *Political Geography* 88.
Stimmatini, Sofia and De Gourcy, Constance (2022) 'Missing in the Mediterranean: A perspective from Tunisian mothers' in Natalia Ribas-Mateos and Saskia Sassen (eds) *The Elgar Companion to Gender and Global Migration*. Cheltenham: ElgarOnline.
Stover, Eric and Peress, Gilles (1998) *Graves: Srebrenica and Vukovar*. Zurich: Scalo.
Taylor, Diana (1997) *Disappearing Acts: Spectacles of Gender and Nationalism in Argentina's 'Dirty War'*. Durham, NC: Duke University Press.
Taylor, Diana (2003) *The Archive and the Repertoire: Performing Cultural Memory in the Americas*. Durham, NC: Duke University Press.
Taylor, John and Lee, Helen (eds) (2017) *Mobilities of Return: Pacific Perspectives*. Canberra: ANU Press.
Tervonen, Taina and Autio, Anna (2019) *Hukkuneet* [Those Drown]. Helsinki: S&S.
Torpey, John (2018) *The Invention of the Passport: Surveillance, Citizenship and the State*. Cambridge: Cambridge University Press.
Triandafyllidou, Anna and Ricard-Guay, Alexandra (2019) 'Governing irregular and return migration in the 2020s: European challenges and Asian Pacific perspectives', *Journal of Immigrant & Refugee Studies* 17:2, 115–27.
Turner, Victor (1977 [1969]) *The Ritual Process: Structure and Anti-Structure*. Ithaca, NY: Cornell University Press.
Van Gennep, Arnold (2004 [1909]) 'The rites of passage' in Antonius C.G.M. Robben (ed.) *Death, Mourning and Burial: A Cross-Cultural Reader*. London: Blackwell.
Van Hear (2005) *New Diasporas: The Mass Exodus, Dispersal and Regrouping of Migrant Communities*. London: Routledge.
Verástegui Gonzáles, Jorge (2022) 'The right to search in the case of disappeared persons: A right constructed from below' in Silvana Mandolesi and Katia Olalde Rico (eds) *Disappearances in Mexico: From the 'Dirty War' to the 'War on Drugs'*. London: Routledge.
Verdery, Katherine (1999) *The Political Lives of Dead Bodies: Reburial and Postsocialist Change*. New York: Columbia University Press.
Vigh, Henrik (2009) 'Wayward migration: On imagined futures and technological voids', *Ethnos* 74:1, 91–109.
Vigh, Henrik (2008) 'Crisis and chronicity: Anthropological perspectives on continuous conflict and decline', *Ethnos* 73:1, 5–24.
Wagner, Sarah (2008) *To Know Where He Lies: DNA Technology and the Search for Srebrenica's Missing*. Berkeley, CA: University of California Press.
Wright, Melissa W. (2018) 'Against the evils of democracy: Fighting forced disappearance and neoliberal terror in Mexico', *Annals of the American Association of Geographers* 108:2, 327–36.
Wright, Thomas C. (2007) *State Terrorism in Latin America: Chile, Argentina, and International Human Rights*. Lanham, MD: Rowman & Littlefield.
Wylie, Neville, Oppenheimer, Melanie and Crossland, James (2020) 'The Red Cross movement: Continuities, changes and challenges' in James Crossland, Melanie

Oppenheimer and Neville Wylie (eds) *The Red Cross Movement: Myths, Practices and Turning Points*. Manchester: Manchester University Press.

Zagaria, Valentina (2020) *'Burning' Borders: Migration, Death and Dignity in a Tunisia Coastal Town*. Unpublished PhD thesis, London School of Economics.

Zemon Davis, Natalie (1984) *The Return of Martin Guerre*. Cambridge, MA: Harvard University Press.

Zia, Ather (2016) 'The spectacle of a good half-widow: Women in search of their disappeared men in the Kashmir valley', *PoLar: Political and Legal Anthropology Review* 39:2, 164–75.

Index

Note: 'n.' after a page reference the number of a note on that page. Page numbers in *italics* refer to illustrations

absence 1–3, 5–7, 19, 25, 27–8, 34n.2, 72, 74–8, 87–90, 97–8, 115, 134–6, 138–40, 144, 146–9, 151, 153, 157–8
 anthropology of 5
 history of 16–18
Abuelas de Plaza de Mayo 109, 130n.7
aerial photography 21, 47, 111
Afghanistan 12
Africa 9, 12, 13, 20, 66, 68–70, 72–4, 76, 79n.7, 120, 128, 129, 152
Agamben, Giorgio 53
Algeria 20, 60, 70, 76
Anstett, Èlisabeth 22, 42–3, 53, 103, 128
anthropology of absence 5
anthropology of death 25–8
anthropology of disappearance 29–31, 158–61
Aragüete-Toribio, Zahira 102
Argentina 6, 13–14, 35n.21, 24, 27, 28, 32, 33, 38–43, 50–6, 88, 102, 105–10, 117, 130n.6, 136, 138, 141–2, 146–8, 152, 154
armed conflict 1, 4, 5, 8, 10, 11, 13, 14, 21, 32, 34, 38, 43, 45, 51–2, 56, 75, 110–11, 126
 see also Bosnia-Herzegovina; 'dirty war'; First World War; Second World War; Spain, Civil War; war
art 14, 24, 33, 40, 84, 110, 139, 157
 as reappearance 146–8, 153
artefacts 136–8, 140, 143, 161
Australia 61, 64, 113

Balkan Investigative Reporting Network 129n.1
Bennett, Caroline 126, 132n.23
biometric identification 21, 63
 see also DNA
Black, Julia 68, 129
Blejmar, Jordana 147–8
Boats 4 People 124
border control 15, 62, 63, 70, 78
border enforcement 21, 69, 70, 78
border regime 32, 61–3, 65, 78, 125, 138
 see also migration order
Bosnia-Herzegovina 3–4, 9, 11, 13–15, 24, 27, 28, 32, 33, 34n.3, 37–9, 43–52, *44*, 53, 58, 59n.7, 67, 87–8, 100–4, 110–19, *116*, *117*, 129, 131n.9, 135–9, 142–3, 146–7, 149–51, 153, 159
Britain 20, 82, 83, 89
burial 4, 24–9, 33, 42, 46–8, 52, 54, 55, 60–1, 72, 76, 88, 100–12, 107–9, 111, 117–19, 121, 129, 130n.3, 133, 142–5, 148, 151, 152, 154, 160
 denial of proper 42, 46–7, 150
 see also funeral; rite of passage; ritual
Burundi 55, 126, 144
Butler, Judith 18

Cambodia 14, 24, 55, 126, 144
Ca-minando Fronteras 124
Cannell, Fenella 152–3
Cattaneo, Cristina 122

Centro International Para La Identificación De Migrantes Desaparecidos (CIPMID) 124
Chile 6, 12, 42, 55, 56
citizenship 17–20, 43, 49, 53, 55, 57, 70, 80–3, 89–98, 108, 127–8, 132n.24, 159–61
civil society 68, 92, 94–6, 105, 111, 112, 123, 125, 139
clairvoyant 95, 151
Clinton, Bill 111
closure 2, 27, 34n.2, 49, 59n.5, 77, 89, 101, 115
Colibrí Center for Human Rights 12, 120, 124
colonialism 20, 23, 56, 126
Cruz-Santiago, Arely 127–8
cultural
  context 2–3, 24–8, 72, 152
  frame 25–6, 40, 78, 97
  scripts 88, 126
Cyprus 30

Dayton Peace Accords, Dayton Peace Agreement 44, 110, 130n.8
Dean, Amber 7, 81
death certificate 67, 77, 107
De Genova, Nicholas 30
de León, Jason 64, 69, 74
Derrida, Jaques 150
desaparecidos 6, 11, 18, 19
'dirty war' 39–40
disappearability 18, 30, 32, 57, 62–6, 68, 70, 71, 94, 97, 122, 159
disappearance
  as a category 7
  as a chronic condition 27–8
  as a strategy 11–12, 18–20, 38–43, 52
  as a travelling concept 55
  see also enforced disappearance
Disappearance Convention 6–7, 19, 34n.6, 53
disturbed intimacies 30, 32, 51, 58, 62, 72–8
DNA 21, 22, 47, 50, 55, 67, 102, 104, 108–19, 121, 127–9, 130n.5, 131n.12, 133, 136
Douglas, Mary 2, 34n.5
Dreyfus, Jean-Marc 53
Dziuban, Zuzanna 55

Ecuador 74
Edkins, Jenny 80, 94
enforced disappearance 6–7, 14–15, 18–20, 28, 31, 37–59, 70, 78, 106–7
  definition of 37
  as an ideal form 53–4
  modernity of 57–8
  see also disappearance
Equipo Argentino de Antropología Forense, the Argentine Forensic Anthropology Team (EAAF) 58n.1, 105, 107–9, 112, 130n.5, 130n.6
Etkind, Alexander 141
Europe 12–13, 15, 23–4, 30, 64–6, 68, 73, 74, 81, 93, 113, 120–4, 139, 140, 148
European Union (EU) 61, 67, 70, 74, 82, 95, 96
excavation 19, 45–6, 110–19, 126, 137, 142
exhumation 19, 22, 101, 102, 106–19, 126–9, 130n.3, 154–5, 160
exile 16, 136, 145
exposure to death 28–30, 57, 62–6, 78–9, 81, 97, 124, 159

Families of the Missing 10
family
  and definition of 'missing person' 7–10
  and enforced disappearance 16–18, 40–1, 55–7
  and identification 103–4
  and 'individual missing' 84–90, 94–6
  as liminal personae 27–8
  and missing migrants 69–78, 122–5
  outreach program 113, 114, 121–3
  and remembrance 135–7
  and the theoretical frame of the book 29–31, 158–9
  see also disturbed intimacies; kinship
fatal accident 1, 5, 15, 94
Ferrándiz, Francisco 18, 22, 29
fingerprinting 21, 22, 108, 121
Finland 11, 35n.12, 13–15, 27, 45–6, 50–1, 67, 81–2, 84–95, 98n.7, 103, 104, 110, 111, 114, 131n.9, 133, 135, 148, 150–1, 154
First World War 23, 152

Index

forced disappearance *see* enforced disappearance
forensics 22, 23, 31, 62, 68, 101–3, 104, 107–9, 110–19, 122–9, 130n.3, 132n.23, 132n.24, 137, 140, 148
   citizen-led 104, 127, 128
   community 124, 132n.24
   counter 132n.24
   lay 124, 127
   vernacular 132n.24
forensic turn 22, 102, 126
Foucault, Michel 20, 28
Frey, Barbara 6–7
funeral 3, 23–4, 28, 50, 53, 73, 76, 77, 101, 108, 114, 115, 117–19, 124, 143
   see also burial; rite of passage; ritual
Fyfe, Nicholas 93

Gammeltoft-Hansen, Thomas 66
Gatti, Gabriel 6, 11, 24, 31, 34n.5, 43, 46, 57, 71, 101, 105, 130n.7, 136, 141, 146, 147, 152, 155n.9, 158
gender 71, 81, 97, 160
Geneva Conventions 7
Germany 96, 103
ghosts 2, 3, 19, 25, 33, 49, 87, 88, 134, 135, 146, 149–54, 157, 161
grandparenting index 109
grave 3, 18, 19, 24, 60, 61, 88, 118–20, 123, 143, 145, 150, 158
   family 24
   mass 21, 22, 45–7, 50, 55, 100, 106, 111–19, 127, 129n.1, 130n.2, 131n.12, 132n.23, 137, 142, 143, 151
   N.N. 24, 107, 108, 120–1, 148
gravestones 24, 143
Greece 62, 120, 124
grievability 18
Guatemala 55, 70, 139, 141
'Gukurahundi' violence 56, 126
Gulag 19, 103, 128

Halilovich, Haris 45, 48
harga 74
Hertz, Robert 26
Hijos de los Desaparecidos 109
Hinzel, Max 148
horror 1, 28, 33–4n.1, 41, 52, 55, 56, 146, 147

Hukanović, Rezak 146–7
human remains 22, 23, 56, 102, 103, 120, 129, 133, 145, 148
   see also burial; funeral; grave
human rights discourse 16, 18, 20, 83
human rights forensics 102, 105, 107, 126, 129, 130n.3

identification 3, 4, 7, 14, 16, 21–3, 28–31, 33, 47–8, 50, 52, 56, 58, 58–9n.1, 63, 65–8, 74, 94, 100–29, 130n.5, 131n.14, 132n.23, 133, 136, 140, 142–4, 153–61
   of the dead 22–3, 110–19
   history of 20–3
   of living persons 21
India 56, 90
indigenous people 18, 23, 55, 70, 81
'individual' missing person 14, 15, 25, 32, 35n.10, 51, 80–99, 103
International Commission on Missing Persons (ICMP) 4, 8–9, 12, 15, 39, 46, 67, 102, 111–19, 124, 130–1n.8, 131n.11, 131n.12, 131n.16, 132n.23
International Committee of the Red Cross (ICRC) 8, 12, 21, 35n.22, 66, 67, 103, 110, 112–15, 124, 130n.3, 130–1n.8, 146
   see also Red Cross Movement
International Criminal Police Organization (INTERPOL) 7, 93
International Criminal Tribunal for the Former Yugoslavia (ICTY) 111, 131n.10, 143
International Organisation for Migration (IOM) 12–13, 66, 67, 79n.6, 124
Iraq 12, 56, 126, 132n.23
irregular migration *see* undocumented migration
ISIS 35n.21
ITAKA 95–6
Italy 61, 73, 120, 122–3, 125

Jugo, Admir 45, 137

Kashmir 56
kinship 30, 66, 69—78, 83, 110, 158
   see also family
Kivilahti, Saila 34n.4, 62, 89

Kobelinsky, Carolina 121
Kovras, Iosif 121

Laakkonen, Ville 30, 34n.4, 62, 94
Laczko, Frank 68
Lampedusa 120, 122, 148
Langford, Jean 27
Laqueur, Thomas 23–4
Last Rights 140
Latin America 6–7, 11, 18–20, 38, 39, 43, 56, 70, 127, 128, 147
    see also Argentina; Chile; Ecuador; Guatemala; Mexico; South America
Lebanon 12, 56
Lesvos 121, 131n.14
Lewicki, Pawel 96
liminality 1, 2, 26–7, 29, 36n.27, 46, 47, 55, 61, 72–3, 76, 77, 88, 89, 101, 105, 118, 119, 135, 139, 148, 149, 158–9

M'charek, Amade 122, 129
Madres de Plaza de Mayo 106–10, 112, 130n.6, 138, 141, 154
Majke Srebrenice 138, 142, 155n.4, 155n.5
Managing Search Operations (MSO) 91
Martin Guerre *see Return of Martin Guerre, The*
mass grave *see* grave
Matyska, Anna 34n.4, 81, 95–6, 149
Mbembe, Achille 28, 29, 38, 41, 51–3, 65, 80, 97
media 67–9, 84, 138, 143
    as reappearance 148–9
    social 35n.21, 93, 95
    spectacles 148–9, 153, 157
Mediterranean 9, 12–15, 33, 60, 62, 64, 66, 68, 69, 73, 103, 119–25, 140, 148, 159
mementoes 135, 137, 138, 143, 153, 157
    see also artefacts
memoirs 24, 41, 146–7
memorials 3, 23, 24, 33, 117–18, 126, 141–5, 153–4, 158, 161
Mexico 12, 13, 15, 56–7, 59n.10, 68, 69, 119, 120, 123, 124, 127
migrant disappearance *see* missing migrants; undocumented migration

migration industry 66, 68
migration order 62–5, 79n.3
Minnesota protocol 23
Missing at the Borders 12, 60–1, 72–8, 125, 138, 151
missing in action (MIA) 11, 23, 51
missing migrants 11, 15, 60–79
    numbers of 13, 66–9
    see also undocumented migration
Missing Migrants Project (IOM) 12–13, 66–7
missing person
    definition of 7–9
    in international humanitarian law 7
    vernacular terms for 11
Missing Persons Institute 112
Moisseinen, Hanneriina 84–90, *85*, 91, 98, 146, 147, 151
Moon, Claire 22–3, 129
Morocco 27, 60, 77, 122
mortal remains 19, 23–4, 29, 33, 34n.2, 100–32, 134, 144, 154, 160
Mothers of Plaza de Mayo *see* Madres de Plaza de Mayo
Mothers of Srebrenica *see* Majke Srebrenice
museums 23, 24, 33, 126, 141–5, 151–4, 157, 161

natural disaster 1, 5, 10, 12, 13, 160
Nazi regime 19
necropolitics 6, 19, 28–9, 32, 33, 38, 41, 42, 51–7, 65, 80, 97, 100, 101, 117, 153
Nepal 141
Nunca Más 41, 107, 110
Nyberg Sørensen, Ninna 66

'organized irresponsibility' 65, 78
osteobiographic methods 22

Pakistan 12
Parr, Hester 27, 46, 72, 89, 93
Parrot, Fiona 135, 136
passport 21–2, 63, 65, 93, 121
Penchaszadeh, Viktor 130n.6
Perl, Gerhild 29, 65, 77, 119–20
Petrović-Šteger, Maja 112–13, 115–17
photography 21, 33, 47, 60, 118, 123, 133–40, 142–4, 147–8, 153, 155nn.2–3, 161
    see also aerial photography

Physicians for Human Rights (PHR) 112
Platform for Transnational Forensic Assistance 124, 140
Poland 11, 14, 15, 82, 95–6, 149
police 9–10, 21, 32, 35n.10, 41, 67, 82–4, 86, 89, 90–8, 98–9n.8, 104, 106, 108, 110, 120, 121, 148, 159
politics of care 29, 128–9
Potočari 24, 117–19, 142–5
prevention through deterrence 64–5, 79
Prijedor 37, 44–8, 100, 115, 146, 151

racism 65, 81
reburial 33, 44, 108, 118, 129, 154, 160
Red Cross Movement 8, 21, 35n.22, 39, 46, 103, 110, 111, 146
    in Finland 4, 91–2
    see also International Committee of the Red Cross (ICRC)
Rehn, Elisabeth 111, 131n.9
Reineke, Robin 120–2, 127, 130n.3
remembrance 19, 141
    history of 23–5
Renshaw, Layla 18–19, 154–5
Restoring Family Links 8
Return of Martin Guerre, The 16–18, 21
rite of passage 26, 88, 101
ritual 2, 25, 28, 36n.27, 47–8, 55, 71, 76, 88, 101, 117, 118, 140, 144, 154, 157
Robben, Anthony 22, 29, 36n.27, 39–42, 58–9n.1, 105–6, 130n.5, 130n.7
Robins, Simon 121
Rosenblatt, Adam 29, 54, 129, 130n.6, 132n.23
Russia 1, 103, 141
    see also Soviet Union (USSR)
Rwanda 14, 55, 126, 144

Samarah, Tarik 142
Sant Cassia, Paul 30
Schindel, Estela 19, 151–2
Schwartz-Marín, Ernesto 127–8
search 4, 7–9, 25, 29–33, 47, 48, 52, 67, 68, 72, 74, 75, 80–6, 89, 90–8, 98n.7, 98–9n.8, 100–34, 137, 140, 142, 149, 154, 157–61
    history of 20–3
Second World War 11, 22–3, 48, 110, 133, 154

Sen, Atreyee 90
Singleton, Ann 68
smuggling 69
Snow, Clyde 107, 130n.6
social disappearance 71
Sonoran Desert 9, 64, 72
South America 19–20, 38, 39, 55, 68, 74
    see also Argentina; Chile; Ecuador; Guatemala; Latin America; Mexico
Southeast Asia 27, 94, 126, 129, 152
Soviet Union (USSR) 19, 42–3, 128, 133, 148
    see also Russia
Spain 62, 119–22, 124, 139
    Civil War (1936–39) 18–19, 154–5
Srebrenica 24, 44, 45, 47–52, 100, 103, 110–19, 135, 137–9, 142–4, *144*, *145*, 153
Sri Lanka 126, 139
Stalin, Joseph 19, 43
state
    complicity 9, 57
    emergent 14, 43–5, 50–2
    and enforced disappearance 1, 6–7, 37–41, 51–4, 108
    as guarantor of citizenship rights 20, 83, 90–4, 159
    and 'individual missing' 83, 94–8
    and missing migrants 63–6, 69–72, 123–5
    and remembrance 141–2
    and the theoretical frame of the book 29–31, 157–61
state of exception 41, 53
Stepputat, Finn 25, 29, 42, 125
Stevenson, Olivia 27, 72, 89
Stover, Eric 130n.6
Syria 12

terrorism 57, 94
    9/11 attack in New York 139–40, 145
Timor-Leste 56, 126, 128, 141
Tomašica 47, 100
Torpey, John 22
tracing service 4, 103
    see also Restoring Family Links
transitional justice 102, 141

Tunisia 24, 60–1, 73, 74, 76, 120, 125
Turkey 12, 51
Turner, Victor 2, 47

Uganda 152
Ukraine 1
undocumented migration 4, 9, 12–13, 15, 17, 18, 22, 32, 57, 60–79, 91, 94, 97, 119–25, 139, 140, 159
United Nations 7, 34n.6, 37–8, 111–12, 131n.9, 131n.10, 138, 143
    see also International Criminal Tribunal for the Former Yugoslavia (ICTY)
United Nations Declaration on the Protection of All Persons from Enforced Disappearance see Disappearance Convention
United Nations Working Group on Enforced or Involuntary Disappearance 20, 110
United States (USA) 9, 47, 61, 64, 67, 82, 98n.3, 107, 110, 113, 118, 120–1, 124, 130n.6, 139–40, 149
Unknown Soldier 23
Uruguay 6
US–Mexico border area 12–13, 15, 69, 119–24

Van Gennep, Arnold 26–7, 36n.27
Vapaaehtoinen pelastuspalvelu, Vapepa 92
Verdery, Katherine 30
Vietnam 56, 126
Voluntary Rescue Service (in Finland) see *Vapaaehtoinen pelastuspalvelu, Vapepa*

Wagner, Sarah 155n.3
war 1, 3–4, 21, 23, 35n.12, 37, 43–6, 50–2, 113–14, 126, 143, 149–51
    on drugs 56–7
    see also armed conflict; Bosnia; 'dirty war'; First World War; Second World War; Spain, Civil War
Wastell, Sari 45
Woolnough, Penny 27, 72

YouTube 75, 118–19
Yugoslavia 4, 8, 9, 11, 12, 45, 46, 52, 102, 113–15, 129n.1
    dissolution of 38, 43–4, 51, 110

Zagaria, Valentina 24, 74, 120
Zemon Davies, Natalie 16–17, 22
    see also *Return of Martin Guerre, The*
Zimbabwe 14, 56, 126–8, 152
zombies 2

EU authorised representative for GPSR:
Easy Access System Europe, Mustamäe tee 50,
10621 Tallinn, Estonia
gpsr.requests@easproject.com